THE WAY IS
IN TRAINING

By Matthew S. Little

DEDICATION

To my wife, Angela. My training partner, my lover, my best friend, my business partner, and my muse. It took me half a century to find you, and it was worth every bit of the wait to have you by my side. I love you.

FOREWORD - "TIME"

Time.

It is the one thing that all of us cannot stop. We can prioritize, we can allocate it, but we cannot get more of it. So, what we do with it is of supreme importance. A teacher should be able to impart knowledge in such a way as to condense their experience into not just information, but into how the knowledge came to be. Feed a man a fish, he eats for a day. Teach a man to fish, he eats for a lifetime.

Sooner, not faster. In this book, Matt has distilled thirty plus years of government service into six books/147 chapters/439 pages. If you notice it resembles *The Book of Five Rings* and *The Art of War*, then you are already on your way to understanding why and how this book is written. I recommend this book to all who are looking to improve, but are not sure where to start, or to those who are already training, and seeking to get better. Matt has taken the guesswork out of developing training, the gear you need to be efficient in your training, and how to be deliberate about your practice. By following these guidelines, you will reach your goals sooner in your training, allowing you to be more effective for a lifetime of service.

Read this book three times. Read it first, from cover to cover, to understand all that Matt provides. We often do not know what we don't know. Then read it a second time, using the parts you need, when you need them. This can be a reference for your training, whether it is a martial skill or a mental skill. Once you have read it, used it, referenced it, and built from it, set it aside. Let your training in all of your areas develop, experimenting with the principles Matt has illuminated. Then, after you have developed, practiced, and executed your training, read it a third time. See how the different tenets interleave with one another, and how the mental, physical, and technical aspects of your training complement one another.

Training today is far better than it has been at any time in modern history. The information and methodology laid out in this book is an excellent guidebook on your path to mastery of martial skill. Good luck on your journey.

COL Joseph J. Frescura, SF, USA (Ret)

PREFACE - "THE WAY IS IN TRAINING"

"From one way, know all ways." - Miyamoto Musashi

Miyamoto Musashi was a renowned warrior in feudal Japan. He fought sixty duels to the death and saw combat in six large scale battles. In his old age he codified his strategy and philosophy in several written works. The most famous of these, "The Book of Five Rings," is still studied by military strategists, businessmen, and philosophers today. In his writings, he put forth nine precepts. These were his rules for success. The first of these simply reads "The way is in training,"

The way is in training. This is another universal truth. It applies to warfighters and healers, artists and tradesmen, athletes and entertainers. Mastery of a craft requires deliberate practice, focused effort over thousands of hours of training. There's more to this statement though. It has a deeper meaning.

Modern training philosophy, especially police and military, is very much result-focused. A police officer completes a forty hour instructor certification course and is now a subject matter expert. At least according to his chain of command. A soldier completes SFAS and the Q-course and earns his Green Beret. He doesn't realize how little he actually knows of his craft until he gets to his team. A problem with check-the-box training is that it's designed to create a minimum standard through brief immersion. That isn't how you train for mastery.

Training for mastery is process-focused. Look at anyone at the very top of their craft. They have a system of training in place designed to carry them through a career lifetime of steady improvement. That system, that process, becomes their lifestyle. Their way of life. It's the foundation their mastery is built on. It's the bedrock that supports them in moments of defeat, and the touchstone that keeps them grounded through victories. And that focus on the process, day in and day out, is how you achieve mastery. Brief periods of intense effort alone won't do it. It takes a sustainable and dedicated level of training over the long haul.

That process, that system, becomes your way. Your path to walk. Your journey to mastery. And over time the process becomes its own reward. The journey itself is now the destination. The way is in training.

This is not just another book on basic shooting principles, rudimentary tactics, or fundamental weapons manipulations. I plan on exploring how warriors should train and fight, as well as how they should live. We will talk about technique but will also dive deep into fitness, mindset and strategy. We will explore leadership and philosophy as well. This book is primarily written for the armed professional—the person whose job is carrying a gun and going into harm's way, or for the citizen who trains for self-protection. But there are applications of these principles for the athlete and the businessman as well. Training, leadership, and strategy are universal. Every vocation, every pursuit has its way. And the way to mastery always lies in training.

Right as I turned 51 years old, I retired from a long dual career that had me carrying a gun for a living for three decades, both at home and overseas. I have been a special operations soldier or a police officer my entire adult life. I have been in combat, and won gunfights at home. I have been in more high risk situations and physical confrontations than I can count or remember. I have fought for my life many times, and I never lost. Despite this, I did not truly begin to understand training and strategy until in my forties. I feel as if I am only now, well into my fifties, truly mastering my craft. Despite a body broken from decades of accumulated injuries, I am only now realizing my true potential.

I also realize now that most of my early victories were simply due to audacity and aggression, or my adversaries' lack of ability, rather than my skill. There is a learning curve to armed conflict, and surviving your first encounter is so often sheer luck. There are soldiers and policemen who have won multiple gunfights, but don't yet understand how or why they prevailed over their opponents. That is a risky and random way to learn.

I think that these are common truths among our warrior and protector classes. It shouldn't be that way. If I had been given a clear roadmap for progress as a new soldier, I could have reached my potential much earlier in my career and been far more effective. And I could have done it with far less damage to my body. It still takes effort and dedication, but training intelligently and efficiently, avoiding detours and dead ends, would take decades off a young warrior's learning curve.

This is why I started my training company, and this is why I am writing this book. It doesn't have to take decades for an armed professional to master their craft. I want to help you shortcut your learning curve and reach your potential level of skill as efficiently and quickly as you can. This isn't some magic bullet. Training is hard, and it takes planning and consistent effort over time. But hard effort alone won't get you to your goal quickly without an understanding of the way there.

There are lessons from the ways a warrior trains that are universal. There are reasons why businessmen and philosophers throughout history study the ways of strategy and war. The crucible of life or death conflict is unforgiving, and success or failure in that arena tests the validity of concepts and principles in a way that other venues do not. I hope that this book, like others before it, will offer value to people from any path who want to succeed without compromising their character, who want to live authentically and become the best version of themselves that they can be. I hope that the lessons I have learned will help others truly live.

So, whether you are a young soldier, a veteran police officer, a martial artist, an athlete, or simply someone looking for an authentic life, let's examine how the lessons of combat and preparation for it can help us fulfill our potential. Let's learn how the discipline of training can show us our true selves amidst the chaos of life. Let's explore the way together, and build a roadmap for the journey.

BOOK ONE - THE MIND

INTRODUCTION - "THE RAZOR'S EDGE"

"The greatest ideal man can set before himself is self-perfection." - W. Somerset Maugham

People who've never spent time in the close company of warriors often think of them as brutish and unintelligent. Even in law enforcement and the military, support personnel and upper management often think of those who do the actual fighting as "knuckle draggers" or "grunts." Nothing could be further from the truth. Especially at the top of the craft.

The "mental game" is vital to athletic excellence, and this just is as true for "combat" or "tactical" athletes as for any other. In my opinion, there is no other pursuit where the mental game matters more than combat. It quite literally is the difference between life and death, not just for the individual warrior, but for those he fights for and alongside.

This incontrovertible truth is historically why warrior cultures placed a heavy emphasis on meditation, philosophy, and religion, as well as art, literature, and games of strategy. They were sharpening their warriors' minds with these pursuits. This is also why combat sports and martial arts are so often seen as vehicles for self-improvement by devotees who will most likely never fight for their lives.

Technical skill and physical preparedness are both useless without a commensurate development of the mind. And not just an academic or scholarly one. The warrior's mind must ride the edge of a razor like a samurai's zen or a praetorian's stoicism. In the moment, unflustered, and resolute. No attachment to consequence or reward, only process and standards. It is vital that you devote yourself to the development of this, or all of your other training will prove fruitless.

STANDARDS

"You can't have high standards without good discipline." - William Hague

What are the standards you hold yourself to and why?

I went through Special Forces Assessment & Selection (SFAS) as a young man, sure of my abilities but largely untested. I had never wanted anything the way I wanted to pass that test. I devoured every book I could find on Special Forces, prepared myself physically and mentally as best I could, and put every part of my life towards that one singular goal. To the young soldier I was, becoming a Green Beret was like becoming one of King Arthur's knights of the round table, and I would have much rather died than failed.

When I was selected, the sergeant major told us all "for the rest of your lives you will be judged and tested by all you meet, because no matter what else you do in life, you will always be US Army Special Forces. Never betray the regiment. Never let it down. Uphold the standard in everything you do." This resonated with me, much more than any creed or code of conduct. It wouldn't be enough to do the minimum in anything ever again. That wasn't what we did. It wasn't who we were. We were the ones who did more, and did it better. Excellence in everything was the standard, and I meant to uphold that.

The standard was about more than just skill or effort though. The pipeline for Special Forces (SF) is intended to produce experts in guerrilla warfare. Because of the classic SF mission, the training is meant to develop free thinkers who know what rules to break, and when to deceive. But, as a seeming paradox, it also demands nothing less than the highest integrity. As an example, during the unconventional warfare "Robin Sage" training exercise I recruited a resident who was not a role player into our guerrilla force and used him as transport so that we could make our hit times. He wound up invited to our victory feast at the end of the exercise, and our cadre applauded our ingenuity. The harsh counterpoint though is the student who was caught cheating and was released from training, never to return. We were taught to never fight fair, but we were also taught to be honorable despite the ruthless nature of our profession.

This is what enables Special Forces soldiers to accomplish amazing things. A Green Beret would rather die than embarrass the regiment. And he would rather die than let down his teammates. It's not an infallible system. We have our fallen, and our failures. But they are few, and the culture is unrelenting about weeding them out and casting them aside. They become persona non grata, unwelcome among their peers.

SF allowed me into a modern warrior class the equal of any historical one that the world has ever known. I was able to fight alongside heroes the equal of any from legend. The regiment gave me an entry ticket into a world most know of only from books and movies, full of experiences far beyond the norm. And all the regiment asked of me—of any of us—in return was that we always uphold the standard in not only skill and ability, in not only effort and commitment, but in honor and integrity as well.

Find your standards. Find your purpose. Something worth the commitment to excellence and integrity. And then you will find the best of yourself.

EGO

"The more we value things outside our control, the less control we have." - Epictetus

Ego is the enemy of improvement. I don't mean pride of accomplishment. I don't mean the will to win, the desire to accomplish. I'm talking about attachment. Attachment to an artificial self-image. A desire to appear infallible, unflawed to others. Attachment to outcomes. Any aspect of self-improvement requires a willingness to work through errors and mistakes without shying away from them or hiding them. Polishing yourself requires the ability to objectively self-analyze, and ego makes that impossible. If you aren't honest with yourself about where you are, you can't find your way to where you want to be.

There is a reason that all the warrior cultures of the world through history emphasize this in their philosophy. From the zen of the samurai, to the stoicism of the Greeks and Romans, to modern day performance psychology in SOF units, the same lesson is taught. Ego is the enemy of improvement. Attachment destroys performance. One of the great ironies of the human psyche is that the more we desire a particular outcome during performance under pressure, the harder it is to achieve it. How then do we train ourselves to perform without attachment? Without ego?

This isn't easy. Far from it. It takes constant attentiveness. It requires cultivating self-awareness. And maybe most importantly it requires the ability to simply let go and reset

23

when attachment to outcome forms, the ability to recognize when ego rises and circle back around to the process as needed over and over. It's a lifelong process, not a simple decision.

The conscious mind needs a job to do. It needs to be given a task or it will override the subconscious processes that lead to peak performance under stress. Process focus is the key. Focusing on the process in the moment allows the subconscious to perform at the peak of your current skill. Focusing on outcomes causes you to force and push performance. This invariably leads to mistakes under pressure. The more you try and force a particular result, the less likely you are to achieve it. The more you simply observe the process of performance, dispassionately and without judgement, the better you perform and the faster you improve.

This same principle that in micro allows peak performance during the event, in macro applies to the process of training as a whole. Goals and needs analysis are vital to plan the training plan and adjust it as needed, but that dispassionate process focus over time is what leads to improvements in skill and ability. When training, if you are attached to how you appear to yourself or others, to your ego, your training will never be as effective as it could be. If you focus on the process instead, you're much more likely to achieve your best.

There is an important life lesson here as well. The same underlying principle applied to how you comport yourself in daily life will help you be the best person you can be. Focusing on the process of living, of being your best in all aspects of your life, rather than on appearances and on satisfying your ego, will allow you to grow as a person and reach your potential away from training as well. This is the fundamental underpinning of zen and stoicism, the biggest lesson of practical philosophy and ethics. To achieve your best, to become the person you should be, let go of desire and simply work the process with unflinching self-honesty. No attachment, no ego, just the process.

MATH

"There is a beast inside every man, and it stirs when you put a sword in his hand." - George R R Martin.

If you carry a gun, for a living or for self-defense, you need to think through the implications before you need that tool. Your mind needs to be right in advance of a deadly force incident. When the incident occurs is too late for that thought process to happen. It needs to be part of your worldview well in advance.

One of the things that I am proudest of in my dual careers, is that I never used deadly force because I could, or even because I wanted to. I am proud of the fact that I was professional enough to only use that level of violence because it was objectively necessary.

The decision to use deadly force should be as dispassionate as triage in an emergency room, it should literally be a mathematical equation. If the opponent chooses non-threatening action "A" he gets response "B" and is unharmed. If he chooses aggressive action "C" then he gets response "D" and is answered with deadly force. Necessity, not rage or fear or cruelty.

Looking at conflict this way both ensures you act ethically and avoids much of the negative emotional response that can follow the use of deadly force. The decision was his, not yours. Math, pure and simple. Dispassionate and void of anger or hatred. Failing to use this mental paradigm not only makes you vulnerable to the emotional stress of using violence on another human being, it also makes it easier to lose your way. I've seen good honorable men do evil things because of rage or fear. There is a beast in all of us that awakens in conflict. The way to keep that beast reigned in is the mental discipline of this mathematical equation. Follow the math, control the beast, and act with honor.

DISCIPLINE

"You had your whole life to prepare for this moment. Why aren't you ready?" - David Mamet.

Discipline. It's a cliché now. Espoused by athletes, personal trainers, motivational speakers. "Discipline trumps motivation." And it does. But discipline is so much more than going to the gym when you don't feel like it. There's another cliché that says that hard work beats talent. And it does, but what they're really talking about is discipline.

Discipline, or the lack of it, colors the quality of your efforts. It permeates every decision, every choice you make. It is the linchpin of your character, the trait that determines if you possess courage in your convictions, the trait that separates heroes from cowards and strong from weak.

Some of my greatest accomplishments, my finest moments, came about after I thought failure was inevitable. That is also discipline. Staying the course when all seems lost. It is also the ability to endure short term unpleasantness in order to accomplish a goal. To put aside comfort, or pleasure, or ease in order to do something you'd never be capable of otherwise.

Discipline is what allows you to make decisions based on reason and logic rather than emotion. Emotions are valuable, but only if you're not a slave to them. How many fights have been lost because of anger or fear? How much disaster and suffering have been created throughout history because people lacked the discipline to make objective decisions?

Tactics only work if you're disciplined. Will you hit your corner in CQB or be sucked into the threat in the center of the room? Will you burn through your ammo in an engagement needlessly or be calm enough in the chaos to make each round count?

High level application of shooting under stress is only possible if the shooter is disciplined. It's one thing to do a lightning fast draw or reload for Instagram, it's another thing completely to be disciplined enough to stay present in the process of shooting in a gunfight or a 32 round field course at a major match.

Cultivate discipline. Nurture it. It may be the single most important quality to living a successful and authentic life. And in the bad days, your discipline, not just in that moment, but throughout your life leading up to it, will be what separates victory from defeat and life from death.

MINDSET

"Of every one-hundred men, ten shouldn't even be there, eighty are nothing but targets, nine are real fighters, and we are lucky to have them, for they make the battle. Ah, but the one, one of them is a warrior, and he will bring the others back." - Heraclitus

Mindset. This is a word we hear a lot in firearms training. It's supposedly what separates the combative student of firearms from the competitive. And perhaps it is, but not in the way most people mean. Most people who use the term don't even define it. So what is it exactly? What do we mean by mindset? You hear instructors and students of defensive pistol craft throw the word around like a cure all. What mindset definitely is not is some magical attribute that will somehow be there when it's needed and overcome a lack of technical or tactical skill. What is mindset then, really? And how do we develop it?

At different times I've heard the word used to mean anything from situational awareness to willpower, from aggression to decision making under stress. It's more correctly a broad category of attributes rather than a particular one—the cognitive and psychological aspects of combative shooting. What every aspect in this broad category has in common is this: you don't train them the same way you train physical skills. And you don't train them at the same time as you train for skill development. At least not if you want to train either your physical skills or your mindset as effectively as possible.

28

This runs completely counter to the old saw of "train like you fight." And with good reason. Training *for* the fight is entirely different than training like you fight. It is important to periodically test skill in realistic scenarios, but that's not how you build skill. Conflating these two different types of training events is perhaps the most common mistake made in the tactical industry. You can't build mindset on the flat range. And trying to do so leads to all kinds of unproductive training.

We've all seen, and most of us have done in training at some point, the exaggerated post shooting sequences following a flat-range drill meant to replicate the actions you would take immediately after a lethal force encounter. Like some stylized martial arts kata devoid of real meaning, shooters "follow" targets to the ground that aren't actually falling, and snap their heads left and right to "scan and assess" and "break their tunnel vision." You aren't cultivating awareness with this sort of range theatrics, merely eating up time better spent working on shooting skill. This applies to a short step while reloading or clearing malfunctions as well. Not that movement isn't essential, more that it needs to be correctly done in training,

Then there are the instructors who yell and scream at their students during drills meant to develop skill, in order to somehow replicate the stress of a gunfight. Skill is best built through deliberate and focused practice. Once skill is developed it can and should be tested under stress, but testing is not training, and yelling is not the same stress as a gunfight, far from it.

Another popular training gaffe is the combination of functional fitness with shooting drills. Once again, this can have real relevant value as a test of skill, especially for those whose job involves infiltration to a target in ways that essentially are endurance events, but it's not the best way to develop skill. And just like yelling to induce stress, the stress of exercise is not the same as the stress of a gunfight. I am a strong proponent of cultivating and maintaining a high level of functional fitness, but that should be separate from skill development. If you look at the way high level athletes train, skill work is optimally done fresh, not fatigued.

If none of this is how we train the mental aspects of our craft, how do we then? That is not as simple a question as one might think. What we refer to as the single quality of "mindset" is more a collection of related but disparate skills and attributes that have to be considered separately. Let's look at each element and explore efficient ways to develop them.

Let's look at situational awareness first. This can be further broken down into three component skills. First there is preventative or preparatory awareness. The ability to discern pre-attack cues and identify vulnerable points in your surroundings can often enable you to avoid conflict. If conflict can't be avoided, this awareness can set you up for success when violence starts and greatly enhance your chances of prevailing.

This is something you can practice every moment of your everyday life. Make the self discipline of awareness a habit. Cultivate it. Play "what-if" games in your head to build a mental database of appropriate responses. Develop sound practices regarding where you sit, stand, and walk in public. Watch and study body language, and learn to truly observe those around you. Research and study the works of experts in this field like Tony Blauer and Craig Douglas. View online videos of violent encounters and learn the lessons they teach. Like technical improvement, this is an area of lifelong study and practice.

Next is situational awareness during conflict. Tunnel vision is not the absolute and unavoidable biological response some would say it is. This is the place for training under appropriate and realistic stress. You don't build physical skills that way, but it's the only way to cultivate this mental ability. The best way to train this is realistic force-on-force training. This sort of training stress inoculates you to gunfighting and allows you to avoid the crippling hyper focus known as tunnel vision.

The analogy I use with special operations personnel when talking about stress inoculation is parachuting. The first time you jump from an airplane in flight, the mind goes into a kind of sensory overload. You remember freeze frames, snap shots of what occurred. The moment you stood in the open door, the moment the parachute popped open, the moment you hit the ground. By the hundredth or two hundredth jump, you are calmly aware of everything throughout the entire event. You've become inoculated to that specific stress. Research shows that this inoculation is to a degree stress specific. My hypothetical veteran skydiver will probably be cognitively overloaded in his first gunfight. This is one of the many reasons why force-on-force training is so invaluable.

Then there is post-event awareness. What Japanese martial artists refer to as "zanshin" or "continuing mind." We see all sorts of exaggerated and robotic range theatrics meant to simulate and train this. These sort of "range kata" are meaningless. They don't replicate realistic post-shooting procedures and are "dead" techniques, to use Bruce Lee's terminology, devoid of any real intent or meaning. Post-event awareness, like situational awareness during the armed confrontation, is best developed during realistic and stressful scenario-based training. Seek out this training and you will develop this attribute.

Let's discuss will and aggression next. What martial artists refer to as "fighting spirit." There's a flip side to this coin as well. Blind aggression or rage is counterproductive. You need an indomitable will and an overwhelming aggression, but both need to be controlled and deliberate. You have to also cultivate a sense of calm within the chaos. These attributes are best developed by working with a noncooperative partner. You can, and should, work this in force-on-force training as well. Mentally though, fighting is fighting. Any combative endeavor can develop this ability. If you aren't doing some sort of fighting sport in addition to your firearms training, you should be. Conflict is a continuum, not a set of discrete boxes independent of each other and should be addressed as such.

Will is also developed throughout your life by challenging and testing yourself. Hardship is a necessary part of the process. Seek it out and embrace it. Use it to strengthen your will. If you don't, when crisis comes to you it will find you unprepared. One tactical cliché that does ring true is that we never rise to the occasion, we fall to our level of training.

Decision making under stress is developed the same way. Putting ourselves in stressful and realistic scenarios requiring judgement is the only way to build this skill. And the more diverse our training base of scenarios is, the better prepared we will be. To sharpen our decision making, we have to develop a broad and deep experience of correct choice and action under stress.

For all that it isn't "tactical," action shooting competition is one of the best and most accessible ways to work on your mental attributes. Not only will it force you to make decisions and solve problems under stress through the application of shooting and movement skills, it is also a very effective way to work on an aspect of mindset we have yet to discuss. Martial artists call it "mushin," or "no mind." Modern sports psychologists call it the "zone" or "flow state." What it is, most simply put, is embodying the process of performance at a subconscious level of competence without interference from the conscious mind. Not only is this essential for optimal performance under stress, it frees up the conscious mind to do its job, heightening situational awareness and allowing sound decision making. And the best mechanism involving shooting I've found for this by far is "run and gun" action shooting competition.

Mindset is crucial. Indisputably so. And it is without a doubt one of the things that separate the combative application of shooting from the flat range development of shooting skill. But changing our shooting training to add in mindset is not the answer. That will not build mindset, and will in most cases it will hinder our technical development. Build mindset off the flat range, make it a part of your every day life; and when you need it, if you've done the work it will be there.

ATTACHMENT

"Think of yourself as dead. You have lived your life. Now take what's left and live it properly." - Marcus Aurelius

The other day at an industry get-together, my old teammate from my 2004 Iraq deployment, Jim Erwin, and I were having a conversation about that trip. We were laughing and joking about all of our close calls, and Jim compared one to the scene in the movie *Pulp Fiction* where John Travolta and Samuel Jackson somehow impossibly survive an ambush at close range and liken it to divine intervention. Don't get me wrong, Jim and I enjoy our memories from that trip. The laughter and joking is real, but so is the reality of it. We almost died but beat the odds many times together.

The Roman emperor and stoic philosopher Marcus Aurelius famously talked about considering yourself as already dead in order to divest yourself of ego and attachment. For many in the modern age this may seem morbid or fatalistic, but it's actually the opposite. What does this mean then? What lessons can it teach us?

Every day is a gift. That's a cliché, a platitude. Dismissed by most. It's also true. No one lives forever, and few choose the time and manner of their passing. We can rail against the random capriciousness of death, or we can choose to truly live. Every day, every hour, every minute that we are given should be put to good use. This isn't a license to not strive for improvement or work hard. It's an admonition to never take any of it for granted.

I've had many close calls in the years since, but in 1999 I almost died in Honduras. Nothing glorious, an accident during a mission mostly spent training locals and doing sick calls in remote villages. Most of the significant achievements of my life came after that. Once I seriously started looking into stoicism and zen, I consciously adopted the perspective that my life had ended that day, and that every day after was a bonus day, a gift from the universe. Knowing that each day is extra, how do I use that bonus time? How do I live each day to the fullest?

That mental exercise has stood me in great stead down through the years. I've had many close calls and managed to achieve many goals. I've also had setbacks and defeats. At this writing, I'm beginning a long course of physical therapy and resharpening skills after my joint implant got infected and I landed in the hospital. If I was attached to things as they were before this latest setback, this event beyond my control could easily be upsetting. Instead, learning to look at each day as extra time, instead of time I'm owed, allows me to enjoy this process almost as much as enjoying when I'm on top of my game.

Zen scholars attribute emotional suffering to attachment. A desire for the world to be what you want it to be rather than what it is. The stoics talked at length about the only variable truly in our control was how we react to reality, and that reacting with negative emotions to events we cannot change does us nothing but harm. This simple truth is one of the keys in my opinion to living an authentic and rich life.

This doesn't mean we don't set goals or want certain outcomes. Far from it. I plan on being a better athlete and shooter than I was before this setback. What it does mean is that with a simple perspective shift, we can learn to enjoy the process of self improvement for its own sake, rather than being discouraged or despondent if goals prove illusive or if we suffer setbacks in our path. To use modern psychological parlance rather than the ancient philosophical ones, this simple mental exercise gives us a growth mindset rather than a fixed one. Divesting ourselves of our attachments to how things should be gives us the power to change ourselves in ways we never could otherwise.

33

LEVEL OF PARTICIPATION

"Strength does not come from physical capacity. It comes from an indomitable will." - Mahatma Ghandi

What is your level of participation? This question is of vital importance for the combat arms soldier or street cop, especially those serving in a special operations capacity. It's also of vital importance though for the armed citizen or hobbyist. Actually, regardless of the pursuit, this question is a central one. What is your level of participation? What amount of effort are you willing to put towards your goals?

All too often, people's goals and expectations don't line up with the efforts they are willing to contribute towards them. I've known martial artists who thought their academic knowledge could somehow make up for a lack of hard training or proper conditioning. Competitive shooters who seldom practice dry fire or live fire yet expect to place well in matches. SWAT cops who care more about their golf game than their shooting or tactics yet think they will somehow rise to the occasion when a critical incident occurs.

But we don't rise to the occasion. The cliché is that we fall to the level of our training. The reality is actually that we fall below our best abilities. Skill doesn't magically appear when you need it. It's the converse actually. Skill degradation is a very real thing. When I need it the most, the skill I have built will never be at its best. When I do my needs analysis and decide what level of skill I have to have to be successful, I have to understand this, and plan my training accordingly.

What matters just as much as my needs analysis when I set my goals though is this. What is my level of participation? How much time and effort am I willing to put in? Deciding that I need or want a certain level of skill or accomplishment is meaningless without dedicating the amount of time and effort it will take to achieve it. And depending on your profession and goals, a lower level of participation can be ok. But be realistic about your expectations. If lives depend on your professional expertise, choose your level of participation accordingly or run the risk of forever regretting your choices when you are found wanting and lives are lost.

STRESS

"That which does not kill us, makes us stronger." - Frederich Nietzsche

Calm, cool, and collected under pressure. There is a reason that is a cliché. It is one of the most important attributes of a warrior. It is also a vital attribute for success in any endeavor. How we handle stress doesn't just determine our success in moments of conflict, it determines our happiness and success in life. Because of the physiological effects of stress, it may also partially determine our long-term health, perhaps even to a degree our longevity.

The key to handling large amounts of deleterious stress (or distress - as opposed to positive stress or eustress) is two-fold. The first half is triage. When combat medics or emergency room doctors do triage, they evaluate which patients to work on based on who can be helped vice who is too far gone, and then by who needs their services the most. This same principle works very well when addressing multiple concerns or problems. Can you fix it or mitigate it? If it's outside your control then simply accept that and move on to the problems you can influence through your efforts. Then you simply pick what needs to be addressed most urgently and work through the issues in order of importance as best you can.

The second half of the solution is to remain process-focused. Worry about outcomes can paralyze you, prevent you from applying whatever remedies are needed as effectively as you are capable. Simply do what needs to be done to the best of your ability. Anything beyond that is once again outside of your control.

How we manage positive stress matters as well, especially over the long term. Eustress, correctly applied, is the sole mechanism by which we improve our strengths and abilities. It's the last few difficult repetitions of an exercise that make us come back stronger or faster after the appropriate amount of recovery. Learning to balance work and rest, to manage self-applied stress, is the single most important principle of self-development in every area of our lives. Master that, and reaching your potential as an athlete and as a human being becomes possible. Fail to understand it, and you will never become who you could otherwise be.

TIME PRESSURE

"Fast is fine, but accuracy is final. You must learn to be slow in a hurry." - Wyatt Earp

Time pressure. Performance degradation under stress is a very real thing. And few stressors affect us more than time pressure. We have to incorporate time pressure into our training and inoculate ourselves against the stress it creates. We must learn how to be calm in a hurry, or as Wyatt Earp famously said, "Make haste slowly."

The way to do this is by deliberately and purposefully practicing it. But how can we do that? Through several approaches, each working from a different direction to teach us to create a flow state, what some athletes call the zone, and Japanese martial artists call mushin, or "no-mind."

The first approach is stress inoculation. The first time I jumped out of an airplane I was hardly in the zone. I remember standing in the door, my parachute opening, and hitting the ground. Everything between these three snapshots of time was an adrenaline soaked blur. By the hundredth jump, I was so inoculated to the stress that everything was as calmly done as walking down porch stairs and standing on the ground.

Stress inoculation requires some degree of specificity. There is a general carryover effect, if you're excellent at handling one specific stressor, you'll be somewhat better at all stressors. But for the maximum benefit, you should have as close a representation of the actual event in training to provide that inoculation. Force-on-force training, done right, is a fantastic "dress rehearsal" for a real use of force. For competitors, local matches are the best preparation for the stress of major matches.

For general carryover, the best and most readily available training modality for learning to shoot well under time pressure is competing in action shooting. No, it's not tactics. But you are learning to shoot well and solve problems under a huge amount of time pressure. This has tremendous carryover to applying your shooting in a real situation.

So, we have the ability to expose ourselves to the stress of time pressure in training. This will create huge improvements over time. But simple exposure isn't enough to reach our potential. We need to approach the development of this attribute in other ways as well.

This is an area where focused visualization works well. Run yourself through the processes of shooting or tactics in your mind, over and over. See it with clarity and detail. Under stress your subconscious will act out that mental movie you made. This helps keep the process subconscious.

Where we make mistakes under the stress of time pressure is when our conscious mind tries to speed up these processes. The time to build speed is in isolation training, not in application. If your mind is in the right place, the process will feel timeless, neither fast nor slow, but will actually be very fast.

The third way we can learn to enter the correct mental state is by developing that ability when we work skills in combination. This is where we develop the mental "transmission" we need, and learn to have one "gear" for pushing and another for application. Then when we perform under stress we can select the proper mental "gear" for optimum performance.

This brings us to our last tool for learning to enter a flow state. In training develop a simple cue that you do before every combination drill or test that helps put you in the zone. A simple calming breath combined with emptying the mind of conscious thought works well. This becomes associated by your subconscious with entering the proper mental state. Then, when you need that calmness under stress, giving yourself that cue helps you create it.

The time to learn this is in training. Lack of doing so is why people with high levels of technical skill fold under pressure. Explore these concepts in your training, and you will learn to excel under time pressure, not crumple under its weight.

TENSION

"The less effort, the faster and more powerful you'll be." - Bruce Lee

Why is a section discussing excess physical tension in the portion of my book focusing on the mind? The answer is quite simple. Apart from instances of learned technical affectation, excess physical tension is born of excess mental tension. The two are inextricably linked. When the mind is tense and in a hurry, the tension in your body builds. If you have excess tension in your technique, it causes mental tension.

The flip side of that coin is the relationship between physical and mental tension can be exploited to our advantage when we start feeling the effects of excess tension, whether physical or mental. This is the mechanism we use when we take a deep centering breath, or when we "shake out" the tension by consciously relaxing and moving our hands.

If I feel too much tension in my body, I will look at a point (usually the first target I need to shoot in a stage or drill) and then allow my awareness to widen out, calming my mind. This in turn helps me to lower the physical tension I feel, relaxing my body. If I feel too much tension in my mind, I'll take a deep, calming breath, and if possible situationally, shake the excess tension out of my limbs. This allows me to positively change my mental state.

Obviously you'll usually need to combine the physical and mental approaches to lowering tension. Experiment with different mental cues, breathing patterns, and physical movements until you find the best combination that works for you. Develop a short routine you can habitually follow and create the habit of using it in training, so that when you need it in application, you'll have a proven technique for managing your physical and mental tension.

CONFIDENCE

"You have to expect things of yourself before you can do them." - Michael Jordan

Confidence. It is essential for success in any endeavor, but especially in conflict. It doesn't take much viewing of the myriad of gunfight videos on the internet to see what happens to a combatant who's confidence crumbles. Just like when one MMA (Mixed Martial Arts) fighter gives the other their back, that lack of confidence inevitably preludes defeat. The difference between predator and prey is obvious in every line of body language.

Overconfidence however can be just as fatal a flaw as lack of confidence. The cocky fighter getting his comeuppance is so common an occurrence in fighting sports that it's become a cliché. Overconfidence and arrogance breeds complacency. And that sin causes carelessness. And carelessness in combat is a potentially fatal error indeed.

Shun overconfidence and arrogance. Avoid them at all costs, but you have to build an unwavering faith in your own ability. The way to do this is through preparation. As in all other aspects of warriorship, the way is in training. Train hard enough and prepare yourself thoroughly enough that your knowledge of your ability is as certain as your belief in gravity. Cultivate an unshakeable confidence.

If you do this properly, it will positively impact every area of your training, and have huge benefits for real-world application as well. Do this poorly however, and you will never perform in training or in application to the level you are potentially capable of.

EMOTION AND WILL

"There is no weapon more deadly than the will." - Bruce Lee

Emotion. It's both extremely valuable if harnessed correctly, and extremely damaging if allowed unchecked by reason. Decisions born of emotion are rarely correct ones, and physical and mental acuity are negatively impacted by strong emotions such as anger or fear. Our reactions to events, especially in the moment, should be dispassionate in order to be effective.

What emotion is valuable for is giving us motivation and determination. Giving us our "why" for our priorities and actions. We can use emotions to feed our will, and will is an incredibly potent thing. Will enables us to overcome the odds and triumph when the weak-willed would surrender to their emotions and give up. Will is what enables people to perform seemingly superhuman feats of heroism. People like my life-long friend Ryan Ahern, who held off overwhelming odds and kept his team alive until QRF arrived, or another friend Jared Reston, who was shot seven times, including once in the face, and still killed his attacker.

Will matters as much or more than technique, even fitness. I've seen technically proficient and highly fit operators crumble under the pressure of combat. Use your emotions to build your will. Rule your emotions and put them to good use rather than serving them. Cultivate an unshakeable desire to achieve and win. Make no mistake, skill matters, as does physical preparation, but without a fierce and indomitable will, they are useless in conflict.

CHALLENGE

"Today is victory over yourself of yesterday; tomorrow is your victory over lesser men." - Miyamoto Musashi

Biologists, really scientists in general, talk about stasis. A steady state, involving neither growth or degradation. But the truth is, in life there is no stasis. There is no steady state. You are either growing and learning or you are diminishing. Challenge is the key to personal growth, the stimulus required to stave off entropy.

Far too often, people think they have "arrived." This leads to complacency. Skills degrade and excuses cascade, and the downhill slide begins. You never arrive. The moment you think you have, you've ended your growth. And once that momentum is lost, it can be very hard indeed to regain it.

Challenge. Always find new ways to test yourself. New goals to achieve, new landmarks and personal bests. This is different than rights of passage. For some reason many people can work single-mindedly to earn a place in a unit or profession, and then abandon that drive once they are on the "inside." A police academy, SWAT school, Ranger school, SFAS and the Q-course. These things are rights of passage but they are beginnings, not finish lines. No one is valuable to an organization if they are stagnant. And more importantly they lose value to themselves.

This continual growth that challenge brings has importance and benefits far beyond just professional development or skill improvement however. Especially as we grow older, it keeps us vibrant and young. It keeps us alive. Truly alive, not just existing. No matter our age, no matter what point we are at in our careers and lives, the willingness to embrace challenge is a catalyst for growth and accomplishment.

Challenge. It motivates you. Tests you. Seek it out. Rank in BJJ (Brazilian Jiu Jitsu), tactical shooting skill awards, classification in action shooting sports, fitness coaching certifications, competition victories of all kinds. All these things can serve as catalysts for personal and professional growth. Embrace challenge. Seek it out in all things. Never stop growing, learning, and achieving. As long as you live.

MAKE READY

"Chance favors the prepared mind." - Louis Pasteur

SOF soldiers, SWAT officers, and defensive-minded civilian shooters often mock the five minute stage walk-throughs and elaborate "make ready" rituals of competition shooters. And their disapproval is understandable at first glance from their perspective. After all, when they get in a gunfight, there won't be time to halt the action and take five minutes to devise a plan, or call "time out" to take a minute to mentally prepare themselves and rehearse.

This disdain is misplaced however. There are valuable lessons from the make ready process that can be applied across the tactical shooting world, whether Law Enforcement, Military, or civilian. The best in the business on the LE and Mil side utilize much of this already, and armed civilians should take note.

How does the artificial gamesmanship of the competition world's stage planning and make ready apply then? What are the real world applications from the sport's preparatory rituals and processes?

Special Forces soldiers and SWAT officers already do mission planning and rehearse actions on the objective. This is in essence no different than a competition shooter's walk-through. Burning your plan into your subconscious ensures that your conscious mind is free to observe the situation and make needed adjustments on the fly efficiently. Rehearsals ensure you perform your tasks correctly under stress and are often the last thing done before infiltration.

How would this apply though to civilians or beat officers? In your day-to-day routines play the what-if game with yourself. Come up with plans for situations you might face, then in your training walk through those plans. Do rehearsals.

When I was a young patrol officer, one of my common drills in dry and live fire was based on just such a mental "what if." Then as a brand new sergeant, I found myself in the situation I had mentally and physically rehearsed countless times. This allowed me to respond correctly under stress, and I won the gunfight without being injured myself. My rehearsals ensured my victory that day.

What about the make ready though? The elaborate pantomime and mental checklist competitors do at the last minute? In truth, that is actually a ritual that puts the competitor in the correct place mentally and allows for one more mental rehearsal before the action begins. This happens in the military and law enforcement world as well, just in a different form. Last minute gear checks before infil are a part of it, running through your plan in your head in the chinook or bearcat during infil, that last calming breath to clear your head at the LCC or breach point. These things are functionally no different than a make ready.

If you're an armed civilian or a patrol officer, you can take advantage of this as well. Have a gear check and dry fire routine you do before leaving your house for the day or your station for the shift. It can be short, but use it to get your mind right just in case this is the day it needs to be. In your range training develop a short ritual involving a calming breath and a mental preparatory cue for performance. When you suspect that something may turn violent, you can use that short breathing and thought sequence to prepare yourself for performance if you need it. That then, is your make ready. And it will help you if things go south.

Develop your processes that ensure your best performance. Burn them into your brain. Make them habits and they will stand you in good stead should the day come you ever need them. Make ready.

PRE-MISSION CHECKS

"Luck is where opportunity meets preparation." - Seneca

Pre-mission checks. In Special Forces and on my SWAT team, these were customary and considered absolutely essential for success. Prior to leaving on any operation, time permitting, every piece of gear was inspected, tested, and checked. Everything from vehicles and crew-served weapons to radios and flashlights. And woe be unto the team member who didn't do this properly and caused comms failure or a vehicle breakdown because he didn't check the equipment that was his responsibility thoroughly enough.

Adopt this principle in your life and make it a habit. Professionally, it's easy to get complacent, especially if you have a high operational tempo. In your personal life this is a temptation too, especially if you're busy and have competing demands on your time. But you should resist the temptation to become complacent and skip over the pre-mission check process.

This principle applies to everything from cross-country driving to your EDC (Every Day Carry) gear. Making these checks a habit, part of your mental operating system, will go a long way towards avoiding potential failure of your equipment when you need it the most.

CUES

"The power of coaching is this – you are expected to give people the path to find answers, not the answers." - Tom Mahalo

Coaching cues. This is a topic that I continue to learn more about with every class I teach. They can be literal statements reminding the shooter of a technical point to focus on in a drill, like looking at the magwell during a speed reload. They can also be describing a feeling that ensures proper technique, even if it's not possible in actuality, like telling a lifter to bend the bar during a bench press. Or telling an operator that when he's the number two through a doorway he should try and be back-to-back with the number one through the threshold. Coaching cues can have a powerful effect on a student's performance when used well.

Even if you aren't responsible for teaching others, it's important to understand the use of cues and develop a library of them that resonate with you. To a very large degree, we are all our own teachers. The use of cues is immensely valuable in practice. I mentally recite a cue I know to be effective in my practice before every repetition of a skill in dry fire and live fire. Cues are extremely individual, one that speaks to another individual may not help you. It's vital that you understand what types of coaching cues help you and that you utilize them.

Research and experiment thoroughly with this in your own practice, and you will accelerate your improvements in skill. Become your own coach and be diligent in cueing yourself and you will reap the benefits.

AWARENESS

"Drop as deeply as possible into stillness, into whatever is unfolding in the present moment."
- John Kabat-Zin

Awareness. This mental attribute is essential for anyone who wishes to excel at shooting, tactics, or combatives. Awareness is not attention. Attention is active, focused on something specific. Awareness is diffuse, non-specific. Once you have internalized the fundamentals of technique, the more you are simply aware, the more effective you will be, both technically and tactically.

In shooting, you should be aware of every piece of input the gun is giving you. The feel of the recoil impulse and trigger reset and break. You should know in great detail how the sights move throughout the entirety of the recoil arc, and still be aware of the empty brass tumbling out of the ejection port. And at the same time be aware of your surroundings and those of your target.

In tactics, you need awareness not just of your field of fire, but your teammates' movements and positions, as well as the details of the environment around you. The best teams almost never talk in CQB except for radio calls to higher. Their awareness of each other is developed to the point that they can read each other's nonverbal communication, apply the proper tactical principles to their environment and just flow through a structure.

In combatives, lack of awareness makes you vulnerable to feints and susceptible to environmental hazards, not to mention other combatants. Proper awareness allows you to exploit those same factors against your opponent instead.

Cultivate your awareness. Strengthen your internal observer. Train yourself in this well and it will dramatically improve your performance in any aspect not just of conflict, but also of life in general.

LOOK FOR WORK

"Opportunity is missed by most people because it is dressed in overalls and looks like work."
- Thomas Edison

Look for work. It's the most often repeated mantra of the shoot house. That isn't just a truism of CQB though. It's a mind set that is valuable in every aspect of life. What needs to be done right now? What work should I be doing in this moment?

This isn't an endorsement of busywork. Sometimes there simply is nothing that can be done in the moment. And sometimes the work that needs to be done is in fact rest and recovery. But we have to be brutally honest with ourselves about what needs to be done right now, making sure that we do just that without fail, regardless of our desire to put off unpleasant tasks.

Like everything else, this is a habit. Build the habit, cultivate it, and it will stand you in good stead. Look for work. Do the work. And earn the rewards.

PROCESS FOCUS

"If you can't describe what you are doing as a process, you don't know what you're doing." - W. Edwards Deming

Process-focused. In the middle of a shooting drill or a stage in a match, or for that matter a fight for your life, if you focus on the desired outcome, you set yourself up for failure. If instead you focus on the process you need to follow to prevail, you'll let the subconscious skill you've developed in training take over and carry you through. If you've developed a sufficient level of skill in training, you'll win.

The key to this, like everything else, lies in the level of your training. You have to develop processes in your isolation exercises that you can follow when you need to apply your skills. Pay attention to the details. Be aware and observe every aspect of every repetition you do in training. Over time you will have developed a subconscious "program" to play when you need a particular skill. No one can create these for you. They can guide and mentor you, but they can't do the work for you. Be diligent in your training, and develop your own process.

Once you've developed a sound process, learn to apply it in ever more difficult and complex combinations, and under greater and greater levels of stress. The more thoroughly you do this in your training, the more sound your process will become. Remaining process-focused despite the chaos of conflict is essential for performance. The more effort you put into this in your practice, the more likely you'll be to win when you're tested.

AFFIRMATION

"If you are proactive about controlling the direction of your life, then you must control the way you think." - Lanny Bassham

Self-talk. That inner dialogue inside our heads. It affects our performance in every area. The words we choose and the statements we make color our picture of ourselves, our self-identity. This is more important than most people think. Visualization and affirmation of achievements work, if they are realistic, and we've done the requisite work.

There are a number of ways we can incorporate this into our training. Many sports psychologists recommend a visualization and affirmation routine done mentally, either first thing upon awakening or at night immediately prior to sleep. It's important to have an organized set of these that is repeated daily. Over time this will help you grow your skills, physically as well as mentally.

Another mental affirmation technique we can use is silently repeating to yourself a simple phrase whenever you are preparing to perform. The phrase needs to be short and simple. The key point isn't so much the phrase itself, but that in your mind this phrase now stands for how you feel when you perform at your best. Over time, the phrase becomes a mental cue to enter what sports psychologists call a flow state, or the zone, where your optimal level of skill is performed with a subconscious level of competence.

A third technique is primarily used when training for a specific goal. Called a directive affirmation, it's a short statement, several sentences long, used to create a calm expectation of success. In the statement, you describe yourself as having already accomplished the goal, detail why you've accomplished it (focus on training here), and then close by once again describing yourself as already having accomplished the goal. You then place notecards with the directive affirmation in places you'll see throughout your day. Whenever you see the cards, you recite the affirmation to yourself. This is extremely powerful when used properly. I have used variations of this technique many times with success.

As "action guys," we tend to be dismissive of things having to do solely with the mental side of performance. That's a mistake. Visualizations and affirmations have the power to profoundly affect how we perform under pressure, and how we train every day. Use them to your benefit and get better at your craft.

ACCEPTANCE

"I don't get PTSD, I give it. I'm the carrier." - Matt Little

That was my joking response whenever anyone would ask me about the mental cost of what we did. In retrospect it was arrogant and defensive. It was also flawed thinking in some ways, and correct in others. Everything has a cost. And sooner or later it has to be paid or it will continue to accrue interest and color everything you think and feel.

I did the math prior to ever taking a life. For me that decision was always dispassionate, logical, and without guilt or remorse. I feel no trauma to this day from any of the violence I dealt to others. And I truly believe that my peace with this is appropriate morally and healthy mentally.

My personal belief is that post-traumatic stress (PTS) arising from doing violence to another happens when one of two conditions is met. One is that you weren't properly prepared mentally prior to the event. You hadn't "done the math" ahead of time. The other is if you compromised your ethics. If the violence was unnecessary or cruel then that can reverberate through your psyche and have serious negative consequences.

In my case I had in fact done the math. I had wanted to be a warrior as long as I could remember, and I come from a military and law enforcement family. I had thought through this well in advance, paid the cost up front before it could accrue mental interest. I also had thought long and hard about the right and wrong of it, the ethics of violence. I can honestly say that while I am proud of everything I have done, what I am proudest of is that I was never needlessly violent or cruel.

The cost I hadn't counted on however, has nothing to do with the things I've done or the people I've hurt and killed. What affected me was the people I couldn't save. The friends I've lost and wasn't able to protect. The victims I was too late to save. That's what haunted me and that's what I had to learn to live with.

I've learned acceptance there as well. Survivor's guilt doesn't honor the dead. It's at its heart self-pitying and counterproductive. I've learned to honor our dead by living the life they should have had. The way to honor those lost is by accepting the loss and attacking life. Pay the cost, accept the loss, and learn to truly live.

SETBACKS AND OPPORTUNITIES

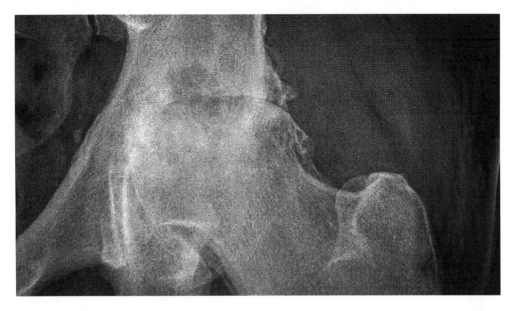

"Do not pray for an easy life, pray for the strength to endure a difficult one." - Bruce Lee

At the time of this writing, I'm waiting on my second hip replacement surgery. Both were scheduled to be done by now, but when they replaced the right one, it developed an infection and had to be redone. This then delayed the left one until they could be sure I was infection free. Just my luck, once I had been infection free long enough to schedule the second surgery, the government was more worried about Covid than non life-saving surgeries for veterans.

Because of the life I've led, I'm no stranger to injuries, surgeries, and recoveries. These are setbacks, that's true, but I've learned to look at them as opportunities. I can't work movement right now, and I can't do the big whole-body lifts in the gym, or the conditioning work I like to do. Because I need to preserve my ability to teach classes, I'm not even able to shoot any competitions until after the surgery. But this also gives me the freedom to focus on other things.

I'm going to take this time on the range to work hard on my stand-and-shoot classifier skills. I'm going to take this time in the gym to focus on prehab and rehab movements, so I will be better prepared when I return to hard workouts. And the hours I'm forced to spend resting because of the injury are being spent writing the book you're reading now. When setbacks happen, and they will eventually happen to everyone, it's what you do in response that matters. In every setback there is opportunity, if you're willing to take it.

BOOK TWO - THE BODY

INTRODUCTION - "OPERATOR YEARS"

"Teach us to give, and not count the cost." - Saint Ignatius

I was fortunate enough to remain operational until I was over 50, far longer than most in my line of work. I paid a heavy price physically though. There was a recurring joke between my SWAT medic, Brian Bardsley, and I. One year at the Special Operations Medical Conference, he attended a presentation that likened years as an operator to "dog years" and proposed that every year spent on a team was the equivalent of three years of wear and tear on the body. We did the math and realized that if this theory was correct, my joints were effectively one hundred and fourteen years old. While I am one of the fortunate ones compared to many of my friends and peers who are functionally broken, my joints often feel every day of that 114 years.

It doesn't have to be that way. If I had known then what I know now, a good portion of that wear and tear could have been prevented. Not all of it. The mission takes a toll to be sure, but our training shouldn't make us broken over time, and it all too often does. There are smarter ways to train. Ways that maximize operational longevity while still achieving high levels of fitness. Many SOF careers are ended, not because of combat injury, but because of damage from training. And that is a waste.

Tactical athletes have to maintain a level of fitness commensurate with the demands of combat. This requires training for broad general fitness. They have to be ready to sprint, climb, lift heavy objects, carry heavy loads long distances, run, jump, fight, swim, or a variety of other physically challenging tasks at a moment's notice. For law enforcement, and certain specialized military units, this is further complicated by the fact that there is no off-season. Sports athletes, even most military tactical athletes, can schedule their training to peak for a season, or a deployment, or a specific event, but law enforcement and military special operations cannot. To paraphrase Rob Shaul of the Mountain Tactical Institute, they bear the "burden of constant fitness."

So, how do we balance operational longevity with both the high levels of broad fitness required of us as well as the burden of constant fitness? Like so many other aspects of our craft, I feel like I have only recently started to truly understand how to properly train for the fitness we need. Let's take a look at the underlying principles and explore together how to properly construct an efficient and productive program for operational fitness.

NEEDS ANALYSIS

"Whatever luck I had, I made. I was never a natural athlete, but I paid my dues in sweat and concentration." - Chuck Norris

Not every tactical athlete has the same needs from their fitness program. The gap widens more when you compare the needs of the defensive-minded citizen to those of the professional soldier or police officer. There are fundamental differences as well between the fitness demands of military and law enforcement, even for SWAT officers. People often lose sight of this when they construct their fitness training programs. In fact, people often construct their programs without objectively evaluating their true needs.

The concept of needs analysis will be a recurring theme throughout the rest of this book. Unrealistic and/or unneeded expectations don't have any place in a training program, either for skill development or fitness. What level of fitness do *you* need? And you need to determine this with a fair amount of specificity. Fitness has multiple components, and many of those are at odds with each other at the higher levels of specificity. Strength & power (not the same thing), speed, agility, endurance, mobility, and others depending on which textbook you reference. There is also the questions of durability (incident rate of injury), as well as longevity of fitness.

It's unrealistic to attempt to achieve the highest levels of every fitness component, especially when fitness is not the only training or life responsibility you have. Look at the requirements of your mission set, and determine your needs from there. This applies to civilians also. Your mission set as a civilian isn't determined by an organization or unit, it's your life and goals. Are you a BJJ student and casual competition shooter? A CrossFit or Tactical Games athlete? Or just someone who wants to be able to protect themself and their loved ones?

If your fitness is part of your profession, to a large degree your mission determines your fitness needs. An urban SWAT officer who never patrols in rural settings needs the strength to carry a wounded teammate when both are wearing kit, and to stay on a perimeter position in full kit for extended periods of time, but doesn't need the endurance for twenty plus mile forced marches with heavy rucksacks. A SOF team that focuses on direct action will have a different set of fitness priorities than one that focuses on special reconnaissance.

The areas I feel are most neglected in needs analyses for "tactical athletes" are durability and longevity. This has improved since I was a young man, but needs greater emphasis still. If I could tell my 18 year old self one thing about training for fitness, it would be to prioritize those two elements over all else.

Durability is lowering the incident rate or probability of injury. This is important for several reasons. Injuries can slow or prevent completion of training, and keep you from being mission capable when needed. Injuries have a way of reoccurring over your operational lifespan, so preventing one in the first place prevents multiple potential reoccurrences over time. Many injuries have the potential to become career ending, and not just injuries due to violence. Acute and overuse injuries from training are often career enders.

Longevity is just what it sounds like. How long can I perform at this level? This is related to durability because of the cumulative effects injuries can have, but is also minimizing the hidden wear and tear on your body. My hips never had an acute injury that I knew of but the training stresses of my three decade career led to me needing both replaced in my early 50s.

Once you've done your needs analysis, then you can properly construct your training program, both to attain your necessary levels of performance, and to maintain them as long as possible.

LEVEL OF PARTICIPATION

"A pint of sweat saves a gallon of blood." - George Patton

Level of participation. How much time, effort, and expense are you willing to commit towards your goals? If the goals don't line up with your level of participation, then you're setting yourself up for failure.

What is your level of participation when it comes to physical preparedness? For the special operations soldier, or the SWAT cop, this should be an easily answered question. If that is your role, you should be all in on your strength and conditioning program. If you're on a different path though, this can become a harder question to answer.

Your needs analysis should have given you sound goals. Then you need to decipher a few things. What is the minimum amount of work I can do to achieve those goals within the timeframe I have? What is the maximum amount of work I can do towards my goals without overtraining? These are rough estimates at best. Educated guesses based on previous training and research into the science of exercise. But they at least give you a starting point.

Then you need to decide how much time and effort you are willing to dedicate towards your goals. You have to be brutally honest with yourself about this.. If your commitment doesn't meet the minimum effort needed, then you have to either scale down your goals or increase the amount of work you're willing to do. The hard truth is that while three hours of dedicated and intense effort a week can work wonders, it won't make you a CrossFit games champion. The flip side of this is that if you put out an effort that is too high for too long, based on your tolerance to exercise and the stressors of your lifestyle as a whole, you can lower performance instead of increasing it. Spend some time figuring your optimal level of commitment, and it will help you reach your goals.

STRENGTH AND POWER

"Strong people are harder to kill than weak people, and more useful in general." - Mark Rippetoe

I'm exploring strength and power first because it's arguably the most important functional attributes to develop, at least where performance is concerned. I'd argue that durability and longevity trump them in the long run for priority, but they impact performance over your career and lifetime, not in the moment. A tactical athlete doesn't need a two thousand pound powerlifting total or a twice body-weight clean and jerk, and their work capacity is crucial, but they do need to be strong and powerful above all else.

When I plan my training I build everything around the strength work. Notice I said training, not "working out." In my opinion that is an important distinction. Athletes train. Every exercise is designed to elicit a performance response. Aesthetics follow function, not the opposite.

If strength and power are vital, how do we develop them efficiently? Let's examine strength first. Large multi-joint exercises build strength the best. The basic movement patterns are squats, hip hinges, pushes, pulls, and carries. We'll discuss exercise tempo, repetition ranges, and exercise volume more in later sections. But for now what you need to know is that strength is best developed by performing three to five sets sets of one to five repetitions at 80% or better of your one repetition maximum.

Power is a bit of a different beast. Power is also called speed-strength by some exercise physiologists and coaches. That's in many respects a more precise term. For power, it's not just how much weight you move, it's also how fast you move it. The Olympic lifts are unparalleled for power gains, although plyometrics (jump training) and medicine ball throws are effective as well. For most tactical athletes, the power variations of the Olympic lifts are more than sufficient and much easier to learn than the full versions. In my opinion, three to five sets of one to three repetitions are best for this purpose.

Exercise selection. There are endless productive variations of strength exercises. As a general rule, unless you are trying to induce hypertrophy as an additional goal, avoid isolation exercises. The exceptions to that are prehabilitation/rehabilitation movements and exercises chosen to correct a muscular imbalance. Apart from that, construct your strength program around the movement patterns above plus the power variations of the clean, snatch, and jerk. A few representative examples of exercises are shown in the table below, although there are many more.

Squat	Hip Hinge	Push	Pull	Carry
Overhead Squat	Deadlift	Press	Bent Over Row	Farmers Walk
Front Squat	Trap Bar Deadlift	Bench Press	Weighted Pullup	Waiters Walk
Back Squat	Romanian Deadlift	Weighted Dip	Rack Pulls	Yoke
Goblet Squat	Good Morning	Incline Press	Dumbbell Rows	Weighted Lunges
Bulgarian Split Squat	Single Leg Deadlift	Push Press	Pullovers	Sandbag Carries

Work each of these movement patterns regularly. Add in assistance exercises only as necessary, and at a reduced intensity level. Two to three sets of eight to twelve reps for assistance exercises should be fine.

Exercise form is beyond the scope of this book, but it is vital. Seek out coaching if possible, but at the very least seek out information. There are a myriad of resources available to learn proper form. Be very sure of the quality of the information, not all of what's available is sound. There are some excellent resources in the bibliography of this book you can use as a starting point.

Loading progressions will also be discussed more in later sections, but you need to understand the two guiding principles behind planning strength progressions. One is that, over time, you want to be adding weight or doing more repetitions, or both. The second is that you cannot lift maximally every single session without your progress eventually stalling out. This is why athletes have deload weeks programmed into their training. A cyclical approach is best, where you work up to a new best lift, deload, then repeat the process. We'll go into greater detail in the section on programming.

Study strength and its development like you study the other aspects of your craft, and it will have benefits for everything else you do. Not just for your craft, but for your entire life.

CONDITIONING

"The first virtue in a soldier is endurance of fatigue; courage is only the second virtue." -
Napoleon Bonaparte

Conditioning. When I joined the army, the institutional concept of conditioning was long
distance running and road marches. Not only is that an incomplete paradigm, it was ill-suited
to the actual needs of our job. The needs of our job included moving heavy weight long
distances and multiple bursts of intense output interspersed between short periods of active
rest.

Conditioning is basically training the energy systems of your body so that your work capacity
increases. The body has three distinct energy systems used to fuel exercise, the anaerobic
alactic or phosphagen, the anaerobic lactic or glycolytic, and the aerobic or oxidative. Each
needs to be trained properly, and with different protocols than the others.

The phosphagen energy system burns your muscles' creatine phosphate for fuel. This provides
energy for short bursts of high intensity effort. This system is used in strength work, sprints,
throws, jumps, etc. Train this system by resting adequately between intense efforts lasting
less than ten seconds.

The glycolytic energy system burns glucose for fuel, creating lactic acid in the muscles as a byproduct. The lactic acid is what causes the shortness of breath and burning sensation in the muscles felt when using this system to fuel exercise. This system powers medium intensity work performed in the 10-90 second range. The efficiency of this system is what people call "muscular endurance." Thirty seconds or shorter bouts of exercise separated by thirty seconds to a minute of rest are a typical way to train the glycolytic system. The rest should feel insufficient for full recovery. Training this system properly not only increases work output, but will also shorten the recovery time needed for subsequent efforts.

The aerobic energy system burns oxygen for fuel. This powers low intensity and long duration efforts. The forty minute five mile runs of my youth in the army are a perfect example of this. There are some subtleties that can make training this energy system more effective, but that's the heart of it. Sustained lower intensity effort lasting in excess of two minutes, and often far longer. One of my favorite ways to train this energy systems is to perform 400-1600 meter intervals of running, cycling, or rowing with moderate rest in between. The rest should once again feel insufficient for full recovery.

Based on your needs analysis, you have to decide what balance of training these energy systems is appropriate for you. However you set your priorities though, don't completely neglect any of the three, all are important.

SPEED AND AGILITY

"There is no greater fame for a man than that which he wins with his footwork or the skill of his hands." - Homer

This is an area of training sorely neglected by most "tactical athletes." Once I started working speed and agility drills into my training because of USPSA competition, I saw immediate benefits in my performance at work. Work these into your physical training and watch your footwork and movement become more efficient and effective.

An important key point to remember here. Agility and speed work is not conditioning. It should be performed fresh and with sufficient rest to recover between sets. Treat it more like skill development than a CrossFit metcon.

The first type of agility work I recommend is movement preparation drills. Movement prep can be done as part of your warmup on a frequent basis, as it doesn't tax your recovery as much as the other types do. The exercises here include wall marches, quick feet drills, and arm swings.

The second category I like to do is agility ladder drills. These can be done relatively frequently as well, although less often than movement prep work. There are an endless variety of these, and all are valuable for building rapid direction changes and quick foot turnover. The ladders themselves are inexpensive, and there are numerous videos freely available in the internet showing the drills.

Cone drills are the next broad category of speed and agility drills I recommend. Much like ladder work, stackable agility cones are inexpensive and readily available, generally, these are more taxing than ladder work, and should be done with somewhat less frequency. These drills are also widely available on the internet.

The last major category of speed and agility drills I use is sprint work. This is not the same as using intervals for conditioning. Ensure a very careful and thorough warmup, otherwise the risk of a muscle pull can be high. Once warmed up, each sprint is a maximal effort with adequate rest in between for full recovery. Use sprint work sparingly and for low repetitions, varying the sprint length from workout-to-workout between thirty and ninety yards.

Research these drills thoroughly and implement them in an intelligent and structured manner and they will have a profound effect on your athletic performance.

MOBILITY

"Flexibility is the key to stability." - John Wooden

Flexibility or, more properly, mobility, is the ability of your joints and muscles to move freely throughout their range of motion. It's key to powerful athletic movement, and essential for preventing injuries, especially long-term. It's also probably the most neglected area of fitness for "tactical athletes."

The traditional way of thinking of flexibility, now thankfully out of fashion, focused solely on passive ranges of motion, and only addressed muscle length. Functional mobility is dynamic, and requires strength at the end ranges of movement. In order to develop we have to look beyond just a few perfunctory static stretches at the end of a training session. We have to address our ranges of motion with several different modalities.

Rather than endless static stretches, which have been shown to be inefficient for developing lasting flexibility, we can use isometrics to rapidly and drastically achieve long term increases in range of motion. Known by exercise physiologists as proprioceptive neuromuscular facilitation (PNF), this stretching technique is far more effective than traditional static relaxation techniques and takes up less training time. The technique is relatively straightforward once you understand how to do it. Hold a stretch at the maximum range without pain, then tense the muscle being stretched as hard as you can for three to five seconds. Relax and you'll find you can move further into the stretch. Continue until you can't stretch further, and then hold one last contraction for fifteen to thirty seconds. Do three to five sets of this three to four times a week at the end of your strength and conditioning sessions and you will make drastic improvements in flexibility.

Another highly effective protocol for increasing flexibility, strength, and the end ranges of motion is loaded stretching. Controlled repetitions through a full range of motion under light load. Exercises like seated cable good mornings, dumbbell pullovers, kettlebell arm bars, and stiff-leg deadlifts lend themselves well to this. They should be done for 1-2 sets 10-20 repetitions once weekly. Do not do these rapidly or ballistically, the risk of injury is too high.

PNF and loaded stretching will build strength at the end ranges of motion and improve our passive flexibility. We still need dynamic flexibility for performance. That is our range of motion during actual movement, not just in a static position. We build that by performing controlled but increasingly rapid leg and arm swings throughout our full range of motion, leading or lifting the limb rather than throwing it. Single sets of twelve repetitions daily, as part of your warmup before your strength and conditioning sessions or in the morning on rest days are sufficient. In about eight weeks your dynamic range of motion should approximate your current passive flexibility.

The last piece of the mobility puzzle is our joint and muscle mechanics themselves. Using implements to loosen adhesions in fascia, using resistance bands to reset joint position and loosen stiff joint capsules. This is an area I wish I had been aware of in my youth. If I had, I'm convinced I could have avoided much of the joint damage I now have. This is put into your training as a recovery practice, and if need be as a rehabilitation or prehabilitation practice as well. This is a complex topic, and beyond the scope of this book, but the information is out there and freely available if you look for it.

Research and implement mobility techniques. They will improve your performance greatly. But more importantly they will increase how long you can perform at your best. Most importantly perhaps, when your career is done, they will improve your quality of life.

DURABILITY

"Durability is part of what makes a great athlete." - Bill Russell

Managing your durability, your susceptibility to injury, is in my opinion every bit as important as your athletic performance. I've seen many people who perform at a high level when healthy and rested fail out of selection processes because of injuries. I've also seen many operational personnel suffer career ending injuries during training or missions. Durability is essential for anyone operational, but it's also essential for your long-term quality of life.

How do we train for durability? We need to achieve and maintain functional levels of mobility of course, but there's other attributes we need to achieve in order to build our resistance to acute and chronic injuries. We need to develop tendon and ligament strength that matches our muscular strength. We also need to maintain a healthy fascia, preventing adhesions that can impair performance in the short term, and contribute to injury in the long term. Lastly, we need to develop and maintain optimal levels of joint health, addressing joint space and stiffness in the joint capsules. So how can we do all that?

Tendon and ligament strength can lag behind muscular strength, and set us up for injury. To strengthen them, include plyometrics, eccentric work, isometrics, and heavy partials into your strength training. These techniques should be used relatively sparingly, and unless you have a coach, I wouldn't emphasize isometrics or heavy partials. Plyometric work can be done a couple of times weekly, but the eccentric work should be periodized as part of your training cycles. We'll go into more detail on that in the section on programming our strength and conditioning.

The fascia, the membrane of connective tissue surrounding our muscles, can be prone to adhesions, where the fascia no longer allows the muscle to glide free because of scar tissue causing the two structures to stick together. Aggressive massage is the best treatment to break up these adhesions and regain free movement. This can be done yourself using implements like lacrosse balls and foam rollers to put targeted pressure on the adhesion. The implements and exercises can be readily found on the internet, as well as in some of the sources I list in this book's bibliography. No matter how attentive you are though, it can be difficult to maintain fascial health without periodic massage therapy from a qualified practitioner. Seek out a good provider and use their services on a regular basis.

Let's look at the joints themselves. We need to maintain proper alignment so that we avoid impingements and a healthy joint space to allow the tissues inside the joint to stay healthy. There are a set of exercises known as banded distractions that are the most effective way of addressing these issues yourself. You'll need to research these, a good starting point is the works of Kelly Starrett, which can also be found in the bibliography.

Don't neglect your joint health. I am completely convinced that I could have avoided multiple surgeries if I had known about and done these joint health modalities as a young man.

LONGEVITY

"A long life is a life well spent." - Leonardo Da Vinci

Longevity. How long can you perform at your best, and how can you maintain functional fitness and a high quality of life longer into old age? Part of the answer lies in prioritizing mobility and durability as much as we do the other elements of physical training.

Because of the martial arts practice of my youth, I was very flexible. But I didn't stay on top of it, and I didn't have a plan in place to address well-rounded mobility and joint health. I'm convinced that if I had known about and prioritized this as much as I prioritized strength and power, I could have avoided a lot of the injuries I've been through.

Nutrition and supplementation matter for long term health and fitness as well. This is another area I wish I had focused more on when I was younger. You can eat poor food choices and still perform well in the short term, as long as your macronutrients, the protein, fats and carbohydrates you consume, are in the right proportions. Over the long term though, the quality of food you eat and the supplements you take matter a lot.

Rest. This is another area I wish I had paid more attention to in my youth. I got so used to going on small amounts of sleep that it became a habit. There are times in the military and law enforcement trades where that it is essential to perform on low amounts of sleep. If you make that a customary practice though, it has extremely negative long-term effects. Make it a priority to get seven to nine hours of uninterrupted sleep daily whenever possible and you will notice a difference, especially as you get older.

The last area I'd like to touch on is recovery and rehabilitation/prehabilitation practices. I was dismissive of many of these when I was younger, but I shouldn't have been. Physical therapy, massage therapy, meditation practices, all of these things have a beneficial effect. Think of it as having a gunsmith go over your firearm, or a mechanic perform maintenance on your car. We can do a lot ourselves, but we can't address everything without assistance from professionals in those areas.

Prioritize these areas as much as you do strength and power. In the long run you'll be glad you did.

PROGRAMMING

"Wisdom is always an overmatch for strength." - Phil Jackson

Programming our strength and conditioning work is the key to achieving our performance goals. We can work hard, pick the right exercises, get enough rest, fuel ourselves with good nutrition, but if we don't plan and template our training intelligently we will never reach our true potential.

In the early portion of our training careers a linear progression alone—where we simply add more weight, speed, distance, or repetitions each workout—is sufficient to improve performance. Over time though, as we get closer to our athletic potential and require ever more training stimulus to produce further adaptations, gains in strength and performance will flatline unless we manipulate the training variables in a more sophisticated fashion. This planned manipulation of training variables is known as periodization by coaches and exercise physiologists.

Periodization, which has its roots in the general adaptation syndrome theory of Dr. Hans Selye and the athletic training methods of the early twentieth century Olympians, was first codified in its simplest form of linear periodization by Soviet physiologist Leo Matveyev in 1964. Newer more complex models of periodization, including undulating, block, and conjugate have been utilized in athletic training since.

Linear periodization is simply lowering training volume over time as training intensity increases. Undulating periodization involving manipulation of the training variables in waves. The classic example of this is heavy, medium, and light workouts in the same week. Block periodization is exactly what it sounds like, distinct training blocks focusing on strength, speed, power, endurance, or other training goals. Conjugate periodization, popular in powerlifting, is alternating between workouts focusing on two separate aspects of performance, typically strength and power or speed.

Periodization models are all divided into blocks of time known as cycles. The longest is the macrocycle. For a competitive athlete this is typically from the end of one competition season to the end of the next. For a soldier this could be from the end of one deployment to the end of the next. The macrocycle is divided up into mesocycles, which are typically between three and eight weeks long. Each mesocycle is further divided up into microcycles of a week or two in length.

The best periodization scheme for you depends on your needs analysis. An SF soldier during the war could treat his deployments as the "competition season" and use traditional linear or block periodization models with planned periods of detraining much like a football player or an Olympic athlete. A police officer who bears the burden of "constant preparedness" would benefit better from an undulating or conjugate type training template where all the aspects of performance are worked on simultaneously.

Understand too that this level of planning isn't strictly necessary at first. But the closer you get to the limits of your potential performance the narrower the window of effective training for further improvement gets. And the more you understand how to manipulate training variables, the more efficient your training is, and the more rapid your improvement will be.

The best way to master this is to research thoroughly. There is a wealth of information on various programs freely available on the internet, and several excellent books are listed in my bibliography. I'm including my current programming as an example. Right now I'm recovering from surgery, and my current goals are different than those of a prospective SWAT officer, or an SFAS candidate, but the process of programming is the same although the end result training template is different.

In my current program I'm using block periodization based on recovery from injury. Once I'm back at a performance level I feel is appropriate, I'll switch to an undulating or conjugate template. If my only concern was USPSA competition I might stay with a block periodization scheme timed to fit into the competitive season. The variables I'm manipulating in the strength work are set/rep schemes, tempo, and rest periods. Sets and repetitions should be a familiar concept for everyone, and rest should be self explanatory.

Strength & Conditioning Template

	Exercise	Block One				Block Two				Block Three				Block Four			
		Sets	Reps	Tempo	Rest	Sets	Reps	Tempo	Rest	Sets	Reps	Tempo	Rest	Sets	Reps	Tempo	Rest
	Joint Rotations	1	15	—	N/A	1	15	—	N/A	1	15	—	N/A	1	15	—	N/A
	Arm Swings	3	15	—	N/A	3	15	—	N/A	3	15	—	N/A	3	15	—	N/A
	Leg Swings	3	15	—	N/A	3	15	—	N/A	3	15	—	N/A	3	15	—	N/A
	Prehab/Rehab Routine	1	15	2-2-2-2	N/A	1	15	2-2-2-2	N/A	1	15	2-2-2-2	N/A	1	15	2-2-2-2	N/A
A	Movement Prep Drill	3	10	1-1-1-1	30 sec	3	10	1-1-1-1	30 sec	3	10	1-1-1-1	30 sec	3	10	1-1-1-1	30 sec
B	Footwork Drill	1-3	1-10	1-1-1-1	30 sec	1-3	1-10	1-1-1-1	30 sec	1-3	1-10	1-1-1-1	30 sec	1-3	1-10	1-1-1-1	30 sec
A	Sprints	1-3	3-5	—	2-3 min	1-3	3-5	—	2-3 min	1-3	3-5	—	2-3 min	1-3	3-5	—	2-3 min
B	Plyometrics	1-3	3-5	—	2-3 min	1-3	3-5	—	2-3 min	1-3	3-5	—	2-3 min	1-3	3-5	—	2-3 min
	Olympic Lift Variation	5	1-3	1-1-1-5	2-3 min	5	1-3	1-1-1-5	2-3 min	5	1-3	1-1-1-5	2-3 min	5	1-3	1-1-1-5	2-3 min
	Lower Body Pull	2	12-15	1-0-1-0	30 sec	3	8-12	3-1-3-1	1 min	5	5-7	3-1-3-1	2-3 min	5	1-4	3-1-3-1	3-5 min
A	Lower Body Push	2	12-15	1-0-1-0	30 sec	3	8-12	3-1-3-1	1 min	5	5-7	3-1-3-1	2-3 min	5	1-4	3-1-3-1	3-5 min
	Upper Body Pull	2	12-15	1-0-1-0	30 sec	3	8-12	3-1-3-1	1 min	5	5-7	3-1-3-1	2-3 min	5	1-4	3-1-3-1	3-5 min
B	Upper Body Push	2	12-15	1-0-1-0	30 sec	3	8-12	3-1-3-1	1 min	5	5-7	3-1-3-1	2-3 min	5	1-4	3-1-3-1	3-5 min
	Assistance Exercises	1-3X3	8-12	3-1-3-1	1 min	1-3X3	8-12	3-1-3-1	1 min	1-3X3	8-12	3-1-3-1	1 min	1-3X3	8-12	3-1-3-1	1 min
	Conditioning	20 min steady state				8-12 min metcon				5-8 min intervals				1-3 min metcon			
	Mobility	Distract, PNF/LS, Roll				Distract, PNF/LS, Roll				Distract, PNF/LS, Roll				Distract, PNF, Roll			

Tempo is the speed of movement in a given exercise. The shorthand for tempo is a series of four numbers. The first number is the eccentric or lowering portion of the exercise, the second number is the pause, the third is the concentric or lifting portion, and the fourth is the second pause.

I'm also manipulating the duration and intensity of my conditioning work to complement where I'm at in the strength progression and rebuild my conditioning to pre-injury levels. Once I go back to an undulating periodization template the conditioning will be more well-rounded, but for now I'm concerned with building a solid foundation.

This plan is unique to my needs and situation, but the planning process itself is similar regardless of your needs and current level of performance. Like other plans, you have to be flexible in implementation. The data you get from your performance enables you to course correct along the way and optimize it for your situation and goals. Learn to coach yourself and you'll quickly improve.

NUTRITION

"Remember that nutrition is 90%; exercise is 10%." - Vince Gironda

Proper nutrition is crucial for health and performance. This can seem far more complex a topic than it needs to be, primarily because there are so many competing nutritional concepts vying for our attention in our society. Paleo, zone, keto, intermittent fasting, IIFYM, and more are presented as the magical catch-all cures for health, body composition, and performance.

Most of the recent dietary approaches have their merits. Paleo avoids processed foods in favor of fresh ones which is a demonstrably healthier way to eat. The zone has a far better macronutrient (protein, carbs, and fat) ratio than the typical modern high carb diet. Ketogenic diets and intermittent fasting can rapidly improve body composition primarily because they are easy ways to limit caloric intake. Macronutrient counting can ensure that you get adequate protein without overindulgence of carbohydrates or fats.

I've tried all of these approaches, and more. I now believe in a more balanced approach. I count macros, especially protein but carbohydrates and fats as well. The weakness of the IIFYM approach though lies in the name itself. If it fits your macros. In other words low quality food choices are fine as long as your protein, carbohydrate, and fat intake is in the right proportion and amounts. This doesn't take micronutrients (vitamins and minerals) into account though, and for that reason in the long run for health and performance food quality matters. I don't follow either the zone or ketogenic macronutrient ratios anymore, but I know people for whom those approaches work very well. This is an area that appears to have individual variation, so experiment with your intake ratios and determine your best approach.

Regardless of carbohydrate and fat ratios, I strongly believe in a relatively high protein intake for athletes. When I am in hard training I like to get a gram of protein per pound of body weight daily. Carbs and fats can be played with, with either moderate carbs and low fat or moderate fat and low carb approaches being viable, but both need to be kept within reason.

I eat 4-6 meals a day because for me this ensures optimal body composition and performance. Having said that, intermittent fasting (IF) is a very successful approach for many people. My wife Angela has used IF with great success and functions well on it. This is another area where you need to experiment and use hard data to determine the best approach for you.

For micronutrients, while in theory high quality food choices should be sufficient, I rely on supplementation to ensure I get what my body needs for health and performance. I'll talk more about that in the next section.

SUPPLEMENTATION

"Our food should be our medicine and our medicine should be our food." – Hippocrates

There are really three categories of supplements. One is micronutrients taken to ensure proper nutrition. Another is food supplements intended to aid in proper macronutrient intake and timing. The last are supplements that have performance enhancing or therapeutic effects.

For the first broad category, the obvious starting point is a high quality multivitamin and mineral supplement. I also like to take additional vitamin C and D, as well as type II cartilage and Omega-3 fatty acids. That's pretty much it for the first category, it's relatively simple, inexpensive, and easily accomplished.

The second category is also relatively straightforward, although peri-workout supplementation, the supplements taken around your training, can be a bit more complex. In general, protein supplements can help with ensuring you get enough protein to support hard training. Not all protein supplements are created equal, but there are plenty of affordable high-quality options. Peri-workout nutrition can and should be more sophisticated. This is the time where amino acid and carbohydrates combined with complete protein sources can have a beneficial effect. There are numerous quality supplements designed for just this purpose, and while they tend to be more expensive than simple protein sources, their value is worth the expense.

The last category is by far the most complex, and the most susceptible to misinformation and bad science. It includes performance enhancing drugs (PEDs) and other drugs, and designer or naturally-occurring alternatives. It also includes substances we don't normally associate with PEDs that in fact are. The caffeine in a pre-workout drink is in fact a drug. This doesn't mean we should avoid caffeine or other substances necessarily. The more honest we are about the nature of these substances though, the more informed our decisions about their use are.

I use a pre-workout drink, but only as needed. Over-reliance on stimulants in my experience is counter-productive. Used sparingly they can aid your training, but if used habitually they can contribute to fatigue and lessened training intensity. Creatine and nitric oxide products are popular, but in my experience they do not provide much benefit. What does help if needed, done legally under a doctor's care of course, is testosterone replacement therapy, thyroid supplementation, and, if you can afford the expense, growth hormone replacement therapy. There are effective grey-market and off label alternatives that work as well, but that's beyond the scope of this book, and I am certainly not giving either legal or medical advice.

The most fascinating part of this third category to me is the ongoing research into cutting edge nootropics and life extension therapies, in particular support for gene expression and telomere length retention. For this, as well as all other aspects of supplementation for performance, health, and longevity, research critically and well. Draw your own conclusions and implement them. The longer you try to maintain optimal performance, or even quality of life, the more important proper supplementation becomes.

TRAINING EQUIPMENT

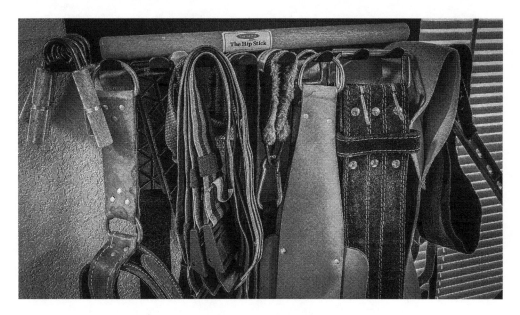

"If you fail to prepare, you're prepared to fail." – Mark Spitz

Regardless of whether you train at home, at a commercial gym, or at a facility run by your unit or organization, there are some items that will help you optimize your strength and conditioning sessions.

Some of these are so useful as to be for all intents and purposes essential. A sturdy weightlifting belt for heavy squats and deadlifts. Weightlifting wrist straps for when you don't want your grip strength to become the limiting factor in an exercise. High quality elastic bands for prehab/rehab and isolation work. A foam roller and some lacrosse balls for self massage.

There are other items that I think are valuable enough to consider keeping in your gym bag. An elastic hip band for squat warmups. Knee and elbow wraps. Heavy duty grip trainers. A dip belt for weighted dips and pull-ups. A "sling-shot" elastic band for bench presses. An agility ladder and soccer cones for footwork drills.

You don't need to pursue every new fad for exercise equipment, but there's a lot out there that can contribute in a positive way to your strength and conditioning work. Be discerning, but don't be afraid to invest in your training.

GYM EQUIPMENT NEEDS

"The iron never lies to you." - Henry Rollins

I'm a big fan of a fully equipped home gym. The initial financial outlay may seem high, but it's an investment into your health and performance. And unlike a gym membership there's no recurring fees. Not to mention the time saved and consistency gained by working out at home.

The absolute bare essentials for an effective strength training program are a heavy duty power rack, a sturdy bench, a good olympic bar, and a sufficient supply of weight plates. The power rack allows for heavy lifts in safety, as well as being a convenient centerpiece to build your home gym around. You can add on to it with accessories like a pull-up bar, dip handles, a landmine attachment, plate storage, and even a high-low pulley setup. You can also hang rings or a suspension trainer from it. For plates, I like a mix of rubber bumper plates for Olympic lifts and iron for power lifts.

I have a lifting platform also, and find it really useful for not just Olympic lifts and heavy deadlifts, but kettlebell work as well. While we are on the subject of kettlebells, you will definitely get a lot of use out of a good assortment of kettlebells and dumbbells. If you can only have one, I'd go with the kettlebells, as they're much more versatile than the dumbbells. Another piece of equipment that is very valuable is a Glute-Ham Developer (GHD) bench.

If you don't have easy access to either a commercial gym, setting up a home gym is essential. Even if you do, I think it's worth it to be able to train effectively at home. Take your strength and conditioning into your own hands, and you'll maximize your performance.

BOOK THREE - THE CRAFT

INTRODUCTION - "THE BLUE AND THE GREEN"

"Policeman are soldiers who act alone; soldiers are policeman who act in unison." - Herbert Spencer

I had a rather unconventional and unique career in many ways. When I went through selection, immediately following the battle of Mogadishu, SOF was basically benched, doing little more than JCETs and FIDs, training exercises in other countries. I had briefly been a cop already, following my time on active duty. I was working in law enforcement when I re-enlisted in the 20th Special Forces Group in the National Guard and prepared for selection. Once I graduated the Q-Course, I had what seemed like a difficult decision at the time. Stay on active duty, or stay in 20th Group and continue a civilian career in law enforcement.

I opted to join the Chicago Police Department and remain in 20th. If this had been after 9-11 instead of before, I'm sure my decision would have been different. In retrospect though, I lucked into the best possible career path I could have ever chosen for myself. I was able to bounce back and forth between the police department and SF, and even took a year's leave of absence to work for the State Department in Iraq as a contractor. This dual career gave me a breadth and depth of experience I never would have had otherwise.

From SF I got the most extensive and comprehensive professional development and training possible, far beyond what I ever received in law enforcement. I got to train US and foreign personnel in a variety of countries. I led American and foreign troops in combat. I learned skills well outside of the normal soldier's realm, espionage and surveillance, breaching, CQB, and so much more. Even more importantly, I was allowed to train and fight alongside giants. Heroes every bit the equal of anyone from Chaucer, Mallory, or Homer. The finest group of people I have ever known.

But I got so many priceless experiences from the police department as well. I enjoyed an autonomy of action that would be hard to find even in the most plum of active duty SF assignments. I was able to work undercover, to investigate homicides and robberies, to conduct a sheer volume of entries and clears that combat experience in the military is hard pressed to match. I worked federal conspiracy cases against gang members and hunted down fugitives. I supervised detectives and SWAT officers. And although the conflicts were lower level than military engagements, I never would have matched the sheer volume of fighting I saw as a cop in the military alone. As the capstone to my police career I was able to bring the lessons learned from both careers to the Chicago PD SWAT team, where I finished up my career as the training coordinator.

Now that my retirement job is teaching firearms and tactics, I am incredibly grateful for the experiences of both careers and the lessons learned from each. It has put me in a unique position as an instructor where I can draw solidly from the lessons I learned from each, and contribute to the next generation of both professions, as well as civilians who depend on me to teach them lessons they have no opportunity to learn otherwise.

EXPERIENCE

"You need experience to gain wisdom" - Albert Einstein

Experience. What kind of experience and how much of it matters? This topic is often a heated debate in firearms and tactics training. And it's really not such a simple question, is it?

We just closed out two decades of the GWOT. Our special operations units have had an unprecedented operational tempo. The lessons learned from that experience have created a level of institutional knowledge in the special operations community that is in my opinion at least the equal of any warrior class in history.

Also, the cold hard truth is that any able-bodied person who wanted to get into the fray has had the opportunity to. There have been Wall Street traders, rock stars, and professional athletes who walked away from their careers to become Rangers and Green Berets. For those with stable careers, there are reserve component Special Forces groups. Anyone who wanted to be a warrior has had ample opportunity.

This honestly gives those of us who chose that path little patience sometimes with people who teach gunfighting who don't have that experience. Sometimes that's fair. And sometimes it's not. Those who chose a different path can still have expertise. I have learned the most about shooting from people who have never been in a gunfight. The same can be said for many other skills. But tactics aren't skills. They are the application of skill in conflict.

So if experience is important for teaching tactics, how do we judge that experience? I had a seasoned SWAT officer who has been in several gunfights as a member of the team argue one of the single most basic principles of CQB in an AAR once. On paper, he was experienced. In reality he hadn't learned the most fundamental lessons from anything he had done. Exchanges like this are also why most SOF veterans, myself included, tend to view police experience as secondary to combat. At least where tactics are concerned. Especially because of the differences in intensity and volume between the two. That bias isn't always fair either. The best CQB operator and instructor on my old SWAT team had no military service, but he intuitively understood tactics, learned from every run he did, and could teach others.

So, experience matters. And not all gunfighting experience is of equal value. But what experience matters for is context. Not all those with experience learned from it. And even fewer can teach others how to do what they can do. Does the instructor have knowledge worth passing on, and can they give you their lessons learned without you having to pay the same price? That's what matters.

CAVEAT EMPTOR

"Let the buyer beware." - Roman Common Law

Thanks to the internet there is a proliferation of open-source material on tactics the likes of which has never before existed. In many ways this is valuable. The serious student of the craft can pick up nuances and details from other's approaches to solving tactical problems. But the serious student has experience and an educated eye. The beginner, or even someone with experience whose professional path has not involved conflict with determined and trained adversaries, can easily be seduced by flashy tactics based on theory. And there is so much out there that is either based in theory or sloppily executed without proper understanding.

The cold hard truth though is that hunting armed men is a time for practicality, ruthlessness, and precision developed through hard-earned skill. There is no shortcut, no "magic technique," no way to stack the odds in your favor without putting in the difficult work required as an individual and a team. Caveat emptor, buyer beware, holds true when seeking out tactical knowledge as well. So how do we evaluate what we see regarding tactics?

CQB, MOUT, or SUT, the principles remain the same. Interlocking fields of fire, 360 degree security, maintaining initiative, communication, movement, and so on. CQB, at its heart, is small unit tactics in a compressed time and space. Finding, fixing, and flanking are as relevant now as they were in Greece and Rome. The one-on-one civilian or LE gunfight is in principle no different than a duel in feudal Japan or a gunfight in the Old West.

Having said that, technically we are probably at the historical height of the warrior's craft. There are individuals with a huge amount of direct combat experience at the highest levels and institutions with a collective amount of experience that is historically unprecedented. So while the principles are historic and universal, the understanding of their application is quite possibly at its zenith.

There is really no reason, given the current amount of legitimate teachers who've actually fought, not to seek out instruction from those who've actually used their teachings in gunfights, whether at home or overseas. Shooting is different, that's an athletic skill. But learning fighting is best done by finding a teacher whose been in a lot of fights. And most importantly, a teacher who understands why they prevailed, what they did wrong, and studied their craft to perfect it.

This applies no less when evaluating information received through the internet. Where did the person learn what their showing? Did they do it for real against a determined adversary willing to kill them? Does it look similar to what you see from those at the top of the craft, SMU and SOF veterans? Because if it doesn't and it hasn't been tested where it counts, it should be evaluated very skeptically and critically before implementing any of it into your personal or professional doctrine. Caveat emptor, buyer beware.

PERSPECTIVE

"Research your own experience. Absorb what is useful, reject what is useless, add what is essentially your own." - Bruce Lee

Experience is extremely relevant to training and instruction. But its relevance lies in perspective. Without the correct perspective it's difficult to discern what is practically effective from what appears sound in theory. Without experience, sub-optimal tactics and techniques can be seductive, leading your training down the wrong path. This is a tale all too familiar in the martial arts world, especially before tests of style such as the UFC became popular. It is also astonishingly prevalent in the tactical world as well, even in military and LE circles. Especially when adapting TTPs to a different operational environment without the proper perspective.

All too often tactics become dogma and technique becomes religion. The principles underlying sound tactics and techniques are universal, but the application of those principles varies depending on the operational environment and the individual applying them. You have to use the perspective of your own experience to develop your own best application of those principles in any given situation.

Individuals and their experiences vary widely. And experiences only have value if they contribute to growth and understanding. I've known plenty of cops who repeated the exact same year without growth or development twenty or more times. That's not twenty years of experience. That is one year repeated twenty times. I've known individuals with multiple gunfights who had no true understanding of why they prevailed and their adversaries did not. They failed to gain perspective from their experience.

The other common failing is assuming your perspective is universal. This is a frequent flaw in highly intelligent and educated people who assume that their expertise in one area of knowledge carries over somehow to all other fields of endeavor. It's no less prevalent in the tactical community though. There is a huge commonality between GWOT experience and police work, but there are also vast differences. Indeed, there are vast differences between one individual's experiences and perspective even in the same profession.

My combat experience is not the same as everyone else's, and neither is my police experience. I am proud of my accomplishments and experiences, and feel I have many valuable lessons to pass on. It would be a staggering act of hubris on my part however if I thought only my perspective was the correct one, only my experiences valuable. And I would forever limit my development if I cut myself off from other's lessons learned or blindly followed one perspective.

Research and learn from yours and others' experiences and perspectives. Put tactics and techniques to the test. Absorb what is useful and valuable, regardless of its origin. Reject what has no use, no matter its source. And add what is yours, what comes from your lessons learned. The hard earned perspective of your own experience.

MASTERY AND INSTRUCTION

"We should remember that one man is much the same as another, and that he is best who is trained in the severest school." - Thucydides

In Special Forces, cross training is prioritized on the team. Medics teach the rest of us TCCC, Engineers teach us breaching, Weapon Sergeants run live fire ranges, and so on. We are all expected to be competent in each area. Competence however is not mastery, far from it. No one person could achieve mastery in as many skills as we were expected to maintain competence in.

I see tactics instructors, some very well known, teaching subjects they have not personally mastered. Performance shooting can be learned without ever being in a gunfight, and in my opinion is best learned from the competitive arena, but tactics is a different story. Mastery requires not only study, but experience.

At one time, before the towers fell, there had been enough time between wars that most tactical knowledge was academic. In our current situation, after two decades of war, that is no longer the case. Academic knowledge can help prepare you, but it is no substitute for experiential knowledge. Would you learn boxing from a coach who had never fought? To learn how to fight, you need to learn from a fighter. Gunfighting is no different.

I personally will not teach something I haven't done operationally at a high level. If I'm contacted for TCCC training, or a sniper course, I'll organize and facilitate it, but I'll hire someone I know who is a subject matter expert to teach it. I've done TCCC but I'm not an 18D and I'm not an expert. I've made long range rifle shots, but I'm not a SOTIC graduate and it was never my job. Now, if you want pistol or carbine shooting, combatives, or CQB, I'm happy to teach any of those, as well as fighting around vehicles. I've studied and practiced these things extensively, and done all of those things in conflict either at home or overseas, or both.

And that, for me, is my dividing line. If I don't have both a deep study of and practical experience in a given topic, I won't teach it. Without personal mastery of a skill, instruction of it becomes purely academic.

EQUIPMENT

"It's not about what the equipment does, it's about what you can do through that equipment. That's where the soul is." - Richie Hawtin

I'm old enough to remember what it was like before the proliferation of gear we have now was available. I remember the days of duct tape, gutted parachute cord, and weak flashlights hose clamped to rifles. When everything had to be heavily modified to function at all. I've watched kit get lighter and more ergonomic, and weapons get customizable and modular. And this is a good thing. As I say in my classes when I'm asked about the custom pistols and rifles I prefer, "You can't buy skill, but you can buy performance." There's a danger in forever chasing performance improvements by purchasing the latest and greatest weapons and kit, however.

It's indisputable that being properly equipped makes you more effective. And I've always believed that a professional in any field should have a professional's tools. Experiment with your kit and weapons just as you experiment in your technical development. Optimize them for you, find your personal best setup.

And much like technical development, this is a never-ending process. You will always be tweaking and adjusting your kit to make it better. Don't be afraid to streamline and be minimal. I've known operators who overloaded themselves with equipment they never needed and impaired their performance by doing so. Mobility and speed matter, and less is usually better than more.

Another hallmark of the professional is their maintenance of their tools. For your kit and weapons to perform for you they have to be properly cleaned and maintained. Take pride in your equipment. Treat its care as if your life depends on it, because it could.

Never forget that capability comes from skill and knowledge, not gear. Software trumps hardware, and highly-developed skill overcomes equipment disparity. Put your efforts into mastering your craft, and seek out new kit and weapons only when there is a legitimate improvement from doing so.

EVERY DAY CARRY

"Man is a tool-using animal. Without tools he is nothing, with tools he is all." - Thomas Carlyle

What I carry everyday varies. Now that I am retired, my needs analysis is different than it once was. When I was still an active law enforcement officer, I needed more items of kit on my person than I do now. Now I can be more streamlined and still be sufficiently prepared for likely contingencies. This is more in line with most civilian CCL holders' needs. With what is going on currently in our country, I may stage more items off-body in my vehicle, or opt for my full-size pistol instead of my compact based on where I will be and what recent events have been. The basics remain fairly constant though.

The basics are, of course, a firearm and a spare magazine. I am large enough to comfortably carry a full size pistol concealed, so my go-to is my carry-comped 2011. It gives me twenty-one rounds of 9mm in a high performing and reliable pistol. I carry AIWB (appendix inside the waist band) for concealment. If I'm going to be driving long distances, running a quick errand, or if I'm dressed for extremely hot weather, I'll sometimes carry my compact 2011 instead. It's a single stack, so it is much slimmer and lighter than my full-size 2011s. The compact also gets worn AIWB as well. It's a comfortable pistol to conceal and shoots well, but it has less performance and capacity than the Staccato XC. I usually carry a spare magazine also. More because of malfunction clearances than the likelihood of a reload being necessary under fire. I use a NeoMag for ease of concealment here.

I also typically carry a small fixed-blade knife. Employing a folding knife under stress while entangled with an adversary can be problematic. A fixed blade solves this issue and is comfortable to conceal when worn properly. My go-to knife at the moment is from Skallywag Tactical. It's a "ring knife" which offers significant advantages for concealment and employment. Another must have EDC item is a small flashlight. There are numerous affordable, small, and powerful options for EDC flashlights available. The last common category of EDC kit is medical. Now that I am retired, I no longer carry any sort of IFAK on my person. I do keep full medical kits in all my family's vehicles.

What is most important to remember, though, is that kit is useless without skill, and both are useless without awareness. Seek out reputable training, practice your skills, and cultivate a mindset of relaxed awareness. Those are the things that carry the day.

AFFECTATION

"Affectation is an awkward and forced imitation of what should be genuine and easy." - John Locke

Affectation. It's an easy and seductive trap to fall into, especially in the early stages of training. I've had to undo its influences on my tactics and techniques myself. Just like the affectation and contrived artificial movements found in classical martial arts vanished once the testing ground of MMA became commonplace, the crucible of the GWOT has eliminated much of it from the higher levels of training in shooting and tactics.

It has taken me years to eliminate it from my shooting. The excess tension and rigidly locked structure I was taught as a young Green Beret has finally given way to a more relaxed and natural way of shooting that is far more effective. In the same vein, the years of putting hands on countless violent people as a cop changed the way I strike and grapple from the stylized Karate, Judo, and Aikido I studied as a young man into a more natural and efficient way of fighting.

I still see artificial movements being taught in the law enforcement community. Unnatural ready positions, rigid shooting structure, an over-reliance on unorthodox shooting positions without a valid context. Avoid these in your practice at all costs. They will invariably lead you down dead ends in your training journey and will take much more effort to eliminate than they did to adopt.

There are myriad subtleties to proper tactics and techniques, but those subtleties make them more natural and effective, not flashy and artificial. Eliminate unnecessary movements and artificial postures at all costs. The act of instilling effective technique is one of elimination and simplification, not complication and excess.

LIVE TECHNIQUES

"A fixed hand is a dead hand; a hand that does not become fixed is alive. It is necessary to master this well." - Miyamoto Musashi

Relaxed, fluid, and adaptable movement is a hallmark of mastery. If either the mind or the body become fixed, performance suffers drastically. Rather than artificially imitating someone's technique, or trying to consciously control your technique, you need to put enough deliberate practice in during training to internalize the principles of proper technique. Then when it's time to perform, your skills flow from your subconscious like a program running in the background on your laptop.

This frees up the conscious mind to be aware rather than focused. This allows you to sustain situational awareness and fosters correct decision making. Let your techniques be alive, adaptable, natural, and spontaneous. Let your mind simply be aware, and you'll perform at the best of your current level of skill. But allow the conscious mind to be fixed on technique, to focus on execution, and you will falter. Your techniques will be fixed and dead, ineffective and inappropriately applied.

In your training, constantly seek to program your subconscious correctly so that your techniques and tactics remain flexible and natural. Live technique instead of dead. This is absolutely essential if you seek mastery of your craft.

READY

"In all forms of strategy, it is necessary to maintain the combat stance in everyday life and to make your everyday stance your combat stance." - Miyamoto Musashi

Ready positions. Fighting stances. Post shooting procedures. All too often these are contrived and artificial things. Lifeless technique devoid of real intent, theatre meant to convince yourself of your ability to prevail in a violent encounter. This is nothing new. The history of martial training is full of the equivalent of modern range theatrics. Artificial ready positions and mindless rituals meant to simulate tactical awareness are a cliché in the martial arts world precisely because of their prevalence. At least their prevalence in the academic study of violence.

Academic study, technique based on theory, is very different than practical and relevant experience, however. And people who have fought for their lives repeatedly against competent and determined opponents have a ruthlessly practical view of technique and training. The trainers and trainees who espouse contrived techniques are the ones who haven't been truly tested.

This doesn't mean that oversimplification of technique is optimal either. That is a trap even highly experienced people can easily fall into. A good example is high vs low ready with a rifle. I was raised in U.S. Army SOF, where I was taught that the high ready was sacrilege. Something the SEALs did, not us. Now, after two decades of cross-pollination in combat, Special Forces now uses both the high and low ready as applicable. As they should, since both positions have value depending on the context.

It also doesn't mean that there aren't subtleties to positioning and technique. But subtleties are different than artificialities. Exaggerated and contrived technique is never optimal, and only effective against the unskilled. Nowhere is this more apparent than in ready positions. If your stance is contrived and tense you will never be able to fight effectively. This holds true for all kinds of fighting, armed or not. If you are still shooting in a "SWAT crouch" or running around in the temple index, you aren't training optimal technique.

Fighting is fighting. Movement is movement. The laws of human physiology and psychology are universal, and the principles of good athletic performance don't change when you put a gun in your hands. Make your stance and structure athletic and natural, and you'll optimize your technique for you. Learn to be ready, naturally.

MOVE

"Movement is life." - Jules Verne

Movement. Mobility is crucial in a fight, and a gunfight is definitely no exception. When it's time to shoot, shoot. When it's time to move, MOVE. And when you need to do both at the same time, you need to have the requisite level of skill to shoot accurately while moving with a sense of purpose.

This is one of the skill sets I see practiced incorrectly the most among tactical shooters. The same mistakes are so common that they almost seem like doctrine rather than errors. And the way movement skills are commonly trained doesn't properly develop skill at either shooting or moving. So, how can we address this in our training?

To begin, we need to train like athletes. For some reason, people seem to think that the rules governing human performance and skill development don't apply when you have a gun in your hand. In fact, nothing could be further from the truth. The body and the mind work the way they work, regardless of whether you have a firearm or not. Sprint mechanics don't change because it's a gunfight. Neither do the biomechanics involved in moving rapidly but smoothly enough to have a stable athletic platform differ when shooting on the move.

Efficiency. How many times on social media have you seen shooters training movement drills with cones or barricades and they come into position nowhere near ready to shoot. Gun not up, stance not yet stable. Regardless of whether you are entering a position and immediately shooting, or setting up behind cover, you should be entering that position ready to shoot. Exiting a position should be explosive. Once you've made the decision to move, that needs to happen right away.

Shooting on the move. All too often shooters wind up moving so slowly that there is no benefit to be gained. If you have a reason to shoot while moving, both need to be done at a high enough level that you get the benefit of both rapid movement and accurate hits. The old heel-toe "duck walk" just won't produce this level of results. Learning to relax and create a stable platform during rapid and fluid movement will. But it has to be trained.

The best shooters to learn these skills from are action shooting competitors. No, USPSA matches aren't gunfights. And they aren't "tactical." But one of the things a USPSA match does have in common with a gunfight is this: fractions of a second can make the difference between winning or losing. And any top USPSA shooter has learned to maximize their efficiency and move like an athlete. If you want to move well, train that skill set like an athlete and you will get better.

SIGHT AND VISION

"The only thing worse than being blind is having sight but no vision." - Helen Keller

"See what you need to see." It's become a mantra for teaching performance shooting, especially competitive. It's a lesson that's hard to learn, but once you do it carries benefits for you far beyond the ability to shoot fast and accurately.

I remember a friend of mine who's a USPSA Grand Master talking about how at a certain point in his shooting career the sights started to look different. After I had been a Master-class shooter for a while, I understood what he meant, because I found myself experiencing the same thing. After enough repetitions spent at the ragged edge of my ability, I started to be able to interpret the input from my sights far more effectively at speed.

Vision drives your shooting. Everything from driving your eyes to the correct spot on the next target, to ensuring you see a correct sight picture for the target difficulty before pressing the trigger, to watching the sights lift prior to shifting the vision away. Vision drives movement. From looking at the spot you need your foot to stop on before initiating movement to looking at the empty magazine well to guide the magazine in during a reload. Vision drives more than just physical skills though.

Vision is more than just sight. Vision is awareness. The ability to process visual information at high speed while under a demanding cognitive load. That is a mental skill that can be trained and developed. And it's a mental skill that is the single most important attribute for managing violent physical conflict. Awareness drives your tactics and your decision making. And it doesn't matter how well you can shoot or how well you can fight, if you make the wrong decision. The OODA loop concept is over-quoted and often misinterpreted, but Boyd had it right. Observation and orientation are the keys to winning a fight, whether between athletes in the ring or fighter pilots in the sky, and everything in between.

So if our vision is so crucial how can we develop it? And I'm not referring to mechanical acuity. This isn't so much about 20/20 vision as it is about interpreting the information our eyes give us. And interpreting it at high speed while performing difficult physical tasks at a subconsciously competent level. How do we train that skill?

Historically, tactical athletes show improvement in perceptual speed through exposure to their event. Runs in the shoot house, real world hits, bouts in the octagon. This works, and the difference in performance is marked between experienced practitioners and neophytes. There is a ceiling to this improvement however, and here is why: there is no "overspeed" component to the experience you accumulate.

The best way I have found to improve perceptual speed is action shooting competition, specifically the US Practical Shooting Association's style of matches. Because you are paying attention to data and performance at a pace where thousandths of a second count, your brain gets acclimated to observing at that pace. No, USPSA is not tactics. And that's actually why you get this benefit, because the pace of a stage is so much faster than the "real thing." Then when you work a tactical problem, the mental bandwidth you've developed by solving problems while shooting and moving at a far faster pace allows you to be relaxed and aware at what would otherwise be your limit speed.

See what you need to see. To make your shot, to process your environment, to make sound tactical decisions. See what you need to see. And learn to see it faster.

EYE DOMINANCE

"In the land of the blind, the one-eyed man is king." - Erasmus

Eye dominance is an issue that in my opinion is given far too much importance, especially given the prevalence of modern optical sights and the increased understanding of what can be accomplished with target focused shooting, even with iron sights.

I have cross-eye dominance, and long ago learned to shoot with both eyes open and using my right eye to align iron sights. The main visual issues when doing this with irons are a "ghost image" of either the target or the sights. The ability to use the correct visual information is trainable without much effort. I've now done this for so long that I find myself using whichever eye is most advantageous based on the context of the shot I am taking. This is even easier with an optic.

If your cross-dominance is too severe to train out, which is sometimes the case, there is still no need to switch the shooter to their support side in an attempt to mitigate the issue. With pistol, the difference in presentation and index is minimal, and shouldn't become a limiting factor. With rifle, it isn't an issue if you select the proper riser height for your optic. My friend and mentor, Mike Pannone, lost his right eye in a breaching accident, and he still shoots rifle right-handed. There is especially no need to shoot pistol with your dominant hand and rifle with your non-dominant side. In my experience this creates more technical issues than it solves. In general, I do not like the typical "solutions" offered up for situations such as cross-eye dominance. Quick fixes almost universally become limiting factors in the long run.

SHOOTING PACE

"There is a rhythm to everything, but particularly in the martial arts, if you do not train in its rhythm it is difficult to succeed." - Miyamoto Musashi

Pace. This is an aspect of shooting that I often see misunderstood and applied incorrectly. And if we are to develop the highest levels of skill at performance shooting, the pace at which we shoot absolutely has to be intuitively understood and correctly applied to a particular shot at a subconsciously competent level. Without this unconsciously competent mastery of pace, our shooting will never find the appropriate instinctual balance between speed and accuracy required of us.

Speed and accuracy are conflicting goals. To maximize them is always a balancing act between doing too much, and shooting too slowly; or doing too little, and not shooting accurately enough. To perform this balancing act correctly requires a true understanding of what needs to be done technically for a particular difficulty of shot.

What happens most often, is a shooter thinks of going "faster" or "slower" and doesn't change how they execute the component tasks involved, and this almost always leads to errors. Especially because subjective judgement of the passage of time is notoriously inaccurate under psychological pressure, even for highly skilled individuals. Instead, changing the technical response based on the demands of the shooting problem at hand changes our speed. Proper pace is a byproduct of correctly applied technique.

I find it helpful to conceptualize shooting pace as three broad categories. Like everything else, these weren't invented out of thin air. Two of the three are used by USPSA Grand Masters, JJ Racaza and Ben Stoeger, in their classes, where they refer to them as "control" and "attack," or "reactive" and "predictive," respectively.

These categories as I use and teach them are Deliberate, Reactive, and Predictive. For me, looking at it this way is invaluable for my shooting. Remember though, this is a way of conceptualizing a spectrum of technical solutions for shooting, not just multiple choice options exclusive of each other. What differentiates these categories is the combining or separating of the component tasks that make up the act of shooting, and the level of care taken when performing them.

Deliberate shooting pace, which is the only one of the three that can be done successfully using solely the conscious mind, is when each component task is separate and distinct from the others and performed with meticulous care. Each task can be "fixed" during execution if needed, dependent on shooter skill of course. Think of group shooting, or extreme examples of low-percentage, high-risk hostage taker shots. This is more akin to how a bullseye competitor shoots than the "typical" shot requirements in an armed encounter.

Moving up the spectrum with our pace from deliberate, we move into the Reactive category. Reactive shooting pace is the category between the two extremes of deliberate and predictive. It is very much the middle ground between combination and separation of our component skills, and has the widest variance of the three. It is also the pace that the overwhelming majority of the shots we take as "tactical" shooters require.

When shooting with a reactive pace, we combine more and more of the component tasks involved. Combining finalizing the grip with establishing sight alignment, or recoil mitigation with trigger reset and prep, as examples, offer significant time savings without overly affecting accuracy. The tasks we don't combine here are sight picture and trigger press with recoil mitigation. We react to the sights being "right" for a particular shot difficulty with the appropriate trigger press. Unlike the deliberate pace, we try and eliminate any lag time between the appropriate sight picture and the appropriate trigger press, but the one still distinctly follows the other.

The final, and fastest, category on our continuum of shooting pace is Predictive. In predictive shooting, we begin our trigger press while the sights are still returning in recoil to our point of aim. This allows us to shoot much faster, but requires us to master the predictive timing required. It also has the highest incident rate of error between the three, and so needs to be used selectively in the actual application of our shooting. Predictive shooting is how competitors burn down a Bill Drill or an El Presidente at blistering speed, and how top-tier tactical shooters blaze on a FAST drill or Gabe White's Turbo Pin Standards.

Truly understanding the variables that are adjusted to create your shooting pace, and understanding how to apply them based on the shooting problem you are faced with, are vital to the development of high levels of shooting skill. Study this deeply, and your raw shooting skill will improve, but even more importantly your mistakes will lessen during the application of that raw skill under stress.

TIMING

"You win battles with timing." - Miyamoto Musashi

There is timing to all things. Simply being fast is no guarantee of victory in a fight. We can develop blinding speed on the flat range or in the gym, and all other things being equal faster is better than slower, but raw speed is not the same as timing. And timing cannot be developed alone.

There is a cooperative timing to team tactics. A rhythm to working together in CQB that can only be polished through countless repetitions until you develop a feel for your teammates' movement and intent. And there is an adversarial timing to fighting. In this respect, gunfighting is no different than any other fight. Learning to capture your opponent's timing and exploit it through broken rhythm is no less an aspect of strategy in gunfighting than it is in the octagon. How then do we learn this, short of a real gunfight?

A fighter learns timing through hours of practice against noncooperative opponents. We have force-on-force training with firearms, and that is exactly what's needed, but with a stipulation: force-on-force is commonly scripted, with the admonition to fight through being "shot" in order to avoid a training scar. The theory behind this is that stopping because you are shot will carry over to an actual gunfight and cause a potentially disastrous hesitation if wounded.

For scenario-based training, I agree. Reps should be done that instill that desire to stay in the fight. But scenario-based training, as valuable as it is, doesn't lend itself well to learning how to truly fight. It is far more valuable for command and control considerations as well as polishing team tactics under added stress. Fights though, real fights, are unscripted.

To learn to fight, there has to be an element of noncooperative conflict. Sparring. No different than a boxer, or a UFC fighter. When I ran the training for my SWAT team, we would periodically have one cell enter the shoot house through one breach point, and another cell through the other. The cells would then fight it out with Simunition marking rounds in the shoot house, unscripted. They would spar in force-on-force. The lessons learned carried over to the real world, and have been used by my teammates in gunfights since with success.

Working against a determined adversary is the only way to understand the timing of conflict. Seek out opportunities to do so. If unscripted force-on-force training isn't an option, seek out other martial training. Learning to fight in any context can carry over to self-defense, armed as well as unarmed. And if your job involves high-risk entries in any context, make no mistake, CQB is fighting. It's team-based, and has its own particular constraints, but it's very much a fight. Learn the timing of it, learn to capture your opponent's timing and use it against him, and win your battles.

SAFETY

"Safety is something that happens between your ears, not something you hold in your hands."
- Jeff Cooper

Col. Jeff Cooper made many contributions to the tactics, training, and culture of combative firearms use in America. Of all his legacies, perhaps the most well known is his four rules of firearms safety. In the original form, they read like this:

I.   **All guns are always loaded.**

II. **Never let the muzzle cover anything you are not willing to destroy.**

III. **Keep your finger off the trigger until your sights are on the target.**

IV. **Be sure of your target.**

The brilliance of these rules lies in their redundancy. They provide interlocking levels of protection against error in such a way that you have to violate two before you accidentally injure someone. If I break any one of these rules by itself, while following the remaining three, my carelessness results in no more than minor property damage at worst. I have to break two or more before I cause serious injury or death. If I have a negligent discharge but do not muzzle anyone, no one is harmed. No one but my own career anyway. If I muzzle someone but my finger remains off the trigger, once again all I have harmed is my own reputation. If I break both those rules simultaneously however, I can seriously injure or kill someone through my negligence. This redundancy is incredibly effective once these four rules are ingrained at a subconscious level.

However, their wording is intended for the conscript, the basic trainee, or academy recruit. The professional should think of these rules in a more nuanced fashion, while remaining true to their original intent. My preferred method for teaching these is as follows:

I. **Know the condition of your firearm at all times and always handle it as if it were loaded.** When you carry a firearm for a living, not knowing it ISN'T loaded is just as dangerous as not knowing it is. Ingrain ammo management and status checks into your habits and rituals, as well as trigger discipline and muzzle awareness.

II. **Never let the muzzle cover anything unless you are prepared to destroy it.** This is a subtle distinction but an important one. I was, in essence, a professional gunfighter, among other roles of course, for over thirty years. I have pointed firearms at plenty of people who were "unknowns" in that moment. I was prepared to shoot them if, and only if, the need arose. Waiting until the other side initiates a gunfight is no way to live until retirement.

III. **Keep your finger off the trigger and positively contacting the frame of the weapon until you are visually connected to the weapon and your target and have made a conscious decision to fire.** Waiting until you have finished aiming to put your finger on the trigger can place you dangerously behind the power curve in a close distance gunfight. If, and only if, you have made the conscious decision to fire as you are drawing or presenting the weapon, the finger can be placed on the trigger the moment both the target and your weapon (not necessarily your sights) are in your field of view.

IV. **Be sure of your target, as well as its backstop, its foreground, and its surroundings.** It's not enough to positively identify your target. You have to know what its backstop is, what's between you and the target, and what's to its sides. Conflict is chaotic and unpredictable. Your awareness has to open up and take the entire environment into account.

These aren't just rules for the flat range. They are rules for every time you utilize firearms in any capacity. Internalize these and make them a constant. Failure to do so can have dire consequences.

MARKSMANSHIP FUNDAMENTALS

"A good archer is known not by his arrows but by his aim." - Thomas Fuller

Marksmanship fundamentals. The classical paradigm for this is to break the process of shooting down into six categories: Stance, grip, sight alignment, sight picture, trigger control, and breathing.

I break these down a bit differently. I don't spend any real teaching time on breathing. Breath control can matter for extremely long range precise shooting, but for shooting fast and accurately at close to medium distances, the only real admonition is to remember to breathe. This is sometimes harder than it sounds, and unconsciously holding your breath impairs performance. I also don't separate sight alignment from sight picture, for reasons I'll explain shortly. The categories I use in my teaching are grip, structure, aiming, and trigger management. Let's examine each of these in detail.

GRIP

Grip is an interesting thing. Especially for a pistol. No two proper grips look exactly the same. Robert Vogel and Ben Stoeger are both world champion pistol shooters, yet their grips look nothing alike. What is the same about both of their grips however is that they follow the same principles. You have to understand and internalize the principles that underpin proper technique, then optimize them for you.

The principles that underpin grip technique are friction, leverage, and pressure. Friction is increased by maximizing the surface area of your hands in contact with the grip of the gun. Leverage is increased by adapting the shape of your grip to maximize it. Pressure is the interesting one. More pressure helps with recoil mitigation, but too much and trigger manipulation suffers. There's also the issue of tension, but we'll get back to that in a moment.

To maximize friction in your grip, experiment with hand placement until you have put as much surface area as possible in contact with the grip of the pistol. This has to be done, though, without interfering with maximizing leverage. Between the two, leverage trumps friction, so shooters with smaller hands may have small gaps in their grip in order to have their proper technique.

For leverage, a couple of things need to be considered. One is a simple matter of physics. The force of the pistol's recoil travels down the line of bore, the barrel of the pistol. The closer the grip is to the bore then the more leverage you have. In other words the higher on the gun, the better, as long as you're not creating a contrived and overly tense structure. The second is that there are a lot of small variables that can positively impact leverage such as where the fingers of the support hand link up with the ones of the strong hand, placement of the pistol's backstrap against the palm, and many others. You must experiment with all of these in your training.

Pressure. The pressure of your grip assists with friction and the maintaining leverage. Your shooting hand should have as much grip pressure as you can produce without interfering with the relaxation of your trigger finger. This will increase over time with proper practice, especially if you focus on the pinky and ring fingers doing all of the gripping. Your support hand should literally grip as hard as possible without creating excess tension. It's especially important to learn to localize the muscular tension to the hands and forearms. If you allow the tension to extend to your upper arms and shoulders, it will negatively impact your index and transitions.

The same principles apply to unsupported rifle shooting, but it is far easier to grip a carbine. Separating the support and firing hand as much as possible allows for much more leverage than you can achieve on a pistol. That combined with more points of contact on a weapon with less felt recoil makes it a much simpler proposition to shoot a carbine at speed.

It is vital to explore all of this in your own training, and don't be afraid to experiment. Mimicking the outside appearance of someone else's technique, no matter how accomplished a shooter they are, will never be as effective as optimizing your technique to suit your own physiology.

STRUCTURE

Rather than stance, I like to think of how we stand and move combatively in terms of structure. Stance makes people think of a static rigid position and focuses on our lower body. Conflict is dynamic and chaotic, and it requires fluid powerful movement. None of that comes from static, contrived positions that utilize muscular tension. What we need is proper structure in a relaxed and athletic posture. The principles behind this are universal, although the application is contextual.

We need a slight forward weight bias. This doesn't come from an exaggerated forward bend at the waist. Think instead of having your weight on the balls of your feet. A coaching cue I use myself for this is one I stole from the writing of Bruce Lee who said you should feel as if there is a sheet of paper between your heels and the ground.

Feet should be generally between hip and shoulder width apart, although there are exceptions to this for some applications. In a static position, it is optimal if your strong side foot is about one-half to one-and-a-half foot lengths to the rear, but it's best not to be attached to this because of the necessity for fluid movement.

Your hips and knees should have some bend. How much is again contextual, but it's best not to change levels unnecessarily. Because of this, a good rule of thumb is to keep the hips the same height they are when you run, rather than raise them when still and drop them to move.

The core should be engaged, but not unnecessarily tense. Relaxation is essential for fluid athletic movement, and tension will severely impair that. The core has to be engaged, however, so that force can be transmitted from the hips into explosive movement.

Shoulders should be down and relaxed. For most, myself included, the "tell" for excess tension is high shoulders. The other common error is rounding the shoulders forward and ducking the head. This not only creates excess tension and impairs movement, but it adversely impacts field of view as well.

Elbows should be slightly bent. The degree of bend varies from person-to-person and situation-to-situation, but they should never be locked. Along with the degree of bend, the angle of the elbows is also contextual and individual. It's important to experiment with all of these variables in your training until the principles become internalized and subconscious. Then your structure will be not only efficient, but uniquely yours.

AIMING

The classic breakdown of marksmanship fundamentals has two separate categories for aiming, sight alignment and sight picture. Classically, with irons, you're told to center the front sight blade within the rear notch the same height as the rear sight with a crystal clear front sight focus and a blurry rear sight and target. You're then told to place the tip of the front sight where you wish the round to go.

I believe this to be an insufficient way of articulating what actually needs to happen when you shoot accurately at high speeds. First, sight picture implies a snapshot prior to trigger press, as if no other visual input matters to shooting. Nothing could be further from the truth. What you need is a sight *movie*. You need to learn to track the front sight or dot throughout the entire recoil cycle in great detail. The second error inherent in this way of conceptualizing the aiming process is this: sight picture and alignment aren't separate tasks. They are different visual aspects of the same task, aiming.

Aiming is nothing more than aligning the firearm with the target. But like so many other things, the devil is in the details. How much visual confirmation do I need to place an acceptable hit on a particular target? This can vary drastically and is a continuum. But I find it's helpful to have a set of categories to describe that continuum, so that shooters can understand the process better. These are the categories of visual confirmation I use to describe that continuum:

1. Index Confirmation - Solely body alignment. Target is in vision, and the firearm may be visible, but there is no visual confirmation of sights at all. Used on extremely close range wide open targets, typically seven yards and in for pistol. A flat range example of this could be the first round on an extremely fast Bill Drill, where you might fire before the pistol reaches eyeline. In real world application, this would most commonly be used for retention shooting at arms-length engagement distances.

2. Outline Confirmation - Using the actual shape of the firearm as the aiming mechanism. This is done by centering the outline of the firearm in your vision within the acceptable scoring area on the target. With an optic, using the shape of the housing is extremely effective and more precise than the overall shape of the gun. Also used on close range wide open targets, typically ten yards and in for pistol. On the flat range this is my normal level of focus for the first round off the draw at ten yards or closer on an open target. I may very well see the dot in my optic, but I'm not looking for it prior to my trigger press. Then I'll find the dot during the recoil arc, and use it for subsequent shots. For actual application, this is how I might aim if there were no cover, a solid backstop behind the threat, and speed was essential, so that I could put effective hits on the threat before he was able to put them on me.

3. Flash Confirmation - With the target in clear visual focus, seeing a flash of either the front sight fiber for irons, or a streak of red for an optic, centered in the acceptable scoring area of the target. For open targets inside of fifteen yards with a pistol, this is the level of confirmation I use almost solely, whether on the flat range or in application.

4. Partial Confirmation - With the target in clear visual focus, for iron sights the front blade is relatively centered and level within the rear notch, although it can be moving more than just the natural arc of movement you have when trying to keep the gun perfectly still. For optics, the dot is no longer a streak although like with irons it doesn't need to be as still as possible. I think of the dot as needing to be a "squiggle" for this level of confirmation. This is my level of confirmation with a pistol that I use for open targets from fifteen to twenty-five yards.

5. Full Confirmation - With irons, this is the classic "hard front sight focus, equal height, equal light" confirmation that everyone is taught as a new shooter. With an optic, this is a still, calm dot. With a pistol, this is my level of confirmation on open targets at twenty-five yards and beyond.

The distances above are examples of when each confirmation is effective for me. This changes as your skill increases, and your grip, index, and structure improve. You must continually experiment with this in your own training, so that you instinctively understand what level of confirmation you need under stress for a particular shot.

Bear in mind two other factors as well. The distances given above are for open targets, in other words an unobscured torso. Partial targets, movement, non-standard shooting positions, and other factors can drastically increase target difficulty for a given distance.

Target difficulty isn't the only factor to consider when choosing what level of confirmation is needed for a particular shot. The other factor is target risk. In a match, a target partially obscured by a no-shoot will be given more care than one partially obscured by hard cover. The reason is that the penalty for hitting the no-shoot is far higher than the penalty for hitting hard cover.

The same principle applies to real world application as well. If I am engaging a threat in the open at seven yards, and they are standing still in front of a brick wall with no windows, then my penalty for missing is minimal. The same threat standing in front of a playground full of kindergartners at recess would require a much higher level of visual confirmation for the shot because of the much higher level of risk.

Without learning to intuitively apply the appropriate level of confirmation for a particular shot difficulty and risk, you will never reach your potential level of skill as a shooter. This needs to be continually explored in your training, since it changes over time as your technical skills improve.

TRIGGER MANAGEMENT

Trigger control. I don't like the customary phrase. It's rooted in the traditional wisdom in firearms instruction that would have you believe that the root cause of all success or failure in marksmanship is the correct performance of a meticulous trigger press. Especially when shooting at speed, this is simply not the case. Despite what the old "diagnostic charts" would have you believe, too little or too much trigger finger has little to do with shots being significantly left or right.

I prefer the term trigger management. I feel that does a better job of conceptualizing what you need to do to shoot fast and accurately. Rather than a rigid concept of one meticulous style of trigger press, you need a more flexible approach. You need to manage the trigger as a part of your overall shooting process.

Much like I break down aiming into different types, I do the same with trigger management. Just like all the other aspects of the shooting process, this is really a continuum, but the divisions help me conceptualize what I need to do with the trigger for a particular shot difficulty and risk.

One important commonality among all three types is that the trigger reset, and prep if needed, happens during the recoil cycle. Pinning the trigger to the rear while the gun recoils is counterproductive for both speed and accuracy when shooting. Study this in live fire until

126

you can bring the trigger to the wall and no further during the recoil cycle with 100% consistency. Understand also that in application this assumes that the conscious decision to make a follow-up shot has already been made.

1. Slap - just what it sounds like. The finger comes completely off of the trigger during the recoil cycle and aggressively moves the trigger through its full travel with no thought given to the wall or break. Actually, when I shoot using this style of trigger management, I literally don't think of the trigger at all. Once I get the needed level of visual confirmation for the shot, the gun fires with no awareness of the trigger.

2. Rolling Break - The finger remains in contact with the trigger, and preps it to the wall during the recoil cycle, but does not pause there. Assuming the correct level of visual confirmation is there, the finger smoothly but rapidly moves the trigger through the remainder of its travel. Mentally there is an awareness of the trigger breaking, but no attempt to influence when it breaks.

3. Prep and Press - The finger remains in contact with the trigger, and preps it to the wall during the recoil cycle, and pauses there while the needed level of visual confirmation for the shot is achieved. Once the sights have sufficiently settled, the trigger is pressed through the break and then once again reset in recoil.

Despite everything I said above, there are nuances of trigger finger placement and trigger press that do impact marksmanship at speed. They are a small part of the equation however, and are far overshadowed by proper grip. Having said that, you will eventually need to explore them in your training in order to develop your own best technique. A personal example of this is my trigger finger placement when shooting a pistol. When I shot Glocks, I got my best results from burying my trigger finger as deep as possible on the trigger. Shooting a 1911/2011 style pistol I get my best results from the more traditional fingertip placement style. These sorts of technical subtleties are very individual and have to be derived from your own personal experimentation and study.

WEAPONS MANIPULATIONS

"Learn to draw quick and shoot straight, the former being even more important than the latter." - Theodore Roosevelt

Weapons manipulations are simply the set of necessary firearms skills that aren't the actual shooting. Draws, reloads, malfunction clearances, and so on. It is of immense importance that our weapons handling is fast and consistent under stress. In a drill or in a match, any time you're not shooting points is hurting your score. In a gunfight, any time spent not scoring hits on your opponent is potentially time they can be using to score hits on you.

The counterargument to this is always that draws and especially reloads under fire are relatively rare, statistically speaking, as winning factors in actual engagements. While this may be true, they do happen. And when they do, your skill at these tasks is very important indeed. I've never had to reload a pistol during a gunfight, but I have reloaded a rifle. And though it's not common, I have actually had one "Wild West" style quick draw pistol gunfight, and when it happened, I was very glad I had put effort into developing my draw. I tend to think of draws and reloads as "reserve parachute" techniques. You probably won't need them, but when you do, you REALLY need them.

As far as malfunctions go, the only personal experience I have ever had clearing a stoppage during an engagement was with an AK-47. But pistol malfunctions under fire can be seen on numerous body cam videos from officer-involved shootings. Mechanical devices can fail, and firearms are machines. When they fail, you need to be prepared to remedy it skillfully and intuitively.

Let's look at weapons manipulations for carbine and pistol, as well as malfunction clearances, and go over some important concepts.

PISTOL

The manual of arms on the overwhelming majority of modern semiautomatic pistols is basically the same, although there are differences in control placement and grip angle. There are some outliers like paddle mag releases, but for the most part any of the popular modern duty pistols are manipulated essentially the same.

The two pistols I have extensive experience with as a cop and a soldier, and the ones I've been in gunfights with, are the Beretta 92 and the Glock 17/19. However, my personal favorite has always been the 1911 platform. Now that I am retired and can carry whatever I want, I carry and compete with 2011s which are essentially a 9mm 1911 with a double-stack magazine for higher capacity.

The weapons manipulation techniques I use for pistol are based on my experience with these three platforms. The principles I espouse apply regardless of the pistol you are shooting, but don't be afraid to experiment in your own technique, especially if your pistol's manual of arms is significantly different than those I have used.

The Draw - Strong Side Overt OWB

My preferred method of overt carry is strong side, outside the waistband (OWB). This allows for the fastest and most consistent draws under stress, and apart from vehicle operations, is the most accessible when wearing kit. When retention is needed, I prefer a Safariland ALS holster, modified with the Nub Mod from Oregon Trail Defense to present a larger surface and better angle for the thumb release. I am not a fan of hood-style retention devices or any retention mechanism activated by the trigger finger.

I've seen multiple overly complicated and inefficient draw strokes being taught. The one that is still widely prevalent is the "press-out" draw. In this draw stroke, the pistol is brought up to eye level then extended out to full presentation, cleaning up the sight picture along the way. This does have some practical value if the shooter is not going to practice enough to develop a proper index, because it combines the action of aligning the sights with a portion of the draw stroke. But if the shooter has a properly developed index, which is the ability to look at a point and then bring the weapon in line with the eyes so that it is aiming at the point being looked at, then this technique will quickly become a limiting factor due to its inefficiency. No one with a truly fast draw presses out in that fashion. The most efficient path between two points will always be a straight line.

The other argument I sometimes hear for the press-out draw is that your retention draw stroke then matches your regular draw stroke. The problems with this argument are this. It's not an efficient or effective technique for either circumstance, and there is no logical need to make these techniques match. If you can't tell the difference between a threat at arm's length and one at 10 yards, you have need of further training.

My draw goes like this: whenever possible, depending on the position my hands are in, I use the inside of my elbow as a physical reference point. I do that by touching a specific point on the pistol's magwell with a specific point on the inside of my arm. This repeatable motion will "calibrate" my subconscious to the exact position of the gun in its holster. From whatever position my hands start in, they move as rapidly as possible, the strong hand driving to a master grip on the gun, and the support hand moving to the center of your waistline.

Several important points here, first is that the faster I move my support hand, the faster my overall draw becomes. The support hand should be positioned to meet the strong hand as gun as soon as possible, without being in a position where it will be flagged by the muzzle. The strong hand stabs onto the backstrap of the gun, ensuring that the web of the hand is as high on the backstrap as possible. To ensure this I use a physical reference point for my technique. I memorize the feel of the web of my hand as it contacts the beavertail in a proper grip and learn to drive that point to the same location on the gun every time. Whatever retention mechanisms your holster has must be defeated as the strong hand drives down onto the gun, not after.

Once you establish a grip on your pistol, rapidly accelerate as you draw it from the holster. The cue I use for this, stolen from a practical shooting world champion, is "grip it and rip it." The gun should move in a straight line from holster to eye level. As soon as you won't flag yourself doing so, the support hand meets the gun. Two important points here. This is another place I use a physical reference point for my technique. I memorize exactly where my index finger on my support hand meets the bottom of the trigger guard for a proper grip. When I mate up the support hand with the strong hand, I drive that point to where the trigger guard meets the middle finger on my strong hand. This ensures I have the correct placement of my support hand as I finalize the grip.

131

The second crucial point is that I do not try to finalize the support hand grip here. When the hands meet, the only contact point is that physical reference point. Then the support hand "rolls" into place as the pistol extends, finishing this process and finalizing its grip about three quarters of the way to full extension. The reason for this is tension. If I try and finalize the grip too soon, I will have too much tension for a fast and accurate draw.

From the moment it clears the holster, the gun moves in a straight line to your eyeline, arriving with the sights in correct alignment between your dominant eye and the point you are looking at. This ability to look at a point and then bring the gun into alignment with that point is called your index, and the draw is the best way to develop it. In the draw, your movement should accelerate for 80% to 95% of the draw stroke, depending on target difficulty, and then "coast" into place for the last 5-20%. This allows your sights to settle smoothly into position rather than vibrating like they do if you finish the draw stroke at full speed.

Another performance point is disengaging the safety. If your pistol has an external safety, it should be disengaged relatively early in the draw stroke. My rule of thumb is as soon as I clear my lower body with the muzzle, I disengage the safety.

A related point is when to place the finger on the trigger. My rule for this applies to all firearms. If I am visually connected to both my target and the firearm, and have made a conscious decision to shoot, I can put my finger on the trigger. I don't have to be looking through the sights at the target, but I have to be visually aware of both the pistol and the target I intend to shoot.

Especially when drawing at the limits of your current speed, it is vital to avoid excess tension. The more stress you are under, the easier it is for tension to creep in. Relaxed movement is always faster and more precise, and most importantly, more consistent. The other common error to avoid, especially under stress, is excess motion. Guard against unnecessary movement of the hips or shoulders especially. Video review of your training can greatly assist in simplifying and streamlining your technique so that it is as efficient as possible.

The Draw - AIWB Concealed

My preferred method of concealed carry is an inside the waistband holster, carried at about the one o'clock position just to the right of the bellybutton, and concealed under a closed-front outer garment. This is known as appendix carry, or AIWB, which stands for appendix inside the waistband. Except when wearing business attire, this is the method of carry that best balances concealment and speed.

There are two common start positions for the draw from AIWB concealment, hands naturally relaxed at sides, or hands at chest height in a defensive posture. The strong hand movement is the same regardless, but the garment is cleared differently by the support hand. Obviously these are not the only two positions to start from, but training both of these extensively prepares you well for drawing from other less common positions.

From hands relaxed at sides, the support hand forms a "C" shape, and the fingers scoop the bottom hem of the cover garment. The support hand then moves to sternum height to ensure enough space for the strong hand to establish a grip on the pistol. The strong hand moves directly to the pistol using what is called a "claw grip." In a claw grip, the thumb rests on the backplate of the gun rather than wrapping around to the support side of the grip. For a 1911 or 2011 pattern pistol this has to be modified due to the length of the beaver tail on the grip safety. In that case the thumb settles just to the support side of the gun without yet wrapping around the grip.

The strong hand then rips the gun from the holster, wrapping the thumb into a proper grip the moment it clears. Because of the holster placement and the necessity of clearing the cover garment, the support hand meets the pistol in a slightly different place than in a strong side OWB draw. Once the index finger of the support hand meets the bottom of the trigger guard though, the mechanics are almost identical. The pistol then moves in a straight line directly to your eyeline as the support hand grip rolls onto the gun.

From hands at chest height, the initial mechanics are different. The support hand grabs the front of the cover garment roughly at navel height in a thumbless grip. The key point here is that the fingers should be vertical not horizontal when you grasp the fabric. The hand then again raises to sternum height as in the draw from hands at sides. The strong hand then stabs down onto the pistol in a roughly vertical path. The exact angle varies slightly from gun-to-gun. With striker-fired pistols, the hand comes from the twelve o'clock direction or close to it. With 1911/2011 pistols, a more angled direction is better, roughly from the one o'clock to one-thirty direction. Most other pistols will fall somewhere in this range.

Once the strong hand rips the pistol from the holster, the mechanics are identical to the draw from hands relaxed at sides. It is vital in your training to practice this from a variety of clothing and internalize the optimal technique. With practice, this draw can be every bit as fast as the draw from an OWB holster without active retention. Because of the cover garment though, it will always be more prone to error. If you're going to carry concealed this way, put the time in to training it, and watch your speed and consistency improve.

The Draw - Strong Side Concealed

Drawing from a concealed strong side holster can be categorized into two very different techniques based on the type of cover garment, open-front or closed-front. With the current state of AIWB holsters and the technical evolution of the appendix draw, I could never recommend concealing a holster on the strong side under a closed-front garment.

Open-front garment concealment is still a necessary carry mode for many, such as detectives, agents, and supervisors who wear a suit to work. Special operations personnel in certain low-visibility roles need to be conversant with this method of carry. Even uniformed personnel in extreme cold weather are often de facto concealing under an open-front garment even though concealment is not the aim. Civilians may carry concealed under an open-front garment for the same reasons, or personal preference. While AIWB is my preferred method of concealed carry, it doesn't lend itself well to concealment under an open-front cover garment. Strong side, either OWB or IWB is better suited to these circumstances.

With an open-front garment, the draw stroke is almost identical to that of an overt strong side holster. The only difference is that as the strong hand moves towards the gun, it forms a C shape with the fingers and sweeps the cover garment out of the way. This requires experimentation in training. Too much of a sweeping motion, and you waste valuable time. Too little, and you run the risk of fouling the draw. The force needed varies from garment to garment as well, so if this is a regular form of carry for you, experiment with this in training so that you learn to be both efficient and effective.

Presentation From Ready

My preferred ready position with the pistol is the compressed high ready. When bringing the pistol into a compressed high ready position, if you relax the support hand grip, only keeping the same physical reference point on the weak hand index finger we used to establish the grip during the draw, touching the firing hand middle finger and bottom of the trigger guard, then we can establish a relaxed and mobile ready position with the pistol around chin height. Attempting to assume this position without relaxing the support hand in this fashion creates far too much tension in the shoulders.

From this relaxed position, presentation of the pistol is very similar to the last part of the draw stroke. The firing hand extends out as the support hand rolls into a proper grip, with the movement accelerating until the last 5-15% depending on shot difficulty and then coasting into place with the sights indexed and aligned.

Much like everything else, this technique should be "alive," adaptable and fluid, rather than a static and tense "dead" position. Seek that quality out through your training rather than adopting affected artificial techniques like the temple or holster index, and you will be far more effective applying your training in conflict.

I am not a fan of the classic low or high ready positions either, as I find them stiff and artificial as well. There are times when, based on the context I am employing the pistol in, where the muzzle may be depressed or elevated to avoid flagging non-threats with the pistol, or the pistol may be at arms length downward to appear less threatening. These conditions are again relaxed and "alive," though, not rigid. Presentation here is still much the same if the muzzle is elevated or depressed. If the pistol is down at arms length, then presentation is substantively the same as the draw. Training the draw and the compressed high ready will prepare you for these positions as well.

Speed and Emergency Reloads

I define these as follows: an emergency or slide lock reload is conducted when the slide is locked to the rear on an empty chamber, and there is an empty magazine seated in the pistol; a speed reload is conducted when the slide is still forward on a loaded chamber, and there is a partially depleted magazine seated in the pistol.

The technique for speed and emergency reloads is virtually identical, and should be almost indistinguishable in terms of time. The only difference between the two is the act of dropping the slide forward using the slide lock lever. Which brings us to the first point of discussion. There are still those who teach that the slide would be dropped by grasping it by the support hand rearward of the ejection port and bringing it all the way to the rear prior to releasing it so that it moves into battery. The problem with this technique is that it is significantly slower and less efficient than simply hitting the slide lock with the support side thumb as you roll your grip back into place.

The argument against using the slide lock lever usually runs like this: "Manipulating the slide lock with the thumb is a fine motor skill, and fine motor skills degrade under stress, so all of our manipulations should be gross motor skills only." First, neither is actually a fine motor skill by definition, but if we assume for the sake of argument that manipulation of the slide lock with the thumb is in fact a fine motor skill, and those are unreliable under stress and should be avoided, then how did we get the empty magazine out of the gun? The magazine release is smaller than the slide lock. The second hole in this argument is that the only action in all of shooting that could realistically be accurately characterized as a fine motor skill is our trigger press on the most difficult shots. This is also arguably the most important action in all of shooting.

To conduct an emergency reload, the initial key point is being aware enough of the visual and physical input from the gun to immediately recognize the slide locking to the rear. The strong hand then drops the spent magazine while the grip of the gun is still vertical in order to maximize the assistance of gravity in ejecting the magazine from the gun. The strong side elbow then bends to approximately ninety degrees and about one foot of distance from the torso. The strong hand also rotates so that the magwell of the pistol points at the magazine pouch on the belt. It is vital to be able to see the interior of the magwell.

While this is occurring, the support hand drives to the magazine pouch and snatches the fresh magazine free. In the case of concealment, the support hand first sweeps an open-front garment aside or "plucks" the bottom of a closed-front garment up before securing the new magazine. Then by simply dropping the support side elbow, the magazine is brought in alignment with the magwell of the pistol. The magazine is then inserted into the pistol and driven home by the heel of the support hand. As the weapon is presented to full extension, the support hand grip rolls into place just like in the draw. The support hand thumb disengages the slide lock as the grip is established, bringing the slide into battery and charging the pistol.

The technique for the speed reload is identical to the emergency reload, except that the support side thumb sweeping the slide lock lever has no effect. When trained this way, the time it takes to do an emergency reload is almost indistinguishable from the time it takes to do a speed reload.

For left-handed shooters, if there is not an ambidextrous magazine release on the pistol, the trigger finger can activate the magazine release and the slide lock lever. This technique works so well that in the Beretta 92 days in Special Forces, many of us flipped the reversible magazine catch around so that right-handed shooters with smaller hands activated it with their trigger fingers.

The support hand does the bulk of the work in the reload. It has to move much further and perform more tasks than the strong hand does. The strong hand, as soon as the magazine is ejected, simply relaxes into position. In order to have fast and consistent reloads, focus on the support hand speed and precision in your dry fire and live fire.

One of the tropes of tactical shooting is that reloads are done in the "workspace," an imaginary box in front of the face. The rationale behind this is that you maintain situational awareness of the threat by keeping your head and eyes up and reloading the pistol at face height. There are several inefficiencies in this technique. The angle of the pistol causes problems. If the magazine is not released early enough, it can bind in the pistol, especially with a polymer gun. The angle of insertion with the fresh magazine is awkward, requiring the elbow of the support side arm to raise after the initial drop, wasting time, and creating an unnecessary failure point when performed at speed under stress.

Another unnecessary failure point is created by keeping the visual focus in the distance rather than on the pistol. Our movement is driven by our vision. Consistency under stress is improved when we "look" the magazine into the gun by visually focusing on the inside of the magwell. If we learn to remain aware of our peripheral vision, then this doesn't damage our situational awareness, and it drastically improves both speed and reliability in the reload.

Another point that bears discussing again is how likely is an emergency reload, and how that should inform your training. In the context of civilian self-defense, an emergency reload is extremely unlikely. In law-enforcement it is still very rare, but not unheard of. A pistol reload in the context of a military engagement would mean you were having a very bad day indeed.

In my opinion though, none of that means it should not be trained to a very high level however. First, just because it is improbable statistically does not mean you won't wind up in an outlier situation. I view low probability but high risk techniques like the emergency reload much like my reserve parachute back in my military days. You probably won't need your reserve parachute, but when you do (and I have), you'll be very glad you have it.

Second, the skill carryover for the emergency reload, much like that of the draw, is very high. The emergency reload will make you more competent at malfunctions, increase your ability to diagnose and correct malfunctions, and aid in the development of a proper index. Don't shortchange your training time on this skill.

Tactical Reload

The tactical reload for the pistol is widely taught in military and police circles, and often put on the clock in law enforcement pistol qualification courses of fire. The oft heard institutional dogma is that you should retain the partially expended magazine when topping off your pistol during a lull in the gunfight.

The traditionally taught technique for this is to first secure a fresh magazine into the support hand as you would for a speed or emergency reload. You then shift the index finger around the fresh magazine so that it is held between the index and middle fingers. You eject the partially depleted magazine from the weapon into the support hand, trapping it between the thumb and index finger. Then you index and insert the fresh magazine into the weapon, seating it fully before stowing the partially depleted magazine on your person.

The rationale behind the this technique is that during the aforementioned lull in the gunfight, you top off the weapon so that it's fully loaded, minimizing the amount of time the weapon doesn't have a magazine in place in case you need to employ it. There are two flaws in this way of thinking. First, my personal experience is that pistol gunfights don't usually have a lull. The fight begins, and then it's over, although there is value in topping off your pistol in case of secondary threats. Second, while the traditional technique may minimize the amount of time the pistol isn't fully loaded, it doesn't minimize the amount of time before you can employ the pistol.

While not statistically probable at all, it is possible that you may feel the need to top off your pistol during a space in the fighting created by fire and maneuver, although this is more likely in military engagements with a carbine than in pistol engagements. If there is, in fact, a momentary lull in the gunfight, and you are concerned that you are running low on ammunition in your pistol, then the fastest technique is to simply perform a speed reload and not bother to retain the partially depleted magazine.

The place where I feel that it is valuable, especially for law enforcement engagements, to top off your pistols is immediately following the gunfight. I have faced secondary threats in that context and have done just that. Rather than the traditional method though, I now teach the following technique for that purpose. Eject the partially depleted magazine from the weapon into the support hand and then stow it on your person. Secure a fresh magazine with your support hand and insert it into the pistol as if performing a speed reload. Put on the timer, this technique is faster than the traditional one, which is why it is almost universally used in the only action shooting sport that requires reloads with retention, IDPA, or International Defensive Pistol Association. The other benefit of this technique is that it does not require large amounts of additional dry and live fire practice.

Deliberate Load and Unload

There are a couple of schools of thought on best practices for an administrative loading or unloading of your pistol. One is deliberate load and unload sequences that both double check the status of the firearm and its accessories, and offer additional repetition that reinforces the draw and reload. The other is simple but safety conscious techniques for loading and unloading the pistol.

Which approach is best is in my opinion entirely contextual. Loading your weapon as part of your pre-mission checks or before wearing it as your EDC is a different circumstance than administratively loading a pistol on the flat range. Unloading your pistol at the end of a USPSA competition stage as a high level competition shooter isn't the same as administratively clearing out a firing line of police recruits.

Prior to an operation, I still like to load the way I was taught in Special Forces. This becomes part of my pre-mission checks. Since pistol is the secondary weapon, it gets loaded first so that it's not inadvertently bypassed. I draw the pistol in a safe direction, check the weapon light and adjust the optic. Then I lock the slide to the rear and load it as if performing a slide lock reload. I then perform a press check to ensure the round is chambered, and the pistol is in battery. I then eject the magazine, holster the pistol, top off the magazine to replace the chambered round, reinsert the magazine and ensure it is seated. While this process is long and detailed, it ensures my light and optic are functioning correctly, and that the pistol is loaded correctly. It also gives me one last focused rehearsal for the draw and reload. The idea is to leave as little as you can to chance before going into harm's way.

When making ready for a stage at a match, I ensure I get a good draw to one of the targets, preferably the first one I'll be shooting, checking my optic as I do so. Then I load a magazine into the pistol as if performing a speed reload. I chamber a round then perform a press check and ensure the pistol is in battery. If need be, I'll then "Barney up," exchanging the magazine for a fully loaded one. I then holster the pistol, getting one last solid grip on it with my strong hand before assuming the start position for the stage.

When putting on a concealed firearm for the day it is usually already fully loaded and in the holster. If so, I'll put the holster on with the firearm in it. I'll then draw the pistol in a safe direction without putting my finger on the trigger. I then check the light and optic and do a press check. I'll eject the magazine and ensure it's fully loaded, then reinsert it and check that it's fully seated before reholstering the gun.

When running drills on the flat range I don't do an elaborate, deliberate load sequence. The point is to maximize training time and efficiency. I will say this, however, ammo management in training is crucial. If I have 2 rounds in the gun, and I attempt a Bill Drill, I've just wasted that repetition along with ammo and time. I want every round fired in training to be a lesson learned, not just an exercise in producing gun smoke and spent brass.

Unloading your pistol should have redundant safety checks built in to ensure that the weapon is safe and empty. On the range for practice I tend to follow the same system as a USPSA match. Remove and stow the magazine, cycle the slide to eject the chambered round, aim the weapon safely at the berm, and drop the hammer on an empty chamber. In an organizational setting, the common practice of redundant physical and visual inspections of the magazine well and the chamber after removing the magazine and ejecting the chambered round make perfect sense.

The gist of my viewpoint on best practices for administratively loading and unloading your pistol is simply this—adopt a ritual appropriate for the environment you are in, and perform it mindfully and correctly every time you are unloading in the environment that ritual is appropriate for. This consistency with flexibility will breed good safety habits that are still adaptable rather than rote and mindless.

This philosophy translates well to systems you utilize for safety or preparedness in other areas as well. Rather than mindlessly follow a one-size fits all procedure, use the procedure as an adaptable pattern that fits the circumstances and creates the desired effects efficiently.

CARBINE

My preferred choice of carbine for general purpose and CQB use are AR-15 pattern rifles. They are far superior to both AK pattern guns and bullpup style weapons in my experience. I have used other weapon systems operationally including H&K submachine guns and Soviet block weapons, and I much prefer my M4.

For fighting in the mountains, I've used SOPMOD M14s and they are excellent for that purpose, but the AR platform is a better all around weapon. Precision rifle work is a different beast, but I still prefer an AR-pattern gas gun over a bolt gun for that purpose in the majority of applications.

If your mission or circumstances dictate a different platform, then the details of gun handling will of necessity be different for that weapon's manual of arms. But the principle won't change. Whatever platform you use, seek out the most relaxed and efficient techniques possible.

Presentation - Low Ready

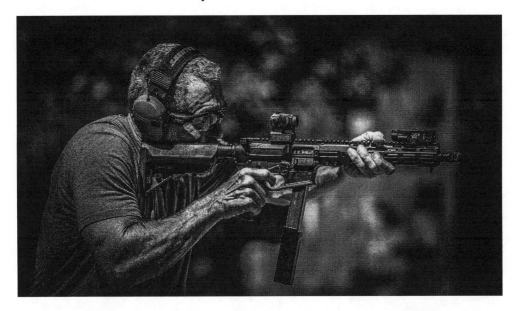

Presentation of the carbine from low ready is a relatively simple skill. The toe of the carbine buttstock should be in the correct place for properly mounting the rifle at the beginning of the presentation so that movement is minimal. If you're moving into a low ready style presentation from a variation such as a more relaxed patrolling position or a vertical indoor-carry style ready, then the toe of the rifle buttstock should move rapidly and smoothly to the correct placement in the pocket of the shoulder at the beginning of the presentation.

The rifle simply rises until the sights are aligned and indexed. Much like the pistol draw the movement accelerates until the last five to fifteen percent, depending on shot difficulty, then smoothly relaxes into position. There should be no unnecessary movement or tension in your body beyond that required to mount the rifle. Common errors are to introduce unnecessary head movement, excessive blading of the body or forward lean into the technique.

The safety should be deactivated as you present, and activated as you return to the ready. Right-handed shooters and left-handed shooters with ambidextrous controls should do this with a simple sweep of the thumb. Left-handed shooters without an ambidextrous safety can manipulate the safety with the base knuckle of the trigger finger. This movement should be practiced until it is automatic.

This presentation can become very quick and precise with the right amount of focused practice. Once it is practiced sufficiently, it should seem as if your optic simply appears indexed on your target without conscious thought. Explore this in your dry fire and live fire training until it becomes subconsciously repeatable under stress.

Presentation - High Ready

The presentation from the high ready is technically more complex than mounting the rifle from the low ready. On the flat range, the presentation from low ready will be faster on the timer. In application this very much becomes a contextual thing. Some applications are better served with the high ready position, so it needs to be developed to a high level as well. One should not be prioritized over the other.

Much like the low ready presentation is really a category encompassing everything from a vertical "indoor" carry through the muzzle slightly depressed version commonly seen in engagements in and around structures, presentation from the high ready includes everything from a vertical high port down to the competition stock on belt position.

The movement starts by "punching" the carbine out so that the buttstock clears the torso and any kit while simultaneously leveling it out horizontally at shoulder height before pulling it back into the pocket of the shoulder so that the rifle is correctly mounted and indexed. As in the presentation from low ready, the safety should be deactivated as you present the weapon and activated as you dismount it. It takes a significant amount of practice to make this motion efficient and consistent.

Although the presentation from the low ready is easier and faster, and can be used in most applications, there is significant value in the high ready positions. Put the training time in to make it proficient. The additional benefit in training both presentations is that if both are developed to a high level, then you learn to naturally mount the carbine from a wide variety of uncommon positions. Study this well in your training, and it will pay dividends in skill.

Speed and Emergency Reloads

I categorize speed and emergency reloads for carbine in a similar fashion to how I define them for pistol. An emergency or bolt lock reload is conducted when the bolt is locked to the rear on an empty chamber, and there is an empty magazine seated in the carbine. A speed reload is conducted when the bolt is still forward on a loaded chamber, and there is a partially depleted magazine seated in the rifle.

Both reloads can be conducted with the buttstock on the shoulder, or by bringing the stock either under or over the firing side arm. Whether you perform the reload with the carbine mounted or dismounted should be contextual, not because you've only practiced one way. With practice there shouldn't be a significant performance difference between the three versions.

Much like the emergency and speed reloads for pistol, the only difference between the two is activating the bolt release to charge the weapon on the emergency reload. Unlike the pistol techniques however, the action of activating the bolt release is a significant enough change that both versions should be practiced independently in your training.

To conduct an emergency reload, the initial key point is being aware enough of the physical input from the gun to immediately recognize the bolt locking to the rear. For right-handed shooters, the strong hand then drops the spent magazine by pressing the magazine release with the trigger finger. For left-handed shooters if they have ambidextrous controls installed on their carbine, the technique will be the same. If not they have a couple of options which I will cover shortly.

As the strong hand activates the magazine release, the support hand drives to the spare magazine. I prefer to do my rifle reloads from a pouch on my belt with the magazine oriented so that the bullets face to the rear. I grab the spare magazine with the bullets oriented towards my fingers. I place the pinky finger underneath the base of the magazine for support, and the thumb extends towards the mouth of the magazine, indexed at or beneath the detent in the magazine for the magazine catch. Looking at the magwell to ensure consistency, I then insert the magazine until it locks positively in place. I then slide my hand up the magazine until my thumb hits the bolt release and activate it. If I'm immediately presenting the weapon the support hand slides from there to its grip on the fore end. If I'm moving, the support hand simply releases the rifle so that I can use proper running mechanics.

For left-handed shooters, the best option is ambidextrous controls. If you find yourself forced to run a gun without ambidextrous controls installed, you have a few options for techniques. The best left-handed rifle shooter I knew in Special Forces hit the magazine release with his support hand as it left the fore end and drove to the spare magazine. Once he inserted the fresh magazine, he wrapped the fingers of his support hand around the front of the magwell and hit the bolt release before sliding the support hand out to its grip on the fore end. Joel Park, a high level competitive shooter friend of mine, secures the replacement magazine with his support hand first and then hits the magazine release with his support hand thumb. Once he inserts the fresh magazine, the support hand goes to the fore end and his strong hand hits the bolt release with his trigger finger.

When performing the speed reload, the support hand goes straight to its grip on the fore end without the necessity of actuating the bolt release. Unlike the pistol, this shortens the

148

movement enough that practicing the speed reload is not sufficient practice for the emergency reload. You need to work both in your dry and live fire practice.

For civilian self-defense or domestic law enforcement engagements, the rifle emergency reload is probably even less significant statistically than the pistol one, although I still believe it should be a staple of your practice for the same reasons I advocate seriously training pistol reloads. For military though, rifle reloads in an engagement are common enough that you should treat them as an absolutely essential task.

Much like pistol reloads, the bulk of your training on rifle reloads can be done in dry fire, with enough live fire work done to confirm that your dry practice is effective. Spend enough time on this skill to make it dependable under stress and executed at the subconscious level.

Transitioning Shoulders

Transitioning shoulders with your carbine is a somewhat controversial skill in the profession of arms. Some view it as essential while others view it as unnecessary. My own opinion lies between the two extremes. In order to exploit the tactical advantages that can be gained by transitioning to your support shoulder, you need to be proficient enough at shooting with your support side. Even if you have built up the requisite skill, whether or not there is an advantage to be gained depends on a multitude of factors. For the general shooter who isn't training for mastery, there are other skills to prioritize.

Having said all that, if you are going to master your craft, then you should put in the effort required to transition to and shoot expertly with your support side. And not just for the times when it can give you an advantage in application. There are also positive carryover effects from training your support side that will improve your skill in general.

The mechanics of the transition are simple enough. Sling setup is important. Single-point slings lend themselves well to this. If I'm running a dual-point sling, I first slide my support arm through the sling so that it is looped loosely around my neck instead of across my back. I move the carbine to my support shoulder without switching hands first. I can fire the weapon from this intermediary step if necessary. Depending on how aggressive my stance is I may have to switch feet in place or step either forward or back as I do so. Then I simply switch hands on the carbine, leaving it mounted. Done correctly, this transition is fast and maintains positive control of the weapon.

Transitions to Pistol

For law enforcement and soldiers engaged in CQB, the transition from rifle to pistol is a far more probable occurrence than a rifle emergency reload. If your primary weapon, your carbine, malfunctions or runs dry, your first instinct at CQB ranges should be to transition to your secondary weapon, your pistol, immediately.

Some decision points here. Especially at distances greater than typical CQB engagements but within effective pistol range—what determines when we should transition as opposed to either performing an emergency reload or a malfunction clearance? Part of this decision should be based on the condition of the weapon. And that brings us to an important point. To be truly competent with firearms, we should be attuned to the output they give us during the firing cycle, not just visual, but physical as well.

On an AR-pattern rifle especially, because of the buffer system, it is easy to tell by feel the difference between the bolt locking to the rear on an empty magazine, a failure-to-fire or extract, or a double-feed or bolt override. There should be no need to visually inspect the ejection port. Understanding this and knowing the condition of your weapon reliably can definitely factor in to the decision whether to transition or take corrective action on your primary.

151

The other factor that should impact your decision is shot difficulty. As I stated above, inside a structure the transition should be automatic. As ranges increase, especially with partially exposed or high risk shots, the decision whether to transition isn't so black and white. If it would take you longer to get an acceptable hit on the threat with your pistol, or if the shot difficulty or risk places it outside of what you can reliably do with your pistol, then you need to get the primary back up and running.

If transitioning to your secondary is the appropriate choice, then it needs to be done very rapidly indeed. In terms of technique, the transition is basically a pistol draw made slightly more complex due to the presence of the rifle.

I always attempt to put the rifle on safe prior to moving my strong hand to the pistol. This is not so much for when the transition is being performed in response to a malfunction or empty carbine, but more for when the transition is in order to search a confined space with the pistol, or there is a need to have one hand free. Attempting to place the weapon on safe costs no time, as you are already guiding the rifle down at the same time, so there's no reason not to train it that way.

As I drive the strong hand to the pistol, the support hand guides the rifle down to your side. Once it has done so it moves to the centerline of the body, and the remainder of the transition is not substantively different than a pistol draw. The one further complication is a need to be aware that your draw stroke may have to be slightly modified depending on where the carbine buttstock winds up.

One other note. I've seen a trend in the last several years to advise people with cross-eye dominance to shoot rifle with their support side even though they shoot pistol with their strong side. I cannot ever agree with this practice. This "solution" to a problem that can be easily trained out of causes far too many issues with weapons handling. Mike Pannone, a friend and mentor of mine who lost his dominant eye to a breaching charge when he was at SFOD-D still shoots rifle with his strong side.

If your job is CQB, work your transitions between your primary and secondary weapons systems extensively. The ability to reliably and consistently execute this skill at a subconscious level is crucial. Work this, especially in dry practice, until it becomes automatic.

152

Tactical Reloads

Tactical reloads with the rifle for law enforcement and civilians are even less likely than tactical reloads with a pistol. They, however, happen with enough frequency in military engagements to be a training priority. This is the only reload I have ever had to actually perform in an engagement, discounting topping off my weapon after the fight to prepare for secondary threats.

My philosophy on the performance of a tactical reload with the rifle is the same as with the pistol. There are various commonly taught techniques where you switch the magazines out at the gun, but I am not a proponent of any of them. They are far too inefficient and lend themselves to too great an error rate.

If time is pressing, I simply perform a speed reload. If I am behind cover and have sufficient time I will simply eject the partial magazine into my support hand, stow it on my person, and then reload the rifle with a fresh magazine. This uses the same efficient mechanics as a speed reload, and requires virtually no additional practice. It also is a much more dependable technique under stress. This is also the technique I use to top off my rifle after an engagement in case of follow-on threats.

This method is far more efficient and reliable than attempting to hold two magazines in the support hand as you switch between the two. It also takes far less focused practice, as it uses

153

essentially the same mechanics as a speed reload. Experiment with this technique in your training and learn to apply it reliably under stress.

Deliberate Load and Unload

Much like the pistol, I believe that your deliberate load and unload sequence for your carbine should be contextual. I use different methods depending on my role at the moment. Just like with pistol, these should be safe, repeatable, and valid for the circumstances in which they are applied.

In practice on the range, I load my carbine as simply and efficiently as possible while following the rules of firearms safety. The point of practicing shooting is to actually practice shooting, not practice my operational or competitive deliberate load and unload sequences.

In competition, the rules require a chamber flag. Once I'm given the "make ready" command, I remove the flag and lock the bolt to the rear. I then present to a sight picture, on the first target I'll be shooting if possible, checking my optic as I do so, and adjusting it if need be. Then I load the carbine as if performing a bolt lock reload, and "bump up" a magazine into my "go-to" pouch. All that's left is to assume the specified start position for the stage.

Prior to an operation, I have always preferred the way I was taught in Special Forces. Since the carbine is the primary weapon, it's loaded second. This is to ensure that the secondary isn't

154

glossed over or forgotten, since it's your emergency backup. First I lock the bolt to the rear, then present the carbine in a safe direction, checking and adjusting the optic, light, and laser. I then load the carbine as if performing a slide lock reload, and "bump up" a fresh magazine into my primary magazine pouch.

For deliberate unloads, the same priorities apply as with pistol. The sequence should have redundant safety checks built in. For competition and in my own live fire training, I follow almost the same procedure. With the carbine pointed in a safe direction, I first remove the magazine then eject the chambered round. Keeping the carbine aimed in a safe direction, I pull the trigger, dropping the hammer on an empty chamber. For competition, I then reinsert the chamber flag. In my own training, I omit that step as unnecessary. In an operational or institutional setting, the practice of visual and physical inspection of the chamber and magwell are entirely valid.

MALFUNCTIONS

"Malfunctions are inevitable. It's important to push through them during practice - versus stopping to fix and restart - so that you're prepared for one mid-competition." - Amanda Beard

All mechanical systems malfunction and fail. We can mitigate this through maintenance and correct use, but we cannot eliminate it. It is vital that we learn to efficiently and rapidly address malfunctions in order to stay in the fight. There are a few points here that apply regardless of weapons system or malfunction type.

You should be conversant enough with the recoil impulse of your firearms to know without looking if the bolt or slide has locked to the rear, or if the gun has malfunctioned. You should be able to tell the difference between a failure-to-feed or fire and a complex malfunction intuitively. Despite what the popular training videos of the 2000's show, there should be no need to visually inspect the ejection port of a carbine to see if the bolt is locked to the rear or if there is a double-feed.

In the beginning, it can be valuable to learn "by the numbers" techniques for clearing malfunctions, but as your skill and understanding increase, this can become a limiting factor. An example is the commonly taught "tap-rack-bang" technique for a failure-to-fire or failure-to-feed/extract. If the weapon has fired more than once, then the cause is something besides the magazine not being fully inserted. In that case, the "tap" portion of the technique is wasted time and can be omitted for efficiency. As your experience increases, these sorts of judgements should be made intuitively and subconsciously so that you can get your firearm running as quickly as possible.

It's important to explore this in your training so that your response to a malfunction is immediate, efficient, and appropriate. If your gun isn't operable, you're not in the fight...

PISTOL

To understand why pistols malfunction, you need to understand how they work. When the trigger is pressed, the hammer or striker falls, causing the firing pin to strike the primer of the chambered round. This causes the round to fire. The force of the round firing causes the slide to move to the rear. The extractor in the slide pulls the empty case from the chamber until it hits the ejector in the frame, which causes the brass to tumble out of the ejection port. Once the slide begins to move forward again, it strips a fresh round from the magazine and feeds it into the chamber. Once the round is seated in the chamber and the slide is all the way forward into battery, the pistol is ready to fire again.

A failure-to-feed occurs when the new round is not stripped from the magazine and fed into the chamber. The most probable cause for this is a failure to seat the magazine completely when loading the pistol. It can also occur when the magazine follower sticks in the magazine tube, either because the magazine is fouled by dirt or the magazine spring has worn out and is too weak. The last cause is when ammunition is out of spec and does not completely feed into the chamber, causing the pistol to be slightly out of battery.

If the magazine wasn't seated properly but doesn't drop from the pistol when it's fired, the best remedy is the classic "tap-rack-bang" taught to beginning shooters. When racking the pistol. I find it is much faster and more efficient if I manipulate the slide by pinching it in the web of my thumb forward of the ejection port. This allows me to regain my proper support hand grip on the pistol much faster. If the magazine drops from the pistol when it's fired, the automatic response should be to immediately perform a reload and manually cycle the slide, since it won't be locked to the rear.

If the failure-to-feed was due to magazine failure, the classic "tap-rack-bang" won't correct the malfunction. In this case, you will have to perform a reload and manually cycle the slide in order to get the pistol back into operation.

If the failure-to-feed involves a round that doesn't fully chamber due to being out of spec, it can usually be cleared by simply racking the pistol to eject the faulty round and feed a new one. Sometimes the out-of-spec round can become stuck in the chamber, now causing a failure-to-extract. The quickest way to clear this is to firmly grab the top of the slide with the support hand and strike the rear of the grip with enough force to cycle the pistol and extract the stuck round.

A failure-to-fire occurs when there is a properly chambered round, but when the trigger is pressed and the striker or hammer falls, the round doesn't fire. This can sometimes be caused by a mechanical issue with the firing pin but is more commonly an ammunition issue. If the primer is faulty, or seated too high in the shell case, it won't ignite when struck by the firing pin. If this is an ammunition issue then all you need to do to correct the problem is rack the slide and feed a new round. If there is an issue with the firing pin, then this malfunction can't be fixed without disassembling the pistol, and possibly replacing parts.

A failure-to-eject is when the empty case is extracted from the chamber, but is not ejected properly. This is often called a stovepipe, which is what the partially ejected brass sticking out of the ejection port looks like. This can most often be cleared by simply stripping the case from the ejection port with the support hand.

A failure-to-extract is when the spent case remains seated in the chamber. In most cases, simply cycling the slide will extract the spent case. Sometimes you will need to hold the slide firmly and strike the tang of the grip sharply to dislodge the spent case. If the case is damaged or deformed severely enough, then this may require tools to correct.

The next type of malfunction is the double-feed. This is when two rounds are attempting to seat in the chamber at the same time. To clear a double-feed, the classically taught technique is best. Lock the slide to the rear, strip and discard the magazine, cycle the slide, and reload the pistol.

The mechanics of these responses can quickly be developed at a high level through dry repetition. The difficult part is diagnosing the malfunction subconsciously and performing the correct technique to clear it automatically and without hesitation. The only way to develop this ability is through sufficient experience. And the only way to gain that experience is to shoot enough under time pressure where you have to remedy any malfunctions on the clock. The best place I've found to do that is by competing regularly in action pistol matches.

CARBINE

Just like pistol, understanding how your carbine functions is essential to learning how to intuitively and efficiently correct malfunctions. The AR carbine uses a either a piston or direct impingement gas system to function. When the chambered round is fired, both systems utilize the expanding gases from the round to unlock and cycle the bolt in the receiver. The bolt moves rearward, extracting and ejecting the spent casing as it recoils against the buffer and spring inside the buttstock and then cycles forward, stripping a fresh round from the magazine and chambering it as the bolt then locks into battery. The carbine then fires again if the selector is on full auto and the trigger remains depressed, and is ready to fire again if the selector is on semi-automatic.

One advantage the AR carbine has over pistol in this regard is that due to the buffer system there is a very perceptible difference in how the recoil impulse feels between proper cycling, the bolt locking to the rear on an empty magazine, and the bolt stopping out of battery due to a malfunction. This makes it easier to learn to initiate the appropriate response by feel. The disadvantage though is that more complex malfunctions such as double-feeds and bolt overrides can be difficult to clear.

A failure-to-feed is customarily addressed with the traditional "tap, rack, bang" response. If the magazine isn't correctly seated, but doesn't drop free when the rifle is fired, this is definitely the most efficient response. If the magazine wasn't seated properly and does drop free, treat it as an emergency reload where you have to manually charge the carbine rather than just drop the bolt using the bolt release. This is also the appropriate response if the failure-to-feed is caused by a fouled or faulty magazine.

If the failure-to-feed involves a round that doesn't fully chamber due to being out of spec, it can usually be cleared by simply cycling the carbine to eject the faulty round and feed a new one. Sometimes the out-of-spec round can become stuck in the chamber, now causing a failure-to-extract. The quickest way to clear this is usually to collapse the buttstock, put downward pressure on the charging handle, and "mortar" the carbine by striking the ground using the heel of the stock with enough force to cycle the rifle and extract the stuck round. If this doesn't clear the chamber you will usually need tools to get the weapon back into service.

A failure-to-fire is also traditionally addressed with "tap-rack-bang." Just like clearing this on a pistol, if the magazine is correctly seated, and the failure-to-fire is solely an ammunition issue rather than a mechanical issue with the gun, then striking the base of the magazine is an unnecessary step and should be eliminated. In this case the most efficient response is to simply charge the rifle, ejecting the faulty round and feeding a fresh one. If the cause is a mechanical defect, the malfunction can't be cleared without disassembling the carbine and possibly replacing parts.

A failure-to-eject is when the empty case is extracted from the chamber, but is not ejected properly. This can be as simple as a stovepipe, when the partially ejected brass sticks out of the ejection port. This can most often be cleared by simply stripping the case from the ejection port with the support hand. On an AR, this can also cause what is known as a bolt override, which we'll cover in a moment.

A failure-to-extract is when the spent case remains seated in the chamber. In most cases, simply cycling the bolt will extract the spent case. Sometimes you will need to mortar the carbine to dislodge the spent case. If the case is damaged or deformed severely enough, then this may require tools to correct.

The next type of malfunction is the double-feed. This is when two rounds are attempting to seat in the chamber at the same time. To clear a double-feed, lock the bolt to the rear, strip and discard the magazine, manually clear the rounds with your fingers if necessary, cycle the action, and reload the carbine.

The last malfunction we will cover is the bolt override. This is when either a spent case or a live round lodges on top of the bolt in the receiver, locking up the action. There are several recommendations for clearing these, but the best of them in my opinion is the one created by my friend Mike Pannone of CTT solutions. Strip the magazine, and from the kneeling position trap the rifle between your torso and the ground, with the muzzle resting on the sling on the ground to protect it, and the buttstock between your pecs. Use both hands to work the charging handle back until you can lock it to the rear, then strike the charging handle forward using the edge of your hand. Finally, use gravity and your fingers as needed to clear any remaining rounds from the chamber before loading and charging the carbine. Mike teaches the best AR malfunction block I've ever seen. If you get the chance, take a carbine class from CTT Solutions, and learn this from him directly.

The mechanics of these responses can easily be learned at a high level through dry fire training. The hard part is learning to differentiate between the malfunctions correctly and immediately. Just like with pistol, the only way to develop this at a high level is through enough experience shooting on the clock. Once again, the best mechanism for developing this skill is action shooting matches. Seek them out, and use the lessons they teach to inform your training and application.

WOUNDED WEAPON MANIPULATIONS

"If an injury has to be done to a man it should be so severe that his vengeance need not be feared." - Niccolo Machiavelli

Anyone who has done extensive force-on-force training knows all too well how possible it is to take a hit to the hands and arms. The time to sort out how you're going to run your gun using one hand is before this happens, not in the moment. Put some time and effort into rehearsing this in your dry and live practice so that you can work through an injury calmly and competently.

This is usually drilled by the numbers in a very mechanical fashion. There is some value in this approach in the early stages of your training, but as your skill progresses you need to develop responses that are more fluid and adaptable to the situation at hand. Learn to use your sling, your holster, your kit, even parts of your body to assist in manipulating the firearm. Learn to transition your pistol or carbine to your support side without the use of your strong side. Figure out how to address reloads and malfunction clearances using one hand. Explore and experiment with a variety of these techniques in your training so that your responses become intuitive.

TARGET TRANSITIONS

"Everything changes and nothing stands still." - Heraclitus

Efficient and consistent target transitions are a fundamental shooting skill. In an encounter with multiple adversaries, the ability to engage several targets of varying difficulty and risk can mean the difference between life or death. In a match, transitions are the pure shooting task that is arguably the most important for your score. For your training, transitions are not only an important skill for their own sake, but also have a strong carryover effect to single target engagements because they are one of the best ways to develop a proper index.

Index, simply put, is your ability to look at a point and then bring your weapon into your eyeline with the sights in alignment with the point you're looking at. This is one of the most important shooting skills, and is something you absolutely need to develop at a very high level. It is also the essence of target transitions.

When transitioning targets, you need to lead with the eyes. The moment of your last shot on a target that the sights or dot lift, and no sooner, you immediately snap your vision to a precise point on the next target you are going to engage. You then move the firearm to proper alignment with the point you're looking at. Subjectively, it should feel as if the sights or dot simply appear effortlessly in correct alignment with where you are looking.

163

Some important points to consider here. One is that it is extremely important to guard against excess muscular effort in the transition. This feels faster due to the acceleration, but because it's harder to stop the weapon on target smoothly and efficiently, it actually wastes time. Obviously the wider the transition, the more muscular effort is necessary. Even on the widest transitions though, confine the acceleration to the first two thirds or less of the transition, and allow the firearm to smoothly coast into alignment with the target.

Related to over-muscling the transition is allowing excess tension to creep up. This not only prevents efficient target acquisition, it also slows the transition speed. Excess tension never allows for efficient movement, and this is no exception to that rule.

Rather than the old school "tank turret" style of transitions, or even some more recent paradigms such as driving the transition with the hips or knees, I try to stay relaxed and let multiple joints come into play. With a pistol I move the gun in a straight line, and although this is imperceptible in close transitions, it becomes very apparent when the transition is greater than ninety degrees.

I put a strong emphasis in transition work in my live and dry fire training. You need to develop the skill to transition between targets of varying difficulty in random arrays quickly and efficiently at a subconscious level of competence. Put in the work to build that skill, and it will improve your abilities as a shooter.

NONSTANDARD SHOOTING POSITIONS

"Incoming fire has the right of way." - Clint Smith

Effective use of cover often forces us to deviate from our normal shooting stance. This has led to a wide variety of nonstandard shooting positions being developed and taught. This is important both for your training and application. There are some important points we should consider where these techniques are concerned.

The first thing to remember is that it does not take much deviation from your natural balanced posture before the difficulty increases in your shooting. It is not enough to simply learn a variety of cookie-cutter stances. You have to spend time shooting from awkward and unbalanced positions to understand how your shooting changes.

The second important point is to make your positions as efficient as possible from an athletic performance point of view. An example of this is using the muscles of the outside leg to initiate and stabilize a lean, rather than leaning with the upper body. Find ways to assume nonstandard positions that work with your natural structure, not against it.

Lastly, while there is definitely a tactical value to the ability to maximize the use of cover through nonstandard positions, there's a risk as well. Mobility matters, and there is a trade off here. I've seen a lot of people in a training environment assume some exotic shooting position simply for the sake of doing so. Needlessly increasing complexity hinders effectiveness.

MOVING WITH A FIREARM

"The essence of fighting is the art of moving." - Bruce Lee

One of the biggest technical issues I see with "tactical" shooters isn't even a shooting issue per se. It's movement. For some reason most people, even gifted athletes, forget all the rules of athletic performance when you put a gun in their hand. Part of this is the way movement technique is typically taught in military and law enforcement circles, and part of this is how it is typically trained. Movement should be trained athletically, and the movement techniques chosen should be performance-based. There are some general principles to follow to make this happen, regardless of the particular movement skill being trained.

Always be aware of muzzle direction at all times. This can be at the subconscious level once sufficient skill is developed, but it always has to be present. This does NOT mean you need to use some artificial and rigid ready positions when you move. I am very much against moving with the pistol "indexed" against the temple or holster, or in any other static ready position, including "sul." Learn to keep your muzzle pointed where you want without having to resort to over complicated and unnatural techniques.

The essence of movement with a firearm, whether in a gunfight or a match, is the ability to shoot accurately while you are slightly unstable. Practice this thoroughly and extensively, it is absolutely essential for your progress as a shooter.

Movement needs to be relaxed and athletic. This does not mean it isn't explosive. What it does mean is that it shouldn't be tense or rigid. Movement is movement, and the principles don't change from other athletic endeavors just because you are operating a firearm.

Vision drives movement. Even a quick glance at the exact spot you want to set up at will help you be precise with your positioning, even operating at high speed under stress. Much like looking the magazine into the magwell during a reload, this will drastically improve both speed and precision in your technique, and contrary to traditional doctrine will not significantly impair your situational awareness.

The gun needs to be kept high when setting up into position. It does you no good to get into position rapidly if you aren't ready to shoot when you get there. I see this very commonly in "tactical" shooters, and it's a major technical deficiency.

Look at top athletes for examples of relevant footwork technique. The best sources for gunfighting footwork are field and court sports. I came to this realization late in my career once I started USPSA competition. This took some adjustment on my part, as my athletic endeavors had always been either endurance or strength-based because of the fitness demands of my military and law enforcement careers, or combative sports and martial arts. Martial arts footwork is applicable for using a firearm at contact distance or when entangled, but it is not the right way to move in a typical gunfight.

Don't train movement as an afterthought. Drill its component skills dry and live, and emphasize its development at a high level. Just like every other type of conflict, movement is essential for victory in gunfighting.

SHOOTING ON THE MOVE

"Float like a butterfly, sting like a bee." - Muhammed Ali

The famous quote, made as a boast before his fight with Sonny Liston, is a good metaphor for what shooting on the move should feel like. All too often, shooting on the move is done without a clear understanding of why or how it should be applied. To gain any advantage, either tactical or competitive, from shooting on the move, you need to be able to move rapidly enough to make the increased difficulty and exposure worth it.

Rather than the exaggerated short steps and forward lean of the traditionally taught technique, we need to walk in a fluid and relaxed fashion. We do need to bend enough at the knees and hips to smooth out our sight picture, but the shoulders and elbows should help absorb that motion as well. An exercise I like for developing this ability is to fill a glass with water, and to walk rapidly, with changes of direction, while holding the glass in both hands at arm's length like a pistol. Trying not to spill the water while working on movement helps you learn to "float" the gun while walking rapidly.

Moving laterally to your support side is more difficult than to your strong side. I find that angling my foot closest to the target slightly towards it allows me to open up my hip a bit and engage the targets more naturally. Experiment with this in your own training and figure out your own optimal technique.

You need to work on shooting on the move in your dry and live fire practice with varying target difficulties and angles of movement so that you have an intuitive grasp of when you can successfully apply it and when you can't. Sometimes it will serve you better to simply move into your next position and post up rather than attempting to engage targets on the move.

POSITION ENTRY AND EXIT

"Proper footwork is good balance in action." - Bruce Lee

Position entry and exit is simply that. How we leave one shooting position, move to, and enter another. This has to be done as rapidly as possible. What that means though is improving efficiency as much as raw speed. Being ready to shoot *sooner* is infinitely better than coming in "hot" to a shooting position and having to mount the gun and stabilize the sights before you can shoot. In a similar vein, learning to leave a position after the last shot fired immediately and as efficiently as possible matters more than just having an explosive start to your movement.

I categorize position exits into three broad categories. The first of these are "Hard Exits." A hard exit is when your last target is high difficulty, high risk, or both. These means your shooting platform needs to remain as stable as possible until your last shot breaks. The second category is "Easy Exits." An easy exit is when your last target is easy and low risk enough that you can begin your upper body movement while engaging it. The third and final category is shooting out of position. This is for very easy and low risk targets that you can successfully engage after initiating your lower body movement.

The footwork for each of these variations is different. For a hard exit, remain completely stable until the last shot breaks, then immediately explode out of position. Take your support hand off the firearm and glance quickly at the spot you want to set up in for your entry while taking a large step with the foot closest to your direction of travel. Accelerate, driving with the legs and pump your arms. Learn to use the weight of the gun to contribute to your acceleration by "punching" it out as you explode out of position.

For an easy exit, you begin moving your upper body in the direction of travel while still shooting, once you've fired your last shot, you "fall" out of position and initiate the movement with the foot furthest from the direction of travel. As the foot crosses over, turn your hips in the direction of travel and then accelerate using the same lower and upper body technique as the hard exit.

Shooting out of position is simply shooting your targets on the move, then accelerating hard in the direction of travel once the last shot is fired. This often necessitates walking backwards for a few steps then turning the hips towards the direction of travel while explosively accelerating using the same technique as above.

Much like position exits, I categorize position entries into three categories. The first category is "Hard Entries." A hard entry is when your first target is difficult or risky enough that your shooting platform has to be completely stable prior to breaking your first shot. The next category is "Easy Entries." An easy entry is when your first target is sufficiently easy and low risk enough that you can engage it prior to stopping your upper body movement. Lastly we have shooting into position. This is for very easy and low risk targets that you can engage prior to completing your lower body movement.

The footwork for all three entry variations is the same. Utilize a series of short choppy steps to bleed off momentum as necessary. Then take a large step with the foot closest to your target to eliminate the last of your momentum, simultaneously mounting your firearm, followed by a step that brings your outside foot in line with the inside and pointed towards your target. The last step is a slide with the inside foot, finishing up square towards the target with your feet between hip and shoulder width without raising your hips up from the height they were during your run. Done correctly, your sights should be stable before the last step finishes.

For the movement between positions, it needs to be as fast as possible while remaining controlled. You need to factor in the movement distance and terrain to avoid coming into position with too much residual momentum. Remember that the entire point of the movement sequence is to put yourself in an advantageous position while being ready to shoot as soon as you enter position.

Explore all the variations of position entry and exit in your training. Manipulate the variables above, as well as movement distance and direction, until you are able to apply these techniques in any circumstance.

SHORT MOVEMENTS

"According to the enemy's rhythm, move fast or slowly, adjusting your body not too much and not too little." - Miyamoto Musashi

For short movements, three to four steps or less, there isn't enough space to use our position entry and exit footwork. There are a wide variety of footwork patterns for this, each applicable in different situations. In these shorter movements, I do not take my support hand off of the firearm, and may even keep it mounted depending on the context.

For short forward movements requiring speed, I use a quick shuffling run. Almost halfway between shooting on the move and position entry and exit. It is vital to keep the firearm high and ready to mount immediately. It's also vital to maintain the same height as you move, not bounce up and down. For less aggressive forward movements, simply walk forwards as if shooting on the move. This has a wide variety of tactical application.

For lateral movements at speed, there are a few options, depending on context. The first is a dynamic lateral step, pushing off the trail foot, the foot opposite the direction of travel, and stepping deep in the direction of travel with the lead foot, then sliding the trail foot into position. Keep the firearm at the eyeline, even if you dismount it. This is a movement where I seldom dismount the gun.

Then there is a sliding step, where you bring the trail foot into the lead foot then push off, step, and slide into position as in the lateral step. The coaching cue I use for this is replacing the lead foot with the trail. It should feel like your feet are switching places. Another important technical point is to keep the hips level once they are low enough to drive efficiently. You should also initiate your movement with the upper body, driving with the elbow. Done correctly, this footwork is extremely explosive.

There is also the step-to-slide. This is a combination of the previous two. Begin with a lateral step with the lead foot, then immediately continue into a sliding step with the trail foot. The transition should be seamless and aggressive while keeping the hips level. You can string two sliding steps together to make distance if needed, but more than that and you're better off using a position exit and entry.

For less aggressive lateral movements, we can do either a crossover step or turn the hips in the direction of travel and step naturally. The crossover step is faster, and very applicable for moving reloads or short distance shooting on the move on easy targets. Turning the hips and walking normally is suitable for shooting on the move on more difficult targets or pieing off corners and thresholds at speed as well as much of the movement for CQB.

These shorter movement techniques should be drilled and practiced until you can apply them appropriately and efficiently for any given context. Train movement like an athlete.

THRESHOLDS AND OBSTACLES

"The obstacle in the path becomes the path" - Ryan Holliday

Maneuvering around objects is a critical skill for gunfighting. Your ability to do so as efficiently as possible is literally a matter of life or death. This skill should be approached as an athletic one, but I seldom see it trained that way.

The most common error I see when people address thresholds and obstacles is not being prepared to shoot the instant you clear them and are exposed, even partially. If you move past an object without orienting your weapon immediately towards the uncleared space, you are dangerously behind the power curve if your opponent is waiting there to ambush you.

Your footwork should be highly efficient as it serves to orient your presentation to the uncleared side of whatever physical barrier you are negotiating. This could be a door jamb, an exterior or interior corner, a support column, or any other object you need to maneuver around. Develop your footwork with a critical eye, ensuring that it is as effective as possible.

Your ready position with the firearm should be appropriate to the situation and allow you to mount the gun rapidly as needed. It should be relaxed, adaptable, and fluid rather than the stiff and exaggerated positions that are all too popular.

Explore these factors in your training. Constantly evaluate and polish your movement and stack the odds in your favor when it comes time to apply it.

SUPPORT SIDE SHOOTING

"I presume you know the difference between front and back, right hand and left hand?" - Sun Tzu

Support side shooting isn't trained enough by most people. Granted, this isn't something that should receive a training priority, especially for lower level shooters. But for those who want to master their craft, there are several reasons for developing shooting skill with your support side.

The most obvious is the possibility of an injury to your strong side. Also, at least with a carbine, there are some situations where transitioning to your support side offers a tactical advantage as long as you have the requisite shooting skill. In both of those instances, during the event is too late to develop skill. You need to do that ahead of time. Also, and perhaps most importantly, there is a carryover effect. Getting better with support side shooting improves my shooting skill as a whole.

The principles of marksmanship don't change when you switch to your support side. Learn to apply them in a mirror image of your strong side. Train this well and you'll be a better shooter because of it.

LOW LIGHT

"Bright light is injurious to those who see nothing." - Aurelius Prudentius

Low light engagements involve several interrelated skill sets. The first is simply developing an applied understanding of how ambient lighting can be used against your opponent and how it can be used against you. One of my mentors, Ken Good of the Surefire Institute, a pioneer in the combative use of lights, used to talk about how "dark holes hide guns." At its most basic level, you want to work from a darker area towards a brighter one whenever possible. If this isn't possible, and your situation allows the use of white light, you want to light up the darker areas to take the lighting advantage away from any opponents potentially hiding there.

Then there is the use of handheld and weapon mounted lights. White light, when used properly, is a very powerful tool. It can be used for navigation, target location and identification, and as communication. Offensively, white light can be used for subject control, deception, disorientation, and distraction.

When navigating or searching for threats, I believe white light should be used in an intermittent and seemingly random fashion, moving between activations. I have experienced this first-hand as a role player in force-on-force training and used it operationally countless times. I can vouch for the fact that it is more deceptive to the opponent than you might think.

Light can be used to communicate with teammates. You can use the throw of your light to identify a location, signal for a link-up, direct attention, or to show that a danger area is being covered. It can be used to direct potential threats and command their movements. This is also where visible lasers prove their value. In my opinion, a visible laser has far more worth as a communication tool than as a sight.

When engaging a threat, focusing a steady beam of light into their vision can disorient them and impair their ability to process information visually. This can be used to cover a teammate's movement, assist in establishing control of a subject, or make your offensive actions more effective.

Then there is night vision, and the associated tools of IR lasers and lights. With the recent proliferation of affordable night vision, an over-reliance on active aiming tools like IR lasers can be problematic. Gone are the days when we could say we owned the night. Passive aiming through night vision compatible optics is preferable now, and IR lasers and lights should be treated like their visible counterparts.

WEAPONS RETENTION

"Remember the first rule of gunfighting ... have a gun." - Jeff Cooper

Weapons retention is crucial for anyone carrying a firearm. In law enforcement management circles, this is all too often addressed solely through mandating holsters with multiple levels of retention rather than through effective training in combatives. At its heart, weapons retention is a software issue, not a hardware one. Situational awareness and combatives skill trump kit selection where this is concerned. In the military, until relatively recently, weapons retention hasn't received enough attention, especially in conventional units. Now, though there are realistic training programs such as the Jujitsu-based MACP and SOCP systems that effectively address weapons retention. In this though, as in so many other aspects of the profession of arms, it simply isn't enough to rely on the training your department or unit provides. You need to seek out training on your own.

Regardless of whether you are a police officer, or a soldier, or an armed citizen, weapons retention needs to be trained, and it needs to be trained realistically and effectively. I'm a proponent of basing weapons retention techniques off of jujitsu. If you look at the classical development of jujitsu, it developed in a weapons-based environment and included techniques for retaining your weapons and stripping an opponent of theirs. It has been explored for modern application and remains as effective now as it was in feudal Japan. If you combine this with a study and practice of Filipino martial arts such as Kali and Arnis you can develop a solid level of applicable skill.

The SOCP and MACP programs of Gregg Thompson, the ShivWorks training of Paul Sharp and others, the excellent ECQC courses of Craig Douglas, and other training can help provide a framework, but the truth is that skill requires regular practice. Seek out that practice and frame it in ways applicable to your environment and weaponry. Develop a solid foundation of combative skill and it will serve you well. As always, the way is in training.

CONTACT DISTANCE SHOOTING

"Close combat, man to man, is plainly to be regarded as the real basis of combat." - Carl Von Clausewitz

Entangled gunfights happen. There's scores of security camera and LE body camera footage bearing this out. One of the traditional failings of institutional training, especially on the law enforcement side, has been to treat combatives and shooting as separate fields of endeavor. It's rare to see an LE instructor who is both a combatives and a tactical shooting SME. This tendency to compartmentalize these skills doesn't adequately prepare officers for reality.

The truth of violence is that conflict is a continuum. A fight may move up and down the use of force scale based on distance and the opponent's actions. Employing your firearm while grappling is a very real possibility, and has its own technical and tactical considerations.

The two main concerns when shooting at contact distance are putting effective hits on the opponent without conventional sighted fire, and avoiding flagging yourself with the pistol. Both are very real issues when employing your firearm while grappling with your opponent. Because of the obvious safety concerns, extensive dry drilling should be done prior to any live fire training in these techniques. It's all too easy to flag your support arm and possibly injure yourself seriously with your own gun.

Aiming at contact distance is properly done through body index—either from two-handed retention using the same body index developed through more conventional shooting practice, or by using a thumb/pectoral index where the pistol is aligned by resting the firing hand thumb along the base of the pectoral muscle. With a small amount of live fire practice, a functional degree of accuracy can be achieved with either technique. Which method to use is solely dependent on the situation.

When using the support hand and arm to grapple or create distance, the pectoral index is required. It's important to resist the urge to press the muzzle of your pistol into your opponent. That can induce a malfunction. Point shooting isn't ideal either as it can cause poor hits even at contact distance and makes you vulnerable to having the weapon stripped and taken away. Although, there are times when fighting for control of a handgun where this becomes your only option.

To properly perform the pectoral index, extend the thumb of the firing hand straight along the frame of the receiver and use it as a physical reference point for the alignment of the pistol by running it along the outside bottom edge of the pectoral muscle. Ensure you slightly cant the pistol out from your body to avoid inducing a malfunction caused by the slide being unable to cycle properly. With some live fire practice you'll find that using this index to ensure acceptable hits at contact distance is not overly difficult.

The other aiming option I prefer is shooting from two handed retention. This is simply bringing the weapon to the point on your normal draw stroke where your support hand meets the gun, establishing a firing grip, and using the index developed through your normal live and dry fire practice to align the pistol. You'll find that, as long as your conventional index is well developed, you'll be more than accurate enough at contact distance where windage is concerned. Elevation may take some live fire practice to dial in to acceptable levels of accuracy though.

For carbine work while entangled, the cautions for pistol against pressing the muzzle into the opponent do not apply. Although when you drill this in force-on-force or with inert guns while grappling, you'll discover that it's often better to transfer to your pistol in order to put effective hits on an opponent you're grappling with.

It's extremely important to address the combatives portion of entangled gunfights as well as the shooting one. Once you're exposed to it, the shooting element is not particularly difficult. Drill these situations extensively with inert weapons and in force-on-force and learn to manage them effectively. Like all other aspects of combat, it's important to work your techniques and tactics against noncooperative training partners so that you can find and address any deficiencies in your skill.

Spend some significant time learning how to address an opponent at contact distance. This is far too likely and dangerous a situation to be neglected.

STANDING GRAPPLING

"The art of jiu-jitsu is worth more in every way than all of our athletics combined." - Teddy Roosevelt

Many physical confrontations, especially between armed opponents, involve grappling as much or more than striking. In a one-on-one sporting event, prioritizing ground fighting is sound and proven doctrine. In fights where you have to remain alert for other threats I prefer keeping an upright torso whenever possible, although taking your opponent to the ground absolutely remains a priority. Skill at standing grappling, especially in CQB or law enforcement confrontations is vital. It's also important for civilian self-defense when carrying a firearm for a multitude of reasons.

One of the brilliant aspects of Brazilian Jujitsu is the teaching methodology. They approach ground fighting from a positional framework. When teaching combatives to the Chicago SWAT team, I adopted a similar approach for teaching standing grappling. The three basic positions I taught everyone on the team were the post, frame, and clinch.

The first of these is the post. Posting is using an extended, not locked, arm to manage distance between you and your opponent, and to move them into a position that gives you advantage. It's important to understand that the post is not a static position, and that its value lies solely in your ability to momentarily control your opponent's movement. With regular practice you'll learn the lines of force that work best with this technique.

The next position is the frame. The frame is using your forearm, elbow bent, to maintain distance or move your opponent. The bend in the elbow must be less than 90 degrees, and the elbow is flared out to the side. This arm position is seen in numerous martial arts from classical Wing Chun to Tony Blauer's excellent SPEAR system. Done correctly, this is a very strong position.

The third position is the clinch. This can be done with over-hooks, under-hooks, or a mix of the two. It can also be done Muay Thai style, where your hands compress the back of the opponent's neck. You can also have one hand on the neck and one controlling an arm. It can be done at a variety of angles to the opponent. You can use the clinch to prevent or create movement, to prevent your opponent from striking or employing weapons, and to employ your weapons as needed.

Much like the basic guard and mount positions of Brazilian Jujitsu, there are numerous variations of these three standing positions that can, and should, be learned and trained once you have an effective grasp of the foundational ones. This should be explored in noncooperative drilling with a partner in order to understand what variations are effective and which ones aren't.

Explore throws, locks, chokes, and takedowns from wrestling, Judo, and Aikido along with trapping hands from Kali/Arnis and Wing Chun. Work them in noncooperative practice from each of these positions, and their variations. Learn to apply them under stress on a resisting opponent.

These techniques and positions, and their variations, apply in weapons retention and contact distance shooting as well as unarmed grappling. They provide a framework you can use to employ tools, apply unarmed striking techniques, and set up takedowns, throws, chokes, or submissions. Train these techniques, positions, and their variations thoroughly. Explore how to use them in conflict, armed and unarmed, both solo and as part of a team. Do this and your training will serve you well.

GROUND FIGHTING

"The art of living is more like wrestling than dancing." - Marcus Aurelius

Ground fighting is an absolutely essential skill. But there are subtle differences in how this skill should be applied in real world confrontations as opposed to sporting events. In a weapons-based and team-based environment, neither the classic guard nor a mount where your torso is horizontal are ideal. That doesn't mean they won't be necessary, however, nor does it mean they shouldn't be trained diligently. It also doesn't mean that you can totally avoid going to the ground. In fact, it is often ideal to take the opponent to the ground and immobilize him. But when you do so, if you can, it is best to maintain a relatively upright torso. This gives you better situational awareness, and makes it easier to disengage from your opponent if necessary.

The best teaching methodology I have seen for learning ground fighting is the positional approach of Brazilian Jujitsu. Although there are other basic positions, and many variations, the most fundamental and applicable for us are the guard, the mount, knee on torso, and the rear mount. Knowing these positions, and utilizing them properly, gives you a framework for understanding ground fighting.

The first position, the guard, is defensive in nature. Although there are numerous variations and applications, in its basic form you are on your back, with your legs on the outside of the opponent in order to control and restrict their movement. This is an advantageous position in sport fighting. In real world application it is less advantageous because of weapons, additional opponents, and environmental considerations. It is still an absolutely essential skill though. You don't always get to choose how the fight develops, and the opponent gets a vote. I can think of several real world incidents where my ability to work the guard against my opponent allowed me to control and subdue them easily where I otherwise could have been at great risk of losing the fight.

The second position, the mount, is both very dominant in a sport fight and very advantageous in application, especially when the torso is kept upright. In the mount, in its most fundamental form, you are on top of your opponent and straddling them, inhibiting their movement through your weight and your legs. If they have their back to you, this is the rear mount, and is an incredibly dominant position. The mount and it's variations are extremely valuable in the practical application of grappling. Whenever possible, I attempt to maintain an upright torso in the mount in order to maintain situational awareness and make it easier to employ tools.

Knee on torso is a common position in classical jujitsu, although it's often applied somewhat differently than in modern jujitsu. Both the modern sporting versions and the classical ones have significant value in real-world applications. Whatever the variation, the position is assumed by either placing one knee on top of the opponent's torso or pressing it into their side. The other leg is spread out, either straight or kneeling. These positions lend themselves well to employing tools, applying strikes or joint-based submissions, and creating space if needed.

Learn to work these positions, and more, against noncooperative training partners. Research the submissions of BJJ, classical Jujitsu, Aikido, and Western wrestling. Learn to apply submissions and employ tools while ground fighting. Understand how grappling changes when weapons are introduced. If your job involves CQB, understand how that environment affects your priorities for both standing grappling and ground fighting, because it definitely does. You need to research all these things well in your training.

EDGED AND IMPACT WEAPONS

"When in a fight to the death, one wants to employ all one's weapons to the utmost." - Miyamoto Musashi

In today's world, firearms are usually our primary and secondary weapons systems. But soldiers and law enforcement often carry impact or edged weapons as a tertiary. When carrying a pistol concealed as my primary, I'll often carry a small fixed blade knife as a secondary. Edged weapons can be employed very effectively to retain your carbine or pistol, and impact weapons fit into an intermediate area in your rules of engagement (ROE) or use of force policies between empty hand technique and the deadly force of firearms.

The body mechanics and movement patterns are extremely similar between impact and edged weapons. This allows for training carryover between the two types of weapons. There is a crucial difference though. Impact weapons strike with blunt force, while edged weapons cut most efficiently when the blade is drawn across in either a pulling or pushing motion. This distinction creates a subtle but crucial difference in application between the two types of weapons.

Another important difference between the two weapons is targeting. Cutting with an edged weapon is most effective when you target arteries, tendons, and nerves. These tend to run along the inside of our limbs, as well as the front of the neck where you can also target the trachea. If the blade is heavy and long enough you can target musculature also, as well as abdominal organs. Stabbing or thrusting is effective against organs, depending on blade length, and is very difficult to defend against.

Impact weapons can target muscles, joints, and bones, as well as the brain, nerves, and trachea. For civilian self-defense and law enforcement application it's vital to understand which targets are justifiable in a situation that doesn't warrant deadly force. In situations requiring deadly force, you need to know how to target to inflict maximum damage as well.

For striking and thrusting techniques, research the Filipino arts of Kali, Escrima and Arnis. Combine that with the teachings found in classical Japanese martial arts and you have a sound technical foundation. Temper this with eliminating extraneous or flashy techniques and you can create a solid set of applicable and relevant skills.

A quick note on this—Japanese martial arts have a variety of unarmed techniques vs. edged weapons, and the Filipino arts have a large catalog of disarms as well as complicated drills involving knife against knife. As impressive as these techniques can be when demonstrated by a skilled practitioner, in reality disarms are highly unrealistic as anything more than a last ditch effort in a very bad situation. And knife against knife looks nothing like the extended duels seen in action movies. That sort of confrontation happens very fast, usually with both sides taking significant damage. Focus your valuable training time on simple effective techniques that are repeatable under stress.

An often underestimated value of impact weapons, and edged weapons even more so, is their use in grappling. They can be used to augment many throws, locks, and pins, making them far more effective. They can also be used to defeat the opponent's techniques. The best source material for this, apart from experimentation with inert weapons in your training is the techniques of classical Jujitsu.

Skill at firearms has priority, but we can't afford to neglect training with both impact and edged weapons. Especially since skill with these carries over to the use of environmental and improvised weapons.

IMPROVISED AND ENVIRONMENTAL WEAPONS

"You should not have any special fondness for a particular weapon, or anything else, for that matter." - Miyamoto Musashi

In a fight for your life, be aware of how your surroundings can be used as weapons, or how they can be used against you. I think of this as two broad categories, improvised and environmental. This is different than the process of crafting an improvised weapon from materials on hand. In this context I think of an improvised weapon as an object that can be picked up and used as a weapon. Environmental weapons in this context are anything such as furniture, walls, etc., that you can throw your opponent into or pin them against.

Effective use of improvised and environmental weapons requires not just physical technique, which carries over from your normal combatives. It also requires the calm awareness of your environment under stress that can only be created through intense training.

STRIKING

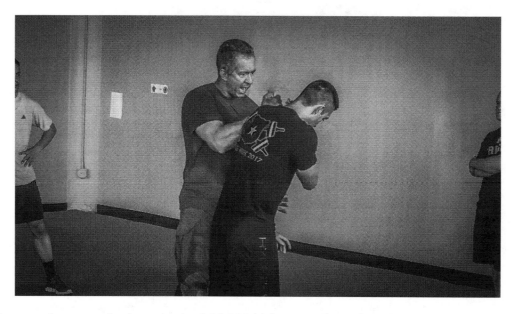

"I fear not the man who has practiced 10,000 kicks once, but I fear the man who has practiced one kick 10,000 times." - Bruce Lee

Striking is an area where traditional martial arts, and even some modern ones have a degree of complexity not needed for most practical application. My original martial art, Shotokan Karate, although it did have grappling elements at the advanced levels, was primarily a striking art. While there was much of value in it, and it was an excellent starting point for my training journey, it honestly is more complex than is needed for our purposes. Given limits on training time, and the large number of skills we need to be competent at, most would be better served by studying a relatively narrow set of strikes and reaching an applicable level of skill at them.

An excellent system for fast tracking striking skills is Muay Thai, otherwise known as Thai Boxing. Since we are researching the techniques of Filipino martial arts already for edged and impact weapons, layering in the empty hand techniques of those arts adds a valuable adjunct to the strikes of Muay Thai. Work techniques and combinations against pads and bags, and learn to hit hard by driving through your target and transferring the maximum amount of energy into your opponent, what boxers call "heavy hands." Spar against noncooperative training partners. Develop a solid repertoire of applicable skills.

Learn to combine striking skills with grappling. The two skill sets should complement each other in application. Learn to use strikes to set up your grappling techniques, to help effect escapes from your opponent's control, or to finish your opponent once they're under control. Train to work striking techniques as part of weapons retention. Learn to use them to assist in employing your tools when standing grappling or ground fighting. Do these things in training, and they will serve you well in application.

MOVEMENT AT CONTACT DISTANCE

"Good footwork can defeat any attack." - Bruce Lee

Footwork for typical gunfight range engagements is different than footwork for engagements at contact distance. Footwork for gunfighting most resembles footwork for field and court sports, but footwork at contact distance is indistinguishable from that of martial arts and combat sports.

For striking, research the footwork of boxing, Muay Thai, Jeet Kun Do, and the Filipino arts of Kali, Escrima, and Arnis. For standing grappling, learn from the unbalancing of Judo, the entries and pivots of Aikido, and the footwork of Western wrestling.

Work agility and foot speed drills and polish the footwork techniques, but that's not enough. Learn to apply them. Drill them against training partners who are realistically resisting your efforts. The angles you take against your opponent, and the distance you create or close are every bit as important as how you move your feet.

Once you understand footwork in an unarmed engagement, start to drill employing and retaining your tools. Experiment with this working with training partners who resist your efforts so that if you need to apply your skills they have a solid grounding in reality. At contact distance, footwork often trumps other elements of skill, so do not neglect it in your training.

VEHICLES

"Nothing is more difficult than the art of maneuver." - Sun Tzu

Vehicle tactics are a hot-button topic in the training community. And in many cases a misunderstood one. Anyone who has seen a wartime vehicle interdiction understands how flawed many things being taught and shown on social media are. Conversely, tactics not suitable in a combat zone, like fighting from the rear of a police vehicle on a traffic stop gone wrong, can make a lot of tactical sense for a solo or two-man patrol car. There are lessons learned from both environments that are valuable, and dismissing either set is arrogant and potentially dangerous.

The first thing to master where vehicles are concerned isn't firearms or dismounted tactics. It's driving. In the military, a downed vehicle can mean the difference between living or dying. In law enforcement, high speed pursuit driving is one of the riskiest tasks to perform. For a civilian, driving skill can not only avoid accidents, but help mitigate vulnerability to road rage and even carjackings.

Performance driving is a complex skill. And there are elements of it that simply cannot be learned by normal driving in regular traffic. I was fortunate enough to attend multiple driving schools in my dual careers. Most soldiers and police officers aren't given that level of training, much less civilians. But there are performance driving schools out there offering training to the public. Seek this training out. It is more likely to save your life, especially as a civilian, than your shooting, tactics, or combatives.

Another set of driving skills, both offensive and defensive, are very different than those used in racing. Ramming another vehicle properly to minimize damage to yours. Executing a PIT maneuver to cause another vehicle to lose control. Reversing directions quickly at speed or in tight spaces with J, Y, or "bootleg" turns. Vehicle placement in traffic, moving and stopped, to minimize risk of being boxed in. Training in these skills can be harder to find, unless your job gives you access. At the very least you should research them so that you understand the principles and how they are applied, even if you have no opportunity for practicing them.

Depending on your profession, motorcade or mobile surveillance operations may be an essential skill. There is a rhythm and flow to driving as part of a team of vehicles. Communication is vital, and position and speed of each vehicle is crucial. This is another skill that is difficult to learn competence in without both training and operational experience.

Fighting from and around vehicles. There are some popular trainers that in my opinion have overcomplicated this topic needlessly. Whenever I teach my vehicle engagements class I can always tell who has trained under one particular instructor by how they perform on their runs. I see an excess of unnecessary positions and movement that slow the student down and keep them on the "X" longer than they should be. This "tactical flair" is counterproductive and risky.

In any sort of competent ambush, the inside of a vehicle quickly becomes a coffin. If the vehicle is drivable, it needs to be driven off the X as aggressively as possible. Passengers can return fire if need be, understanding how difficult it can be to shoot from inside a moving vehicle and adjusting depending on environment and ROE. If the vehicle can't drive off the X, the occupants need to dismount and maneuver off the X on foot. Any fighting from inside the vehicle against a coordinated ambush should only be done in support of one of those two options. There is obviously more detail to this, so seek out training from a competent and vetted instructor in order to learn it properly.

Once dismounted, this becomes a react to ambush or break contact straight out of small unit tactics. There is a tendency to overcomplicate this. Especially if all you have is an academic knowledge. The simple proven tactics are difficult enough in this situation. Making it unnecessarily complicated only lessens your chance of survival.

What law enforcement officers call an ambush is often a very different situation though. It is more likely for police officers to be attacked by one offender armed with a pistol at close range while sitting parked in their vehicle than it is for them to face a military style coordinated ambush. While there are parallels in how these two situations are handled, there are differences as well. It is far more likely that this situation will be over before the officer can dismount from his vehicle. Fighting from inside the vehicle puts you at a disadvantage, but in this instance it may be all you have time to do. This is analogous to a civilian defending themselves in a carjacking as well.

Traffic stops. This is another area where the tactics for law enforcement differ from the military, and rightfully so. Fighting from the rear of your patrol vehicle is absolutely a viable tactic in this context. What is important to understand, though, both in this situation and any other involving a gunfight around vehicles, is that a vehicle not in motion is just terrain. It's also important to have a working knowledge of which parts of a vehicle offer some measure of cover. Any reputable vehicle tactics class should have a ballistic lab component where you can observe the effects of rifle and pistol rounds on a vehicle. Seek out reputable training to gain the knowledge you need for gunfights around vehicles.

Another aspect of fighting in and around vehicles is a struggle at contact distance inside the vehicle. This is a threat in undercover work in law enforcement where many undercover buys are conducted in vehicles. It's an outlier for most military and civilians, but could occur. A fight, especially with weapons, in the confined space of a vehicle can be a dangerous situation. The principles of Brazilian Jujitsu translate well to this. "Rolling" inside a car with a skilled training partner will quickly show you how to use the environment to help you control your opponent.

Vehicle tactics encompass a wide variety of situations, most of which are a very bad day indeed. Do a realistic needs analysis, seek out competent training for the skills you need, and be ready for the bad day if it comes.

INFILTRATION AND EXFILTRATION

"'Hitler made only one big mistake when he built his Atlantic Wall,' the paratroopers liked to say. 'He forgot to put a roof on it.'" - Stephen E. Ambrose

In military parlance, infiltration is the act of clandestinely inserting troops into enemy territory. This is done in a variety of ways, everything from parachute jumps to scuba dives, helicopter flights to boat rides. I've infilled in the back of a HiLux pickup truck. I have a longtime friend who infilled Afghanistan on horseback. I knew a Special Forces sergeant major who once infilled via elephant. Exfiltration is the other half of the process. It's getting your soldiers back out of enemy territory. The classic method everyone thinks of is via helicopter. But soldiers exfil in as many ways as they infil, on foot, in vehicles, by water, and more.

The fitness and skills involved in various infil methods matter. You don't need to be a champion skydiver for HALO jumps, but you certainly need to be competent and safe. The same holds true for climbing, rappelling, SCUBA, etc. Fitness is more important than skill in many cases. I once carried over my own body weight by foot between my own gear and weapons and the gifts we had to hike in for the warlord we were flipping to our side. All of this is important, but the why of it matters as much as the how.

Choosing infiltration and exfiltration methods and routes is a vital aspect of mission planning. It has to be tailored to the operational environment, your personnel's skills and abilities, the enemy's capabilities, even the weather. There are lessons to learn from the military approach to this for law enforcement and civilians. Route selection, terrain analysis, awareness of weather, understanding the importance of fitness. All of these factors and more I carried over into law enforcement from my military experience, and then into civilian life. Learn to use these principles in your professional and personal life, and they will serve you well.

BREACHING

"Once more unto the breach." - William Shakespeare

Breaching, as a craft of warfare, has existed for as long as recorded history. Simply put, it is the art of defeating fortifications. The techniques have evolved over time, but the principles remain the same. Whether mechanical, ballistic, thermal, or explosive, the principles have to be followed to ensure success.

To select the best technique for a breach, and to employ it correctly, you have to have a basic understanding of construction materials and fortifications. You don't have to be an engineer or general contractor, but knowledge of weak points and relative strengths of various structural elements is essential.

You have to have competence with your tools. You need to be conversant with manual equipment like rams, sledges, and Halligan tools. You need to understand how to operate saws and torches, build demo charges and emplace them, and conduct shotgun breaching.

But more importantly, you need to understand the tactical considerations. Security for the breacher. Selection of primary and alternate breach points. Contingencies for contact at the breach point or a failed breach. Understanding the vulnerabilities inherent in the breaching process and how the breach influences the overall operational plan and vice versa.

The time to gain understanding of all these factors is in training. Explore them well, and you will be able to utilize breaching effectively in real world operations.

RECONNAISSANCE

"Time spent in reconnaissance is seldom wasted." - Erwin Rommel

Properly executed reconnaissance can make the difference between victory and defeat. And the principles used carry over from the military to law enforcement, and apply to self-defense and to life in general. Reconnaissance, simply put, is the process of gathering information prior to finalizing and executing your plan. In a military or law enforcement context, this is best done by actually putting human eyes on the objective, almost always in a covert or surreptitious fashion. Barring that, it can be accomplished via imagery from satellites or drones, or at the very least by studying maps of the route and objective.

I've done reconnaissance by wearing local clothing and driving non-military vehicles, or by climbing to the peak of a mountain overlooking the objective. I've stalked through wood lines and crawled through open terrain to avoid detection. I've spent hours in the back of a covert van watching an objective, or surveilled criminals from the top of high-rise buildings, or by sneaking into vacant buildings or through dark gangways.

The principles behind proper reconnaissance can teach us lessons for daily life. No matter what we are attempting to accomplish, gathering data ahead of time improves our chances of success. This applies to self-defense, and to more mundane goals of daily life. Map reconnaissance for route selection can be done on our phones. The internet gives us a wealth of potentially applicable data. Even as simple a mental exercise as habitually identifying exits, choke points, and other tactically pertinent information when we enter a restaurant or other public venue is a form of reconnaissance.

In all aspects of your life, professional and personal, make it a habit to perform some sort of reconnaissance whenever possible. Gathering information on locations and people prior to making decisions and taking action can go a long way towards ensuring success regardless of the context.

PRECISION RIFLE

"The most deadly thing on a battlefield is one well-aimed shot." - Sgt. Carlos Hathcock

I was never a school-trained sniper in the military, and it was never my primary job. Having said that, I have done sniper work on my teams in Afghanistan and Iraq, and I've made precision rifle shots out to 1,500 yards. On the law enforcement side, I've been through sniper schools, but it was never my primary job there either.

Whether it is your specialty or not, the ability to shoot at distance is a crucial skill. Becoming a competent sniper is a specialized endeavor, but every shooter should understand basic wind calls and elevation holds. Don't be afraid to push even a standard AR out to the limits of its effective range in training. If you have a precision rifle, spend enough time with it to learn your dope and use the weapon to its potential.

I personally prefer a high quality gas gun build, such as the ones from Lone Star Armory, over a bolt gun platform. Both have their pros and cons, however, and a quality bolt gun can be run very well indeed. Regardless of the platform, build a sound foundation of long range shooting skill, even if you never specialize in it.

ROOM CLEARING FOR CIVILIAN SELF-DEFENSE

"Tactics flow from a superior position." - Bobby Fischer

CQB. Close Quarters Battle. It's a popular topic on social media and training circles. But contrary to what the "tacti-cool" would have you believe, there really isn't such a thing as solo CQB. Close Quarters Battle is just that, battle. It's small unit tactics inside a structure. The key word being unit. CQB works because it's a tactic for a team to utilize. Those same tactics don't really apply to an individual.

The other reason standard CQB tactics don't apply in a defensive scenario is that they are offensive in nature. There's a reason one of the terms used to describe a CQB professional is "assaulter." A private citizen who has been forced to clear rooms in a defensive scenario has very different priorities of work than an assaulter.

Make no mistake, just as CQB is one of the most dangerous tasks a team can do, clearing rooms as an individual is an extremely high-risk endeavor. There's no way to eliminate that risk, only mitigate it. Unless there is a legitimate need, you are probably better served by either avoidance or, if necessary, taking up a sound defensive posture. But, we don't get to always choose the time and place, and definitely not the manner of the fight. Especially not as responsibly-armed civilians. And sometimes the fight chooses us, whether we want it to or not.

So if we aren't talking about CQB, how should we look at this set of problems and skills? I think we should approach this as fighting inside structures. Once we make this paradigm shift, it's much easier to make common sense choices about our tactics, techniques, and procedures.

Fighting inside structures is primarily a game of initiative and angles. Let's discuss angles first. An early CQB mentor of mine called it "the geometry of tactics." When you're operating as part of a team inside a structure, you mitigate risk by using angles to create as close to 360 degrees of security as you can, and you increase the effectiveness of your offense by creating interlocking fields of fire, much like small unit infantry tactics. As an individual, neither of those options is available to you.

The other important factor to remember is cover versus concealment. Very little inside a modern home offers ballistic protection from small arms fire. This is why many, although not all, teams prefer dynamic over deliberate CQB. As an individual operating alone, however, you have little choice but to use concealment the majority of the time when moving through a structure. It isn't perfect by any means, but it's better than running into gunfire. We'll discuss the exceptions to this when we begin talking about initiative.

We use concealment by playing the angles. Pretty much everyone should at least have a passing familiarity with "slicing the pie," where you progressively take small "slices" visually around a corner. With practice, this can be done far faster and much more smoothly than most people think, without losing effectiveness. This can be applied to doorways as well as corners, and even vertically to the landings of stairwells. If you lead with the muzzle and your dominant eye, it is usually possible to see someone on the other side of the corner before they see you.

199

When done properly at an open doorway, it is possible to clear much of the room except for dead space and hard corners from outside the doorway. As a civilian, whether you enter the room is very contextual, but you have to understand that you cannot completely clear a room without actually going inside it.

And that brings us to the discussion of initiative. If you need to enter that room, you are going to need to seize the initiative in order to mitigate as much of the risk as you can. That's why no matter how deliberate a clearing speed you are using, crossing a threshold has to be dynamic.

To talk about this in greater detail, we need to look at the two basic types of rooms, corner-fed and center-fed. These are exactly what they sound like. A center-fed room has an entrance in the center of one of the room's walls, and has two hard corners that are not visible from outside the threshold. A corner-fed room has an entrance in the corner of the room, and only has one hard corner not visible from outside the threshold.

When pieing off a corner-fed room from outside, there is only one hard corner remaining to be cleared. If the decision to enter the room has been made, the entry is done dynamically and efficiently so that the first thing presented to that uncleared corner is the muzzle of the weapon, and you move out of the doorway rapidly and under control. Then any dead space behind obstacles or in closets has to be cleared by pieing them off as well.

A center-fed room presents more danger to the individual than the corner-fed. Because there are two uncleared hard corners, whichever one you clear first leaves you vulnerable to an attacker hiding in the other. There is no way to eliminate this risk when operating alone. All you can do is pick a corner, then once it's cleared immediately and rapidly shifting your attention to the other. The easy mistakes that must be avoided are not finishing the first corner clear before beginning the second, and standing in the doorway. When you enter the room, you have to fully enter it.

There are subtleties and nuances to this that are beyond the scope of this section, as well as considerations for if and when you are engaged by an attacker while clearing. To truly understand this, seek out valid training from a qualified and vetted instructor, and above all practice on your own until it becomes second nature.

SMALL UNIT TACTICS

"Everything in war is very simple. But the simplest thing is difficult." - Carl von Clausewitz

Light infantry tactics are in my opinion the most fundamental version of armed combat that there is. The principles of infantry tactics haven't changed since before recorded history. Everything I have learned about combat since drilling small unit tactics as a private has been nothing more than an application of those same principles. Even if you aren't a soldier, studying small unit tactics will give you a sound foundation to build upon, whether it's in your CQB as a SWAT officer, or your personal doctrine for self-defense as a civilian.

Read the Ranger Handbook and examine the principles underlying the tactics it teaches, as well as the newer Small Unit Tactics Handbook. Study famous battles of history, from Thermopylae to Robert's Ridge. Become a scholar of small unit tactics, and it will make you a better strategist regardless of the arena.

Look at the classic infantry stratagems. Ambushes, fixing and flanking, support by fire, crossing danger areas, bounding, break in contact, reacting to an ambush, and so on. But then examine the principles that underpin them. If you understand the *why*, then the how becomes obvious. And the how applies to everything you do in conflict.

Internalizing the principles of SUT will also make you a better strategist for life, not just for self-defense or combat. The principles are truly universal, and at its heart, all conflict is in essence the same. The more you can identify and understand the underlying commonalities of conflict, the more prepared you will be regardless of the challenge you face.

MOUT AND CQB

"Speed, surprise, and violence of action." - Anonymous

CQB. Close Quarters Battle. Battle Drill Number Six. A mystique has grown up around CQB during the war on terror that has all but reached the level of a "tactical religion." At least among people that haven't done a lot of CQB against determined opposition. CQB is difficult to do well and is inherently high-risk, but it's not some mystical art.

This especially holds true in law enforcement circles. I have witnessed a myriad of CQB techniques used by SWAT teams that are based in theories rather than grounded in the realities of fighting a determined opponent inside a structure. While there are undoubtedly many reasons for this, I think the two primary ones are the rarity of law enforcement encountering any real opposition, and a resultant tendency to design tactics based around the most commonly encountered threats rather than preparing for the worst potential eventualities.

There is a flip side to this, however. There are differences in how we apply the principles in our CQB stateside in law enforcement operations as opposed to overseas in combat. It is all too easy to dismiss experiences and perspectives other than your own, especially when they come from a lower level of training and application than yours did. But to do so is often as big an error as disregarding real world experience in favor of unproven theory. Tactics must fit the mission and the operational environment, including rules of engagement, to be optimal.

Despite the mystique, CQB isn't some esoteric field of endeavor. It is, in essence, small unit tactics inside a structure. Once you look at it through that perspective, you can identify the familiar tactical elements like 360-degree security, interlocking fields of fire, and fixing and flanking the opposing forces. CQB is very difficult though, make no mistake. What makes it so difficult is the compressed space and rapid pace due to the operational environment. It is an extremely athletic endeavor that requires the highest levels of situational awareness, shooting skill, and well-rehearsed teamwork.

I was raised in US Army SOF, and the doctrine there was dynamic points of domination style CQB. There have been refinements and improvements made from the lessons learned over twenty years of war, but the broad strokes of this style of CQB remain true to its roots, and remain effective. If I only have time to teach one type of CQB to a team this is the one I choose.

I have also been fortunate enough to train with the US Navy's SMU, and DEVGRU has a highly refined and effective system of deliberate CQB. I prefer the dynamic style I was raised up with for hostage rescue and some other applications, but their deliberate style has value as well for some applications, especially in law enforcement. I was convinced enough of its value that I modified their TTPs to work off the same hallway formations as SF-style dynamic CQB so that my SWAT team could seamlessly integrate both methods operationally.

During the twenty years of the GWOT, the high operational tempo and cross-pollination between special operations units resulted in vast improvement to our understanding of CQB best practices, especially in the subtle details. For much of my army career, the high ready was sacrilege and any sort of deliberate movements such as threshold assessments were dismissed as superfluous, but now they are commonplace. At the beginning of my journey, verbiage was overly relied on. Now non-verbal communication techniques like barrel waves and releases, as well as using either visible or IR lasers to signal to teammates, are the standard, and the best teams rarely talk at all.

Our police and military special operations units are the best they've ever been after our twenty years of war and lessons learned. It's up to the next generation of soldiers and SWAT cops to maintain that standard and continue to advance it moving forward. Study tactics in general, and CQB in particular. Master the nuances and subtleties of our craft, and contribute to the further technical and tactical advancement of our profession.

TACTICAL MEDICINE

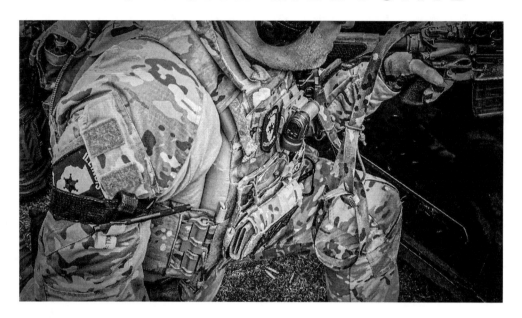

"Do *know* harm." - Anonymous

The birth of modern tactical medicine was the Battle of the Black Sea in Mogadishu in 1993, commonly known as "Blackhawk Down." The frustration of Ranger Regiment medics at the loss of lives that could have been saved led to the creation of the CAT tourniquet, as well as the adoption of hemostatic clotting agents and other technologies that can control hemorrhage. Now, no special operations soldier is without an individual first aid kit, or IFAK, as well as at least one, and usually two additional tourniquets positioned on their kit.

Cross training, while always commonplace in Army Special Forces, has increased across the board, even in law enforcement. I was never a medic, and honestly it's not where my passion lies. But I've done live tissue training, used nasopharyngeal airways, done needle decompression for a tension pneumothorax, tracheotomies, and more. TCCC (Tactical

Casualty Combat Care), or its equivalent is now offered throughout the military and law enforcement professions, and there is comparable training available now for civilians.

Seek out quality tacmed or emergency first aid training. Learn how to treat violent trauma to yourself or another well enough to keep yourself or another person alive long enough to reach professional care. This drastically increases the odds of surviving a life-threatening injury. Once you are trained, stay current on advances in tactical medicine just like you do for firearms and tactics. Buy a quality medical kit for your home and your car. Prepare yourself for handling a catastrophic injury, and if it ever occurs you'll be glad that you did.

PLANNING

"Plans are worthless, but planning is everything." - Dwight D. Eisenhower

Planning. The USPSA competitor running through his stage plan in his head until, when it's time to perform, he just runs his mental movie in real time and dominates his competition. The Special Forces A-team running through every conceivable contingency in their operations order and doing rehearsals before boarding the birds to infil on a capture-kill of a HVT. The SWAT team planning a high-risk search and arrest warrant for a violent armed criminal. The civilian planning and setting up protocols for his loved ones in the case he has to defend them from violence.

All of these are planning. And all of these plans have commonalities, but the hard truth of all of them is that the fight will be what it will be regardless of your plan, and the enemy gets a vote in how that unfolds. To paraphrase Clausewitz's famous words, no plan survives the first contact with the enemy.

So why are plans essential? Why is planning so heavily emphasized by professional warriors worldwide and throughout history? Well thought out and executed plans position us for success, even if we have to deviate from them because of circumstance or enemy action. John Steinbeck once said, "If you find yourself in a fair fight, your tactics suck." Planning is how we set the unfair fight up in our favor.

Plan well, with contingencies in place. But understand the reality of conflict, and realize that your plan is a starting point. It's a framework to build and improvise off of, like a jazz musician playing variations off of a standard melody. Just like technique, your plan must be alive and flexible, not rigid and lifeless. The only way to truly learn this is through experience, so seek out opportunities in your training to gather that experience before you need it in conflict.

OPERATION ORDERS

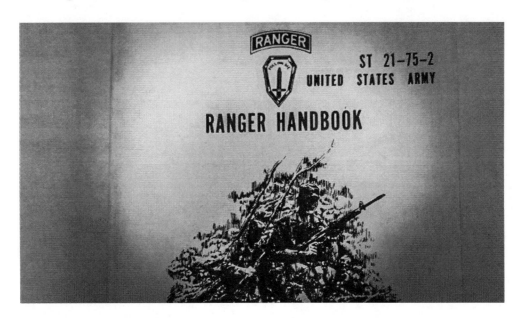

"Rangers lead the way!" - Anonymous

I distinctly remember being a young private and how frustrated I was with the amount of the Ranger Handbook that was devoted to the operations order format, as well as the amount of time we spent learning the format backwards and forwards. I felt this time could have been better spent working shooting or tactics instead. I couldn't have been more wrong. In the years since, I have used the operations order format, and the army's planning process countless times in military and law enforcement settings, and continue to use the principles of the planning process in my business and personal life to this day.

The five paragraph operations order format, and the army planning process in general, is brilliant in its adaptability to a wide range of applications. The best resource to begin learning the orders and planning process is the Ranger Handbook. It's easily available online, and should be owned by everyone with a desire to understand tactics and planning. Get a copy and study it. Learn the principles contained in it. Do this, and both your tactics and planning, regardless of application, will benefit from your efforts.

BOOK FOUR - THE PRACTICE

INTRODUCTION - "BATTLES ARE WON IN TRAINING"

"Every battle is won or lost before it is ever fought." - Sun Tzu

When your skills are tested, whether in conflict or competition, you won't somehow magically perform higher than your training baseline. Your training, preparation, and planning are what carry the day. This applies no less to individual gunfights than it does to large scale military engagements.

So then, what are the implications? How do we structure our training to prepare us for the fight? Not, in my opinion, by trying to replicate the fight in training endlessly. There absolutely is value in the testing phase of training, but it should not be the main component of our training program. No winning football team does nothing but scrimmage. No champion fighter does nothing but spar.

In broad terms, we need to develop attributes and skills, and then learn to apply them. Attributes are the raw physical and mental properties needed to excel. Speed, strength, and endurance are attributes, as are cognition, reaction time, and perceptual speed. Attributes are where GPP, or general physical preparedness, and SPP, or specific physical preparedness, fit into our training template. This is also where visualizations and mental exercises come into play. Although these training modalities don't build skill, they build the foundation for it. The better an athlete you are, the better gunfighter you will be, given equal amounts of shooting skill and tactical acumen.

Once that foundation is laid, we need to build skill upon it. I strongly believe that skills are best built in isolation, without needless layers of complexity or difficulty that don't address the target skill of a particular drill. If you come to a class, you'll find that I put out a system for building skills in isolation as efficiently and productively as possible.

This won't fully develop our skills though. There is performance degradation when you chain skills together, even without stress. The second phase of skill training is working on skills in combination, in aggregate. There are considerations here that I also cover when I teach. The goal of this phase is to minimize skill degradation and build consistent performance with a low incident rate of error. This is important. Fights and contests are won by the individual who makes the fewest mistakes.

The last training phase, and in my opinion the one that should occupy the least amount of training time, is the test. This is where we layer stress on top of running skills in combination in order to find the weak points in our performance. Testing ourselves gives us the data we need to return to the other phases of training and prioritize the areas where we need improvement.

Every battle is won or lost before it is even fought. Battles are won in training. Make sure that when you train, every aspect of it has purpose. Every single thing you do in training should be focused and deliberate. Every rep in training, every bullet fired in practice, should be a lesson learned. Take the effort to learn how to train, and you will improve as rapidly and efficiently as possible. Proper training truly does shortcut the learning curve.

NEEDS ANALYSIS

"First, say to yourself what you would be; and then do what you have to do." - Epictetus

What makes training effective? What makes practice productive? Why do some people progress, and others spin their wheels for years? On a larger level, why do some people achieve life goals and continue personal growth throughout their lifetimes, while others stagnate or regress into ever worse versions of themselves? There are many factors obviously, but one of the most important is that growth and success require purposeful practice.

For practice to be purposeful, it has to be focused and directed. This is the difference between training like an athlete and working out, between training your shooting and plinking, between study and recreational reading. The first step in planning out the next leg of your journey, whatever your goals, whatever your starting point, is a needs analysis. Want to be a Black Belt, a USPSA Grand Master, a Green Beret? Your goals determine your training needs, and an objective evaluation of where you are currently charts your course.

A needs analysis in our context here is a relatively straightforward planning process that all too few people undertake. Want to complete Special Forces Selection? One of the many on demand performance metrics for that process is a twelve mile road march carrying a forty-five pound pack plus food, water, and a weapon in three hours or less. This has to be done hungry, exhausted, and possibly injured. So fresh and uninjured a performance "buffer" should be built in. This same planning process is done for all the known performance metrics for the goal.

Once you've done your needs analysis, your training is easily planned. Then every session is easy to organize so that it advances you efficiently towards that goal. Practice becomes purposeful and deliberate. Anyone who is a champion athlete got there by training, not working out. Top level shooters have organized live and dry fire sessions, they don't plink. To succeed, be deliberate and purposeful in everything you do.

SHOOTING AT THE SPEED OF LIFE

"No second place winner." - Bill Jordan

How fast is fast enough? We have all heard and maybe repeated the familiar tropes of "tactical" pistol training. "Speed is fine but accuracy is final." "You can't miss fast enough." "Slow down and get your hits." How much truth is there to these? In my opinion, while accuracy is important, these truisms are often used to justify a lack of skill.

While it's true that accuracy is very important, speed matters. In my experience, the first combatant to put acceptable hits on his adversary usually wins the gunfight. How fast then is truly fast enough? If gunfighting requires a balance of speed and accuracy, and it does, how important is speed to that balance? How important is speed in a gunfight?

To begin with, this is not as simple a question as it seems. There is more than one kind of gunfight. A military style engagement at more typical small unit distances of 100-300 meters can be slower paced at times, almost methodical. Team based dynamic CQB has a faster rhythm and pace, but movement for the most part is dictated by the speed of the element you're operating in rather than the individual. Although when it's time to engage a threat in CQB, the speed you can get rounds on target is crucial. And then there's the one-on-one gunfight at close range. In my experience, those happen very fast indeed.

The next element of the question is what kind of speed? What matters for tactical applications of performance shooting? Draw speed? Emergency reloads? Target transitions? Fast splits between successive shots on the same target? Malfunction clearances? Physical movement from shooting position to shooting position? Speed while shooting on the move? For the purposes of this article, we'll address these in the context of the one-on-one close range gunfight with a pistol, as that is the most probable type of encounter a civilian in the United States would face.

Let's look at the draw. A sub-second draw from concealment has become a performance standard for defensive-minded shooters. Then there is the crowd that claims that this standard is irrelevant. The argument is that awareness is crucial, and that drawing in response to an attack puts you too far behind the power curve. There is definitely some truth to this, but I don't think it invalidates the need to develop a fast and precise draw.

For one thing, working on the draw is the best way to develop a solid index, which is crucial if you want to become a competent shooter. Simply put, your index is the ability to look at a point, then bring your weapon to where the sights are aligned and aimed precisely at the point without conscious thought. Even if a fast draw was truly irrelevant in a gunfight, it would be worth pursuing in training for this carryover alone.

For another, even if a fast draw in response to a threat only matters in a small percentage of potential altercations, that doesn't mean you might not need it. The analogy I use for draws, reloads, and transitions from carbine to pistol is this. These skills are like your reserve parachute. You may never need your reserve parachute, but when you do need it, you really need it.

This is doubly true of the reload. In a one-on-one gunfight at close range, a reload under fire is extremely unlikely. But if it is needed, speed and consistency with it will be very important indeed. The reload is more complex than the draw, and it takes a lot more repetition to get under a second, but it can be done with diligent dry fire practice. If working from closed-front concealment you can add a half second to that time. This is from shot-to-shot on an open target at seven yards.

Rapid target transitions are another skill that's rarely needed in a civilian encounter, unlike military engagements. On the law enforcement side, they are more likely than on the civilian, but less so than in the military. Once again though, if they are needed, then they'll be crucial to say the least. The thing about fast and accurate target transitions is this. They don't come from muscling or "driving" the gun. They come from a well developed index. So, training the draw and training transitions will also help in fast target acquisition in general. And in my experience, this is of paramount importance. The best way to win a gunfight is to put effective rounds on the other person first.

Target acquisition then is arguably where speed matters the most. This holds true for every type of gunfight I have experienced, from the classic 50-300 meter small unit engagement, to one-on-one close range gunfights in Chicago. And rapid target acquisition is developed by training your index. And your index is best developed by training target transitions and the draw. In my opinion then, target transitions and draws should be prioritized in your dry and live fire practice to a greater degree than their statistical use in armed encounters would have you believe. You get the carryover benefit to the highest priority skill, and you additionally get skills you may very well need despite statistical wisdom.

Let's talk about splits. Splits are the speed of successive shots on the same target. Nothing looks and sounds cooler than a skilled shooter putting a lightning fast string of shots on target. In my opinion though, splits are an area where you should go slower in real world application than in training. There are a couple of reasons for this. One is reaction time. Average human reaction time to a visual stimulus is .25 of a second. With training, many shooters can get their splits down well below .20 seconds, with some competition shooters having splits below .15 seconds. The problem with this in real world application is that each shot should be its own decision, independent of the previous one. That means splits of about .25 seconds are optimal in a gunfight in order to allow that decision process. With high levels of training, I think this could be dropped to .2 seconds as your reaction time gets faster due to subconscious competence.

The other reason I think we should strive for splits between .2 and .25 seconds is that in the real world our accuracy is both more difficult and carries a far greater potential negative consequence for failure. More difficult because our optimal scoring area is a fist-sized group in the upper chest or a credit card sized group in the head. And more difficult still because in a gunfight every target is usually moving, especially once they are being shot.

Malfunctions under fire happen. Body cam video from law enforcement shows this over and over again. Clearing a malfunction under fire needs to be as efficient and rapid as possible. This requires not only a level of unconscious competence with the physical manipulations themselves, but a sufficient level of familiarity with the weapon so that the shooter realizes intuitively and instantly by feel that a malfunction has occurred and what type it is. It's difficult to quantify a metric for this, but automatic and subconscious efficiency needs to be developed.

In my opinion, efficient movement is the category of skills most often trained incorrectly on the tactical side of the house. Movement speed from position to position is contextual to say the least. But if speed is needed, then it should be top speed. There's subtleties to this as well. The speed needs to be controlled so that you come into position ready to shoot. When I watch tactical shooters work movement this is the biggest and most common error I see. Speed is also about efficiency and eliminating lag time, not just about how fast your hand or foot speed is.

Movement includes more than sprinting to a position of cover. Shooting on the move is a high-frequency task in gunfights. What I see too often in tactical training is that neither the shooting piece nor the movement piece is done at the appropriate tempo. People move too slowly *and* shoot either too slowly or not accurately enough, or both. If you're shooting on the move under fire, you need to move rapidly to gain a tactical advantage, either through aggression or displacement. And you need to be able to put acceptable hits on a threat reliably while moving at speed.

So how does all of this inform our training? What performance metrics should we be looking at to ensure sufficient competence with a pistol for self-defense? Let's run through the above skills again and talk about some attainable competency goals for self-defense. Understand, too, that these are not the only skills you need to be working on by any means, but rather a baseline metric of fundamentals.

The draw. It takes some dedicated effort to get a draw from concealment below a second, but it can be done. This is to an open target at seven yards. The accuracy standard for this does not need to be solely the fist sized group in the high center chest that is our optimal scoring area. For this as long as the hit is acceptable it's sufficient. I would say an acceptable hit in this context would be the equivalent of an "A" or close "C" on a USPSA silhouette target. That translates to a solid torso hit on an adversary but eliminates grazing wounds that only damage skin and subcutaneous fat. If you're drawing and immediately engaging an opponent under fire, it's important to get that first acceptable hit on them *fast!* You can then follow up with optimal hits once you've gained the initiative.

The good news about training the draw is that it can be done almost exclusively in your dry practice. Live fire practice on the draw can be just a few reps each session, or within the context of other drills, to validate that you are practicing it correctly in dry fire. Dry fire the draw daily, and you will see it improve rapidly.

The reload, like the draw, is trained primarily in dry fire and validated in live fire. The gold standard set by world class competition shooters is simply that the reload should be roughly as fast as the draw. If conducted from slide lock, it should still be within a quarter second of the draw. This would translate then to 1.25 seconds from shot-to-shot on an open target at seven yards. For open-front concealment add another quarter of a second, and from closed-front add a half second. These times are all for acceptable hits on an open seven yard target. So shot-to-shot from closed-front concealment should be 1.75 or less to the A or C zone of a USPSA target at seven yards.

We've discussed splits at length above. But does that mean splits faster than .2 of a second have no purpose in training? Not in my opinion. If you only train working the trigger at .25 or slower, that is going to remain your maximum processing speed. If you train yourself to process the visual and physical input from the gun at split times faster than you need for practical application, you build in a performance buffer. This is important because your skill will degrade under stress.

Target transitions are an interesting metric to discuss. In application of shooting, whether tactical or competitive, your transitions from target-to-target are dictated by the speed at which you see the visual input required to make appropriate decisions and an acceptable shot. But in order for this to happen rapidly enough for practical application at a subconscious level of competence, speed has to be developed in practice. This can only be developed by pushing the transition speed artificially in your training. On an array of three open targets at seven yards, spaced a yard apart edge-to-edge, you should strive for transitions as fast as your best splits. So if you split faster than .20 of a second, then you should be able to transition under .20 as well on that target array.

Movement is hard to quantify because of the sheer number of variables. There are more than enough subtleties to fill a book this size on movement alone. A good baseline for rapid movement from shooting position to shooting position is two seconds or less, shot-to-shot on open targets at seven yards from two shooting positions ten yards apart. The drill is simple. Draw and fire two rounds on an open seven yard target from one position, sprint to the second position and fire two rounds on another open seven yard target. Regardless of direction the movement time, shot-to-shot, should be under two seconds. This should be trained in all directions until it is easily achieved on demand.

For shooting on the move the metric is a bit less objective. Once a shooter can reliably put acceptable hits on an open seven yard target at a fast walk, they have a solid baseline to work from. It's entirely possible to learn to do this at an extremely rapid movement pace, and that's what a shooter should strive for.

Now that we've determined a set of metrics, we know what we need to achieve for an acceptable level of defensive handgun skill. At least where speed is concerned. Accuracy, although a corollary of these selected metrics, has its own demands in order to prepare us for high risk and low percentage shots. Just like movement though, that's a huge topic best explored in a separate article.

It's vital to realize though, that building our skills in isolation to the levels explored above is only the beginning. We then need to build consistent on-demand performance working skills in combination and test our performance under stress. The standards we've listed aren't enough if it takes a warmup and multiple repetitions to hit them successfully. They need to be available to us on demand at a subconscious level of competence.

To answer our original questions then, how important is speed in a gunfight? Speed is vital for gunfighting skill. Arguably the most important attribute. Knowing that, how fast is fast enough? Probably faster than you think...

PRACTICE

"Practice is the best of all instructors." - Publilius Syrus

There is a pattern I see in many law enforcement, military, and defensive shooters' outlook on firearms training. They look at training as something you do solely in a course or class. Or if your unit or organization sends you to the range. These events are training and are valuable for development as a shooter, but they are not the heart of training.

There are "a-ha" moments that happen in a class, times when a shooter "levels up" due to a personal breakthrough. But these moments are not the norm, and even accounting for them there is only so much a shooter can improve in a few days of training. To reach high levels of skill in any endeavor requires many hours of dedicated practice. What, then, does that practice look like?

Practice needs to be frequent. Fifteen minutes of dry fire six days a week is better for improvement than an hour and a half once a week.

Practice needs to be deliberate. It needs to be planned out to address the shooter's current needs. Training has to change as skill improves, so that you keep improving.

Practice needs to be purposeful. Going through the motions with empty repetitions is wasted effort and time. Each repetition of each skill or drill needs to be done with a clear mental focus on improvement.

Practice needs to be consistent. Consistent effort over time yields results.

Practice needs to be playful. The concept of interleaving practice, or mixing repetitions of several different skills or drills within a practice, has been shown to be a powerful tool for performance improvement. This feels like play, not work.

If you carry a gun for a living or for self-defense, you can't expect to master your craft without practice. Deliberate and purposeful practice that is frequent and consistent. If you are law enforcement or military, you can't expect your unit or agency to do this for you. If you are a responsible armed civilian, no amount of weekend training classes will make up for not practicing on your own.

Training courses are valuable. But they are valuable because they inform your own training, not because they are a substitute. Seek out effective training from quality instructors, and then use what you learn in your own training. Put in the effort and master your craft. Practice.

COMPETITION AND COMBAT

"Men will live and die for points. Competition is bloodless combat." - Jeff Cooper

Competition and combat. At this point, much like the debate over an instructor's experience, you would think we'd have this sorted out. But we obviously do not. On one hand I see guys who've never been in a gunfight claim that competing will somehow be detrimental to their development of martial skill. On the other hand, I know competitors who, because they are fast and accurate with a firearm, think that automatically gives them the ability to apply that skill in an armed confrontation. Neither point of view is accurate, and both examples are doing themselves a disservice.

Nothing spurs the development of shooting skill like competition. Specifically action shooting competition. Once you are exposed to what is possible with a firearm, once you start measuring your performance against those metrics, your skill will increase, provided you put in the work. I have had the good fortune of being exposed to armed professionals of the very highest caliber throughout the three decades I carried a gun for a living. Without exception, the best shooters from those ranks that I have known, whether special operations personnel or SWAT officers, were competitive shooters. And no one who didn't compete, regardless of combat experience or level of training, could match them. And the very best shooters I have ever known are competitors who have never been in a gunfight and probably never will.

Your shooting skill drives your tactics. Without the ability to deliver accurate shots quickly under stress, all the tactical wherewithal in the world will not be enough. But, there is much more to fighting with a firearm than just pure shooting skill. Fighting involves conflict, and the other fighter gets a vote. Without the ability to best utilize the environment, without an understanding of how to press the advantage on a determined opponent or recover from a position of disadvantage, all the high level shooting skill in the world may not be enough to win.

The arguments against competition as training for gunfighting don't hold water when looked at objectively. SMUs regularly bring in world class competitors to learn shooting skills from. Many of the most respected names in the special operations community also advocate competition for skill development. If you carry a gun defensively, one of the best and most cost effective ways to train your shooting skill is action shooting competition. And high levels of shooting skill can overcome poor tactics, while the best tactics cannot make up for a lack of necessary shooting skill. Just don't fall into the trap of thinking that pure shooting ability is the all of it. Gunfighting is still fighting. Just as there is more to winning an empty hand fight than just your striking skill, there is more to winning a gunfight than just your accuracy and speed. Shooting and tactics both matter; we need to train for and understand that.

TEST AND RETEST

"The credit belongs to the man who is actually in the arena." - Theodore Roosevelt

I had an interesting conversation with a group of friends once on the best methodology for training, specifically for pistolcraft. A USPSA GM buddy of mine was of the opinion that you should solely train the myriad of skill elements required to shoot at a high level as a gestalt, and by "feel." Despite his advanced skill level, I couldn't agree with him. I have heard the same viewpoint espoused before, in various disciplines, always by the talented who come by improvements easily.

This is a common approach in the tactical training world. Stress shoots, full mission profiles, shooting in full kit, live fire shoot house runs, all these events have value as tests and confidence builders. I would argue though that these are not good ways to develop skill. Skill is best developed without distractions and in isolation. Then you build consistency and on-demand performance by training the skills in combinations of ever-increasing complexity. Then you test them by adding those physical and psychological distractions back in. Train for the fight, instead of training like you fight.

The great trainers in every endeavor I'm familiar with, from Bruce Lee to Louis Simmons of Westside Barbell to world champion shooter Ben Stoeger, all take a test/retest approach to training. The event, whether it's an MMA bout, a football game, a powerlifting meet, or a USPSA match, is the test of your training. It isn't training itself. You test your skills with the event, simulated or actual, identify whatever component skills or attributes are lacking, and then focus on each in isolation until you build them up. This can be done with simple or more complex training evolutions, but one element at a time is being addressed. Then after working them in combination, you retest at the event or a simulation of it again.

I've made the mistake many times in my own training of working on too many things at once. It's easy to do as an athlete, especially a motivated one. It's often counterproductive though. Especially beyond a certain skill level. As your mastery of your craft grows, the effort required for smaller and smaller improvements increases exponentially. Smaller and smaller pieces of the whole need to be evaluated and improved. One variable at a time gets tested, trained and experimented on, then evaluated with a retest. One by one, weaknesses strengthened, test and retest.

TRAIN FOR THE FIGHT

"Preparation is the key to success." - Alexander Graham Bell

I talk a lot about training like an athlete. I hold fast in my belief that our training methodology is what holds us back from reaching our desired level of skill as efficiently as possible. People confuse events that 100% have value for conditioning or as tests with skill-building. They confuse how things are applied with how they are developed. Units train professionals who are devoted to their craft the same way they train neophytes who lack the desire to excel. Organizations overemphasize large exercises that serve as better tests of command and control than developers of skill at the operational level.

So how should we construct our training? That can be a complex thing as you approach the higher levels of skill, but understanding *why* you are doing a training event is a good place to start. The more skills you try and improve in any particular event, the less effective that event will be at producing any of the desired improvements. Combination drills are essential for building consistent performance on demand, but are a poor mechanism for building performance of the individual skills themselves. The categories I think of when planning training are conditioning, experimentation drills, isolation drills, combination drills, validation drills and testing, and the application of skill.

Conditioning is absolutely important. Success can hinge on fitness. Conditioning, however, is very different from developing skill. Mixing conditioning and skill training has value for testing skill. It is a recipe for blunting skill development though. If you always train a skill under tension and fatigue then your movement patterns become tense and imprecise. Just making training harder doesn't necessarily make it more effective.

Training skill, in my opinion, is best done in isolation. Then once that skill is developed, distractors and stressors can be added in. Performance definitely degrades under mental and physical stress. I believe that the best cure for that is a higher level of skill, and then exposure to those stresses as a test of that skill. When you are working on technique, work on that technique. Combine it, test it, and learn to apply it later. Conditioning supports your skill. The mental game helps you apply it. But neither can make up for its lack.

Working combination drills builds consistent performance on demand. This is an essential component of training and becomes more vital as we progress in our development. This is a step skipped all too often in training and is essential for developing true mastery of our craft.

Testing that skill you've developed absolutely has value. And at some stages in your training, it should be done pretty regularly. It validates and informs your training, exposes weaknesses in need of improvement in future skill building sessions. It helps develop the mental component of performance as well. Testing can take different forms, too. It doesn't have to be a realistic scenario, although it certainly can be. It could also be a stress shoot in full kit or a sparring session.

The application of skill is the event our training is preparing us for. For a responsible citizen, it could be a self-defense scenario or one involving the defense of others. For an armed professional it's going into harm's way. Understanding the nature of what we are training for allows us to prioritize what we train the same way an athlete tailors their training for the needs of their sport.

Despite the often repeated cliché, "train like you fight," conditioning, training, and testing aren't the event. They prepare us for the event. Training like you fight doesn't cut it. There's no champion fighter who does nothing but spar. There's no football team that does nothing but scrimmage. Instead of training like you fight, train like an athlete. Train for the fight.

TRAIN LIKE AN ATHLETE

"Today I will do what others won't, so tomorrow I can accomplish what others can't." – Jerry Rice

From the time I was a young soldier I was determined to master my craft. Especially shooting. I spent countless hours of my own time shooting, dry firing, and researching in my quest to get better. And I did get better. I became a good enough shooter to more than hold my own among my peers. But it wasn't until many years later, when I started competing in shooting sports that I started to understand what good actually was and found my skill level increasing exponentially. The reason for my "leveling up" after so many years was that I was now training my shooting less like a soldier and more like an athlete.

I wasn't satisfied though. My new exposure to high-level competition had shown me what mastery of shooting actually looked like. I now knew first-hand how skilled someone actually was who had truly mastered performance shooting. I wanted that level of skill and was ready to put the work in. Despite intensifying my efforts, I plateaued in skill in short order and couldn't seem to break through no matter how hard I worked. I realized that I needed to be smarter with my efforts, more sophisticated with my training if I wanted to reach my goals.

So, I started researching again. I trained with as many top competitors as I could, read up on athletic performance and sports psychology, studied current research into learning and mastery, and over time pieced together a system of training that gave me steady improvements in shooting skill. I'm now reaching my goals at a record pace because of the way I'm training. Mastery is achievable. It takes not just effort, but effort intelligently applied.

This training system is at the heart of the shooting classes I now teach. There is only so much improvement an intermediate-to-advanced shooter can make in a weekend class. But if that same student learns how to structure their own training more effectively they can continue to improve long after the class is done. I've taught this methodology to numerous shooters and watched them make rapid gains in ability when they put in the work. Shooting is an athletic skill. If you train like an athlete, you will get better.

The first component of this system of training is one that I now think of as crucial, but that I honestly never applied to my shooting until the last couple of years. This is experimentation. No two athletes at the top of their game in any endeavor have technique that is identical. The techniques of top performers all follow the same principles, but they are optimized for their own unique physiology and psychology. The most obvious example of this in shooting is the grip for shooting pistols. No two top pistol shooters have exactly the same grip. Robert Vogel's grip looks drastically different from Ben Stoeger's and so on. But both Vogel's and Stoeger's grips are inhumanly efficient and effective. They have internalized the principles of sound technique and made them uniquely theirs.

We are too often locked into dogmatic thinking in the shooting and tactical worlds. We regurgitate what was taught to us in a forty hour training course or imitate the appearance of someone's technique without understanding why it works. Instead we need to be open enough to experiment with technique and explore variations and variables until we find our own best way.

The second type of training is developing skills in isolation. This is best done without distractions. This is not the time to put on full kit, or do PT-heavy stress shoots. Those types of training exercises can have value as tests of skill, or as gut-checks, but they aren't the best way to develop skill. And before I hear the protests of "train like you fight," consider something. No football team wears full pads for every drill or does nothing but scrimmage in practice. No UFC fighter's training consists solely of sparring. Tests of skill aren't the best way to develop skill.

When people think of isolated skill work for shooting they often think of weapons manipulations. Skills such as draws, reloads, and malfunction clearances. And those are definitely things to be worked on in isolation. But this category also includes much more than just those types of skills. You can use drills to isolate target transitions, movement skills, or any other aspect of performance shooting.

As an example, let's take a classic shooting drill, the Bill Drill. The Bill Drill is typically shot at 7 yards, and is six rounds on a USPSA target from the holster. The gold standard for performance on it is all A-zone hits in under two seconds. What exactly are we working on in this drill? The draw is essential for making that standard, both with speed and establishing a proper grip, but there are simpler and less ammo intensive ways to work on that. When I run Bill Drills, I focus on one of two things: using my grip to mitigate recoil, or tracking my sights throughout the recoil cycle. And only one of these can be focused on in any particular repetition of the drill. One of the easiest mistakes to make in skill development training is trying to work on more than one thing at a time.

How we execute our repetitions for skill training matters. If we stay in our comfort zone, where success is guaranteed, we inhibit our progress. If we do nothing but push for personal bests, especially with speed, our on-demand consistency suffers. So how do we balance these conflicting demands? Whenever I work an isolation drill, my first repetition or two are meant to be my cold, on-demand best. Not a push for new speed and not "hanging back" and shooting below my ability, but an attempt to shoot at my true current level of skill.

Then the real work begins. Now each rep should be an incremental push beyond your comfort zone. This should be repeated until you find a failure point. That last part is essential. Beyond a certain point, you won't improve without giving yourself permission to fail. This runs contrary to a lot of military and law enforcement culture, but it's absolutely essential if you want to reach your true potential as a shooter. You have to set your ego aside and accept that fact if you want to improve. Once you find that failure point, work the issue for several repetitions. This is where you start to correct whatever technical weakness caused the failure. That is the other essential piece of the puzzle. You have to cultivate the awareness to diagnose where your technique is breaking down and work on improving that weakness.

Once you've put some work in and are closing out the drill, there's one more essential part of this. That "push" you've just done to try and break through to a new level of skill is addictive. If you get stuck there mentally, you will absolutely damage your on-demand performance. To prevent that, close out the drill with one or two performances at an on-demand pace. These again shouldn't be lazy reps, but instead right at your on-demand best.

It's important to track the data from these drills. If you have a shot timer, between it and your targets you can collect literally every important data point. You should know with certainty what your times with acceptable accuracy on the targets are for draws, reloads, transitions, and splits for a wide variety of target difficulties and distances. You should have the same familiarity with how long it takes you to move from one shooting position to another. This data drives your improvement on these isolated skills, but it's also important for your training in other ways that we'll touch on in a moment.

In the early stages of your training, experimentation and isolated skill work should be the bulk of your practice. But, as you progress, you will need to start training skills in combination as well. Without adding in this third category of training, you'll see a marked degradation in performance and consistency when you test your skills. The more elements of performance we string together, the greater the cognitive load. Think of your brain as a computer. The more programs you have open simultaneously, the slower the computer runs. Training skills in combination builds up your brain's subconscious ability, the "processor" that allows you to run multiple skills reliably and consistently.

When we work skills in combination, none of the individual skills get pushed like they do in isolation. Instead, they should be performed subconsciously. You should have collected enough data already from your skill isolation practice to know what your current on-demand level of performance on any particular skill is. You should know your baseline performance with acceptable accuracy so that you can compare it to your performance on each element when you combine them into a more complex drill.

Then the goal is to build up longer and more complex combinations of skills while maintaining that baseline performance level on each one. This can be done a variety of ways. One of my favorites is to set up several shooting positions and random target arrays, then work them in every combination I can think of. I typically don't repeat a particular combination more than three to five times, to avoid getting too comfortable with a particular sequence. Over time you can build up to increasingly more complex combinations and more difficult shooting and movement problems. The failure point you're seeking to find and improve on here is the amount of cognitive load you can maintain before your individual skills break down. The failure point can be missing a shot or forgetting a sequence of fire, but it can also be more subtle. If a skill is markedly slower than when in isolation, or if your accuracy degrades significantly, that's a failure point as well.

When you find a failure point, back off on the complexity and then ramp it back up. Over time the level of complexity you can reach without failing will increase. Your brain's "processor" gets more powerful. You'll find that your consistency on individual skills also increases as a result of this mode of training. Your cold on-demand performance gets closer to your best runs, and your incident rate of error decreases so that mistakes become rarer and less significant.

The fourth component of training is testing your skill. Internal tests, or validation drills, should be done frequently to check progress, and see if your training needs any course corrections for further improvement. External testing, whether institutional or competitive should be done periodically as well to evaluate your on-demand performance. This is where team stress shoots and competitions come into play. This is where you evaluate how well your work on skills in combination has built your ability to perform at your current level of skill, under stress and on demand. This is also where you identify technical weaknesses that need focus in your skill isolation drills. Competition is an excellent test, whether it's an action shooting match or an informal competition among SWAT teammates on the range. If you train alone, seek out competition with others.

Without some sort of test under pressure your skills aren't validated. It's much easier to put up personal bests when you know you have endless "do-overs" for your mistakes than it is to perform at your the level of skill on demand and under pressure. Testing your skills creates an essential feedback loop for your training. Identify your weaknesses, focus on them in isolation, strengthen them in combination, then retest and repeat.

The proportion of time spent on each of these three modes of training varies depending on our skill level, goals, and if we are training for a specific event. Complete beginners should spend a significant amount of training time working solely on isolated skills. At least until they have a base level of competence at safe weapons handling and movement with a firearm, and understand fundamental marksmanship. As the shooter progresses in skill, they can begin to add in skills in combination. The closer the shooter gets to "maxing out" on their isolated skills, the more training time should be spent on combined skills.

Another factor to consider when programming training is peaking for a known event. The closer I get to a major competition for example, the more time I spend working skills in combination, and the less I spend on skills in isolation. The same theory could be applied when a soldier is ramping up for a deployment, or when a police officer or civilian is preparing for a difficult shooting school.

The way we combine the training modalities changes as we improve. In the early stages of skill development it's best to distinctly separate each one. This is known as block practice. Block practice is working on one aspect, one "block" of skill, and then moving on to another. This is the best way for beginners to internalize the rudiments of technique.

As we improve, the concept of interleaving practice can be a way to drastically accelerate our progress. Interleaving practice involves mixing skills and modalities of training throughout a practice session. As an example, in my training I'll often throw ten or so repetitions of an isolation drill in between sets of a combination drill. Research has shown that once the fundamentals are grasped, interleaving practice is a far more effective way to reach the upper levels of skill.

Over time, the training template becomes more flexible and instinctive. The ability to practice effectively is in and of itself a skill, and over time we get better at it. The more data we collect, and the more versed we become with applying that data to our training efforts, the easier it becomes to use these modes of practice to improve. This method gives us a system for organizing and directing our efforts into what performance experts call deliberate practice. Deliberate practice is qualitative and focused, incorporating feedback to adjust future training efforts. It's the one thing that researchers believe separates top performers from average ones.

Employed correctly, this system of training gives the shooter a comprehensive plan for improvement. What's even better is that as long as the data is collected and analyzed correctly, the plan is self-correcting. Skills are built through experimentation, honed in isolation, strengthened in combination, and then tested under stress. Weaknesses are identified, then focused on as the cycle starts again. One by one, weaknesses become strengths and strengths get stronger, test and retest, until mastery is achieved. Train like an athlete, and you *will* get better.

DATA

"Technique is the religion of the dangerous trades." - Thomas Harris

Performance shooting is at its heart both an athletic pursuit and a martial one. But like many other skills that are derived from conflict, without objective analysis of performance data, it's easy for technique to become affectation. There are countless examples of this in institutionalized firearms training. Everything from reloading your pistol high in your "workspace" so you can keep your eyes on the threat,\ to slingshotting the slide because the slide lock lever is a "fine motor skill," to many other inefficient and overly stylized techniques.

Suboptimal techniques persist because of two things. The first is a seemingly rational theory justifying why they should be done that way. The second is a lack of objective data to base technical choices on. Anyone who is a martial artist, and old enough, watched this play out in the competitive fighting world with the rise of MMA. Prior to the popularity of the UFC, a lot of stylized and inefficient technique was thought to be effective because of theory. Martial artists now have much more objective evaluation of technique available to them as common knowledge, and as a general rule, now train more like other athletes.

In the tactical shooting community, the persistence of inefficient technique is a bit puzzling for me, and here's why: performance shooting is one of the few endeavors where literally every piece of available data is easily quantified and collected. If you have a shot timer, cellphone video, and targets, you can easily measure every variable affecting performance. This does a lot for us in our efforts to master our craft.

The first thing this does is validate technical choices. If an emergency reload is truly an emergency, then the difference in time between using the slide lock lever and slingshotting the slide matters. If you're reloading an empty weapon in the open and under fire, the slightest technical edge matters, much less a difference as large as this one. If pinning and holding the trigger through recoil were effective, it would produce splits as fast and shot groups as tight as resetting during recoil does. But it doesn't, so that technique should be retired.

Another thing that data does is allow individual technical expression. My grip on a pistol looks drastically different than another shooter's might look, based on individual differences in physiology and psychology. The appearance of a technique doesn't matter only its effectiveness. And the only way to accurately judge technical effectiveness is through objective data.

The last thing that easily collected performance data does is allow us to direct our training efforts efficiently. If every piece of data is observed, we can correct deficiencies and improve strengths in a systematic and deliberate fashion. The cliché that behavior observed is behavior modified is as powerful as it's true. A shooter who can tell me with confidence what their draw would be to a wide variety of targets is, in my experience, a shooter who already has a fast and accurate draw. Keeping track of the data fuels improvement.

So collect the data. Don't be afraid of technical experimentation and validation, embrace it. Find out objectively what works best and adopt it. Use the data to drive your training, take it and make a roadmap to follow. Find the shortcut for your learning curve. If you put the work in, and stay objective, you will get better.

VIDEO

"Truth was never meant to make you comfortable, unless you stand in the middle of it with acceptance." - Shannon L. Alder

The world we live in now is driven by social media, by idealized representations captured in digital video, or photographs posted for the purpose of gathering adoration. In order to market my business, I'm forced to feed the social media machine daily myself. But video footage of our training is valuable far beyond its use on Instagram.

I routinely review video of my matches as well as my live and dry fire training sessions. This review is invaluable for informing my training. With the advent of software apps such as the (now discontinued) Coach's Eye, detailed frame-by-frame video analysis can be done on your smartphone. This is just as applicable to combatives and complex fitness movements such as the Olympic lifts as it is to performance shooting. It's extremely applicable, in fact, to CQB. When I run CQB training, I routinely video runs in the shoot house for review with the students.

What are the considerations for using video for review? How to we maximize the value without becoming over-inundated with information that isn't useful? There are a few guidelines that can help.

Immediacy matters. The sooner the video can be reviewed thoroughly the better. Not only does reviewing it as soon as possible make the feedback more effective for improving as rapidly as possible, but it keeps it relevant, as our technique grows and evolves over time.

The flip side of immediacy is that there is no need to maintain the majority of your video once it's reviewed. It won't be relevant in short order for any reason beyond nostalgia. From a purely practical standpoint, it also takes up a lot of data storage space, especially high resolution, longer videos, and slow-motion ones.

There is coaching value in both third and first-person points of view, so it helps to obtain both. I use a smartphone or tablet on a tripod combined with video glasses. There are a myriad of alternatives available today—GoPro cameras, drones, helmet cams. Use any two of these so that you can obtain footage from both viewpoints.

The third-person footage is best for showing the nuances of stance and movement. This is huge not just for shooting, but also for tactics training. When I ran the training for the Chicago SWAT team, I would routinely set up a tablet on a tripod and video room entries and hallway movements. We could then view the video immediately after the runs. This enabled me to both avoid any conflict in AARs over what actually occurred, and also do a deep dive into the nuances of individual and team movement technique.

The first-person video shows you how your vision interacts with your technique. Vision drives our technique, and with this you can review exactly what you look at. It's also effective at showing you where this breaks down like when we pull off a target on a close fast array because we looked at the next target too soon. Or in CQB how quickly we are actually hitting our corner, not how quickly we think we are.

And if you compete as a shooter, video review of your match and training footage with a critical eye gives invaluable input for improvement. And if you compete and train tactics as well, you'll discover the same thing I did. The better I got at competition, the better I got at tactics. Even though they are very different, there is a huge amount of carryover from matches to be exploited in your tactical training.

So use video. Use it in an organized fashion, and with a plan. Review the footage thoroughly and critically, and you will accelerate your improvement exponentially.

PERMISSION TO FAIL

"Show me a guy who's afraid to look bad, and I'll show you a guy you can beat every time." - Lou Brock

One of the biggest flaws I see in institutional training, both military and police, is a zero-defect mentality. This idea that we can never miss, even in training. I understand where it comes from. It's rooted in the doctrine, fundamental to our professional culture, that we are accountable for every round fired and cannot afford collateral damage. And this doctrine is valid when it comes to the application of our skill. The problem is that, except when testing skill, carrying over that doctrine to the training environment will prevent us from ever reaching our potential.

To improve, we have to push ourselves to the failure point when developing skill. This is especially true when developing speed in our shooting. No one ever became truly fast without training at a pace where they couldn't guarantee success. One of the clichés of institutional firearms training is the admonition to "slow down and get your hits." The problem with this is that when you slow down you are no longer challenging your skill. You don't get truly good at anything by staying in your comfort zone.

Instead of "slowing down to get your hits," maintain that challenging pace and learn to make your hits without backing off the speed. Continue that process, and in short order you will drastically improve your performance. You'll make a lot of mistakes along the way, but the point of training is to get better, not to feel good about your current level of skill.

CRITERIA FOR SUCCESS

"It is a capital mistake to theorize before one has data." - Sir Arthur Conan Doyle

Everything you do in training needs to have clearly defined criteria for success. This doesn't mean that every drill is a pass/fail, go/no-go exercise. Those who've trained with me know that a sizable percentage of my training time is spent on what I call experimentation drills, where the objective is technical experimentation leading to more efficient technique. But for isolation and combination skill work, we have to clearly define our desired end state before practicing.

There are a myriad of scoring mechanisms used for tactical and competitive shooting, and most of them fall far short of the realities of a gunfight. Especially the typical crutch of institutional training. What usually happens in law enforcement and military range sessions is a large number of students on a flat range line shooting a drill with a generous par time that isn't even remotely challenging by true performance shooting standards. What this creates is a lowest common denominator training environment where meeting a minimum standard is enough, and individual students don't even have a mechanism for gauging progress beyond simply passing or failing.

I understand why par time training can be logistically necessary for large training courses, especially for people entering into a career field or specialized assignment. But the reality is that this will never create high levels of performance shooting skill. So how should we score our drills in our ongoing training? How do we set appropriate criteria for success?

There are two main variables at play when scoring a performance shooting drill, hits on target and elapsed time. Neither is more or less important than the other in a gunfight. Indeed, understanding the balancing act between speed and accuracy and putting it into practice is one of the most important attributes needed for the development of a high level of shooting skill.

I judge hits on target in three categories, regardless of whether we are talking about a drill, a competition, or a gunfight. Hits on target are either optimal, acceptable, or unacceptable. On a USPSA target in competition, this translates easily into A, C, and D scoring zones. For the real world, optimal is about a fist sized group in the high center chest or about an index card sized group in the head, acceptable is about the width of the USPSA C zone and from the hips to the collarbones, and unacceptable is anything else.

Elapsed time is so much more than just a par time. If Shooter A can place the same number of optimal hits on target as shooter B in 75% of Shooter B's time, then Shooter A is out performing Shooter B by 25%. This matters in competition, but it matters even more when an opponent is attempting to put rounds on you as well.

Many scoring systems have been created in an attempt to measure the balance of speed and accuracy needed for performance. Par times with penalties for sub-optimal hits and time-plus scoring with varying degrees of penalties, some emphasizing accuracy more than speed and others the opposite. In my opinion, the best of these scoring systems is minor power hit factor scoring as seen in USPSA. If you reduce the size of the A zone by about half, this has the balance of speed and accuracy needed to train for fighting with a firearm. I'll touch on this in more detail in the next section.

The way hit factor scoring works is that it's points divided by time. Or to sum it up, points per second. A zone—optimal—hits have a value of five points. B/C zone—acceptable—hits have a value of three points. D zone—unacceptable—hits (but not misses) have a value of one point. Misses give you a penalty of ten points. The math is cumbersome at first but soon makes sense when you spend some time scoring drills this way.

As an example, let's take an El Presidente Drill. Draw and fire two rounds each on three targets, reload, then two more rounds on each target. Twelve rounds fired is a maximum of sixty points. If I shoot all As in six seconds, I have a hit factor of ten. If I shoot ten As and two Cs in 5 seconds, I have a hit factor of 11.2. Points per second.

The downfalls of hit factor scoring are that it is less user friendly than simpler systems, and less suited to a group or institutional training environment. But in your own training, if you aren't using hit factor scoring, you're doing yourself a disservice. Learn to do the math, internalize it, and your training will become more realistic and efficient. And you'll be a better shooter.

SCORING

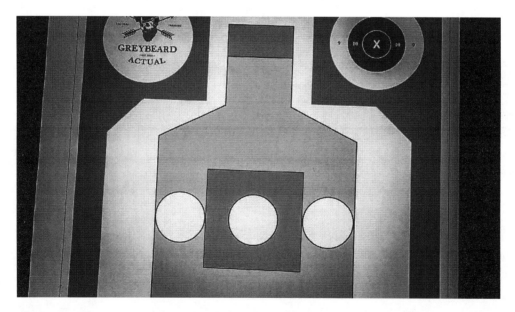

"Good is the enemy of great. And that is one of the key reasons why we have so little that becomes great." - James Collins

I had an interesting conversation with a friend of mine named Bryan Williams recently about what makes someone a good or great shooter from a practical point of view. My friend, a retired chief of police and USPSA Grand Master shooter since the 90's, and I had a wide-ranging discussion about this. We talked about everything from B-8s to Bill Wilson's 5x5 to the FAST coin, and many other widely recognized tests of practical/tactical skill with a firearm.

The conversation helped me solidify something I'd been thinking about for a long time—years really—ever since I ran the training for the Chicago Police SWAT team. How should we measure our skill? How should we score our shooting drills, and for that matter how should we validate the shooting component of our tactics training?

Most "tactical" firearms training—whether law enforcement, military, or defensive—is based around par times and pass/fail accuracy. For initial training in an institutional setting, this makes complete sense from a logistical standpoint. It rapidly becomes a limiting factor in a shooter's growth though. When you're on a line of shooters running a par time drill, you may feel as if you were done faster than most, but feelings aren't data. Even more importantly, once you can pass that drill within the par time, you no longer have a metric for gauging improvement. If I don't know whether or not I ran the course of fire faster than I did before, I not only don't know if I improved, I may not even be aware that I am regressing.

The other popular scoring mechanism I see in "tactical" shooting is some version of time-plus. For this, there are targets with different scoring zones, and your score is your time plus penalties. Penalties range anywhere from a quarter second for less than optimal hits up to five seconds or more for misses depending on which flavor of this system you're using. This takes the time component of shooting skill into account and is easy mathematically, but has one major weakness—the penalties aren't proportional. In other words, a less than optimal hit will cost me the same amount of time regardless of shot difficulty or length of the course of fire.

That's not how the real world works. The closer the threat's proximity, the more important speed is. In practical application, getting an acceptable hit faster than the opponent matters. Speed and accuracy should be a balancing act in terms of priority, and time-plus scoring just doesn't accomplish that very well.

What does a very good job of balancing the speed and accuracy sides of the coin in my opinion is hit factor scoring. This system originated in 1976 with the founders of IPSC competition including the famous Col. Jeff Cooper, and is still used in USPSA competition today. Hit factor is simply points divided by time.

Hit factor scoring is further divided into minor power factor and major power factor scoring. Power factor is determined by bullet mass and velocity but basically boils down to 9mm and

.38 caliber for minor, and, except for custom loads, .40 caliber and .45 caliber for major. This is largely an obsolete distinction now with modern ballistics, but at the time it was meant to reflect the efficacy of the ammunition against an opponent.

The idea was that regardless of major or minor, the most accurate shots are worth five points. It changes as accuracy decreases though. The next highest scoring zone is worth four points for major power factor, and three points for minor. The least valuable hits are worth two points for major, and only one for minor. This was meant to encourage competitors using major power factor ammunition, as it was considered more effective in actual application.

Their intent may have been different, but the balance between speed and accuracy required to shoot well with so-called minor power factor is in my opinion fairly well matched to the demands of a gunfight. The only way it could be a better representation of actual application is in the scoring zones of the targets themselves. The humanoid cardboard silhouette targets used in USPSA have two maximum value scoring zones, called the A zones. The upper or head A zone is four inches by two inches, and the lower or torso A zone is six inches by eleven inches. The upper A zone is a fairly accurate representation of the optimal scoring area for a human head. The lower A zone, however, is far too generous to properly represent the optimal scoring area of a human torso. The body C zone, the intermediate scoring area, is pretty accurate as to width; but is actually not long enough vertically. The head C zone, or what used to be the B zone is too generous as well. The D zone, the lowest scoring area of the torso, has its own issues as well, which we'll come back to shortly.

In my conversation with Bryan, I stated the opinion I've given in my classes many times. That if you cut the A zone in half and made the bottom half part of the C zone, and awarded no points for a D zone hit, then the USPSA classifiers scored with minor power factor would be excellent tests of real-world shooting skill. I still stand by that opinion. If you can score B-class or higher on representative classifiers with the half size A zone and non-scoring D zone, using Production or Carry Optics division hit factors, then you have an acceptable level of applicable shooting skill. If you can score Master-class or better this way then you are an excellent shooter indeed. I would even argue the same for close-range carbine skill using the PCC hit factors as well. The classifier diagrams and hit factors are available for free on the USPSA website, and they are (with some exceptions) easy to set up. Run a variety of them and you get a solid idea of where you stack up against the best in the world in a well-rounded set of shooting challenges.

For those practical minded shooters who don't compete but want to set up classifiers with the changes I've made to the scoring zones, I have designed my own target. It's the same overall dimensions as a USPSA silhouette with the following modifications: the lower A zone is reduced to only the top half of the one on a USPSA target, but the C zone runs to the bottom edge of the silhouette. The D zone on the body is an unacceptable hit, so it's not a scoring area, but you don't get a miss penalty for hits there. For the head, the upper A zone remains the same but now the head has a smaller C zone. It's the same width as the upper A zone, and runs down from the bottom edge of the upper A zone until it meets the lower C zone. Anything else in the head is now the upper D Zone and like the lower D zone is not a scoring area, although you aren't penalized for missing if you hit there. The targets are available for purchase on my website and from National Target Company.

DIFFICULT DRILLS

"I am always doing that which I cannot do in order that I may learn how to do it." – Pablo Picasso

Anyone who's ever trained with me knows I am a big proponent of extremely difficult drills and shooting challenges, what I jokingly call the "soul crushing junk punches of epic proportions." I often have my most productive training sessions focusing on something still mostly out of my reach. Like intensity techniques in strength training though, these sort of drills need to be used when appropriate. Just like too many partials or eccentrics can actually start to lower your strength, too much of this training can damage your shooting.

So how should we apply this in our training? I do these sorts of overreach drills relatively often, although they still aren't the majority of my training. But I also have a psyche conditioned by years of difficult training as well as a temperament suited to grinding away at currently unachievable goals. At the other end of the spectrum, a newer shooter without an athletic or military background, and with a psyche less suited to this style of training might not find value in it at all.

You need to figure out whether you're suited to this style of practice, and if so, how often you should incorporate it. A good baseline to monitor when using this sort of overreach in your training is how you perform in your combination drills. Combination drills place a strong emphasis on consistency, shooting in what competition shooters call "match mode." When you start making more errors than normal in your combination drill practice, you need to back off on the frequency that you use this style of overreach in your isolation work.

When used appropriately, this sort of overreach training can help you break through to new levels of skill. When utilized incorrectly, it can hinder your progress, or even cause you to regress. Explore this in your training, learn to use it correctly, and watch your skill level increase.

QUALITY OVER QUANTITY

"We are what we repeatedly do. Excellence, then, is not an act, but a habit." - Will Durant

It's all too easy to think that more is simply better, especially where training is concerned. This has long been a struggle of mine. That's partially because of my personality type, and partially because of the nature of much of my early training, both military and even earlier in the dojos of my youth. It's a flawed paradigm though.

As others have said, practice doesn't make perfect, it makes permanent. Or at least it makes long-term. I have damaged my shooting and other skills in the past by practicing incorrectly. Especially because of my tendency towards a more is better mindset.

Don't misunderstand my point here. Volume is absolutely necessary as is frequency. No one ever truly masters a skill without a large amount of frequent and focused effort. But it has to be the correct effort and intelligently applied. Simply throwing sloppy effort at a skill will never get you to the level that quality practice will.

Each repetition, each training session, must be purposeful and mindful. Every press of the trigger, every round fired, every step of footwork should be a lesson learned. You need training volume and frequency to improve, but quantity alone won't get you where you need to be without a commensurate focus on quality effort. Quality over quantity.

SUPPORT SIDE TRAINING

"Practice even what seems impossible. The left hand is useless at almost everything, for lack of practice. But it guides the reins better than the right." - Marcus Aurelius

There are typically three reasons for training support side work. It can be for competition. It can be for when the shooter is wounded on their strong side. Or it can be out of a desire to minimize exposure when utilizing cover. There is another reason in my opinion, though, that for the serious student is more important than any of the others.

I'm a big believer that some drills have a training carryover out of proportion to their application value. In my opinion, support side work is one of these. The better I am at a wide variety of tasks with my firearms, the better I can competently address unique situations. There is a phenomenon referred to by sports psychologists as "chunking" where tasks are combined into groups or chunks which are then used to ensure correct and competent responses by the athlete. Chunking allows us to have building blocks of subconsciously competent skills we can apply to unforeseen situations. Then when we are faced with a unique problem to solve, our subconscious can assemble those "chunks" of skill into a workable solution.

There is also a carryover value in my opinion in learning to do things with the "opposite" body alignment. Shooting with my support hand has a carryover value to shooting with my strong hand regardless of how likely it is that I will need to do it in application. The same is true for weapons manipulations. Before I started competing, I never practiced any skills that I didn't think had direct application to gunfighting. And when constructing training for people who have limited time or motivation, I still think that is a valid training strategy. But someone who is going to put in a significant amount of time and work towards mastery can and should take a different approach.

How much training time should be put into support side work? A good rule of thumb is 10-15% of our total firearms practice should be with the support side. If we do that diligently, we will see benefits. For that matter, another 10-15% percent of our pistol practice should be done strong hand only.

Challenging the brain by changing up which side we run the gun with, or otherwise altering motor patterns, can be a valuable skill builder as long as it isn't made a training priority. Do this sort of training too frequently, and it can interfere with your progress. Use these sorts of challenges sparingly though, and you'll see skill improvements.

TRAINING GEAR

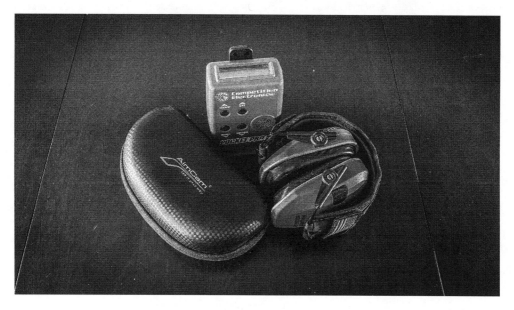

"To be the best, you have to have the right equipment at your disposal." - Hafthor Bjornsson

You need to have the right equipment to train. Too many people go cheap on this and handicap themselves.

For shooting you'll need a few essentials. You should have two of every firearm you carry or compete with. One to train with and one for use. The training one is your backup for carry or competition if the other breaks. A set of training magazines for your firearms. Magazines take a beating in practice, so you don't want to use your carry or competition magazines and run the risk of a malfunction when it counts. A shot timer. I'm always amazed at how many soldiers and policemen don't have one, as they are absolutely essential for improvement. High quality ear and eye protection. For hearing protection, you need electronic muffs or plugs so that you can hear instruction or input from training partners. For eye protection, I prefer the AimCam. It's quality eye protection with a video camera built-in that you can zero to get a true POV recording. This is extremely valuable for gathering data.

For dry fire I like using the reduced size USPSA targets from the Ben Stoeger Pro Shop. They allow you to simulate greater distances in your dry fire practice. There are also some excellent videos for guided dry fire on YouTube that I use frequently on my television. What you don't need are dry fire magazines, laser trainers, etc. if you are honest with yourself about what you see and feel in dry fire, those devices are unnecessary.

For combatives you should have at least a heavy bag, although a top and bottom bag is valuable, too. I prefer the long Muay Thai style bags, so that I can work leg kicks. You'll need inert copies of your carry or duty guns for weapons retention drills. You'll also need inert trainers for any edged weapons you carry. If you have a training partner, I like using focus mitts and kicking shields also.

Set yourself up for success by making sure you have what you need to train properly. Invest in your training, so that you can reach your goals.

RANGE NEEDS

"If I only had an hour to chop down a tree, I would spend the first 45 minutes sharpening my axe." – Anonymous

Let's talk about range equipment from two different viewpoints, individual and institutional. Even before I retired, and despite being an NCO in 20th Special Forces Group and the training coordinator for the Chicago SWAT team, I also practiced on my own every week. So, I had my own set of range equipment apart from the ones I had access to at both jobs. If you're a private citizen, you'll need targetry and other range equipment for your practice. If you have input at an institutional range, there are things most don't have that you may be able to get for your team or unit.

On the individual side, you need to have enough target stands to run all your drills. Three is a bare minimum and I'd recommend six. Steel targets are not 100% essential, but they are very helpful. I have a portable "swinger," a moving target, as well. I'll talk more about that later, but it's extremely valuable for your training. For ease of setup and transportation, I use cones and agility poles instead of walls, barricades, or fault lines. You'll need targets and pasters, of course, as well as target sticks.

At an institutional range, there is certainly already some mechanism for setting up targets, but many only have target hangers immediately in front of the backstop. Without target stands as well, transitions in depth can't be set up for training. Steel targets, both static and reactive, are extremely valuable for training. Most unit's ranges at least have a few barricades, but for optimal training there should be an ample supply of walls and barrels. Moving targets are invaluable too, more on that in a moment.

While it's true that effort trumps equipment for training, don't shortchange yourself. Set up an efficient kit of range gear, so that you can maximize your valuable range time. And if you run the range for a unit or agency, don't shortchange your teammates. Equip your range well, and set them up for success.

MOVING TARGETS

"The right shot, at the right moment." - Eugene Herrigel

Moving targets. In the military and law enforcement worlds we tend to think of expensive automated systems. But the competition shooting world has a variety of inexpensive low-tech options that can provide the valuable experience of shooting at a moving target. Whether you're an individual practicing outdoors, or the range master at a large police department, these are worth looking into. All of these can be activated manually by a firearms instructor, or set up so that the shooter activates them by shooting a reactive steel target.

Drop turners are targets that begin on edge, then face the shooter once or twice on activation, then are on edge again at rest. These are valuable for simulating a threat appearing momentarily then disappearing again behind cover.

Clamshells and Max Traps are movers that place a no-shoot over the shoot target when activated. Good for simulating hostage shots with a moving or struggling hostage.

Swingers are the quintessential moving target in USPSA. Their movement pattern is artificial but the swinging motion of the target is a good exercise in shooting something that moves rapidly.

If you have access to more high-tech options, by all means use them. But these offer inexpensive and easily sustainable options for training. If you practice on your own, look into buying at least an inexpensive swinger. It will pay dividends in skill development for you.

SHOOTING DRILLS

"The key is not the will to win. Everybody has that. It is the will to prepare to win that is important." - Bobby Knight

I've touched in this above, but I believe it's vitally important to categorize our drills in training into three separate types plus an additional fourth category that I don't consider a true training drill. Each has their own purpose and their own best practices. Let's examine each type before giving representative examples that I use in my own classes and training.

Experimentation drills. This is where we optimize and fine tune our technique. Where we make it our own, rather than a literal imitation of someone else's. The principles of sound technique are universal, but the embodiment of those principles is a very individual thing indeed. For experimentation drills to be effective, we need to examine one specific variable at a time and see how modifying it affects the outcome of the drill. An example from my own recent practice is the shape and pressure of my thumb on the safety of my pistol when shooting the Doubles Drill with my strong hand only. By changing that variable I've been able to positively impact the tendency of the second shot to hit low and left when pulling the trigger at speed.

Isolation drills. This is where we polish and sharpen our skills. In isolation work it's best to focus on one element of improvement at a time. Taking the draw as an example, the focus could be as simple as driving down the par time. Or as subtle as the exact and specific placement of the support hand pointer finger on the bottom of the trigger guard at the point the hands meet. There is always an area for further improvement in a particular technique. If you're truly aware in your practice, you'll find the areas for improvement, and they will improve. Isolation drills are the place to push, to allow errors and learn from them. It's also acceptable in an isolation drill to stop a rep and reset if it's not going to be productive.

Combination drills are where we build consistency and lower our error rate. The more component tasks we string together, the more performance on each task degrades, that's just how the human brain works. Proper training on combination drills allows us to perform closer to our personal best on each component skill, and make technical errors less and less frequently. Combination work isn't about pushing, it's about finding the right mental "gear" that maximizes performance and minimizes error.

The fourth category, that we will touch on later, is validation drills or testing. Tests are often used incorrectly as skill building exercises. Testing has an important place in our development, but tests are not training. They are an evaluation of your previous training used to inform your future training. They create a feedback loop, and are vital in that role, but they are poor skill builders.

Let's look at each of these categories in greater detail and give some representative examples of each type of drill.

EXPERIMENTATION DRILLS

"It is what we know already that often prevents us from learning.' - Claude Bernard

Experimentation drills are an important part of my firearms training, but it hasn't always been that way. Up until the last few years, I was hesitant to experiment with my shooting technique. I think subconsciously I was concerned that it would slow my progress if it took me on a technical dead end.

When I began competition shooting, I made Master in USPSA very quickly because of all the work I had put in as a "tactical" shooter. But I did not perform as well in matches as my classification should indicate, and I hit a plateau that lasted longer than it should have. I was finally forced to admit that what had gotten me to the level I was at had become a limiting factor and was preventing me from improving further. I began to experiment with my shooting, deconstructing it, and rebuilding it. Once I did that, I began to improve again.

Now I realize that experimentation is vital for improvement. Rather than imitating the appearance of another's technique, learn to experiment and truly learn the principles underpinning it. Then you can make your techniques truly your own, and optimize them for you.

Number of The Beast

This is a drill I created when I was running the training for the Chicago Police SWAT team. It is designed to allow the shooter to explore marksmanship fundamentals without adding time pressure. The course of fire is simple. From twenty-five yards on a USPSA target, fire six rounds freestyle (both hands), six rounds strong hand only, and six rounds support hand only. The scoring area is the A zone of the target, anything else is considered a miss. There is NO time limit for this drill.

An alternative setup that I now prefer, especially when teaching, is to shoot the drill on a three inch circle at ten yards. This variation is arguably more difficult, but gives immediate feedback without walking down range and back between repetitions.

Use either variation to experiment with aiming and trigger management for extreme accuracy at a deliberate shooting pace. With only one exception, I've never known anyone who could be both fast and accurate that wasn't also extremely accurate when shooting slowly. Experiment in your own training until you have internalized the foundations of marksmanship.

Number of the Beast

RULES: Drill	Created By: Matt Little
START POSITION: Hands Relaxed at Sides	

PROCEDURE:	
Fire 6 shots freestyle, 6 shots strong hand only, and 6 shots weak hand only. There is NO time limit.	**SCORING:** Limited
	ROUND COUNT: 18
	TARGETS: 1
	DISTANCE: 25 yards
	SCORED HITS: 18
	PENALTIES: Any shot outside of A zone is a miss.
	NOTES: May also be shot at 5-10 yards on a 3 inch circle.

25 Yards

Trigger Control at Speed

Trigger Control at Speed is a fundamental drill that can, and should, be done in both dry fire and live fire. The drill itself is simple. Aim at a target without prepping the trigger, and if you are advanced enough, without your finger touching the trigger at all. On the start beep from your shot timer, fire a single shot *before* the end of the beep.

This drill teaches you how to prevent unwanted movement in the gun while moving the trigger as rapidly and aggressively as possible. This skill is absolutely essential for marksmanship at speed. When shooting at maximum speed, everyone slaps the trigger. Put the work in on this drill and your accuracy at speed will improve exponentially. I begin every dry fire session with this drill, as I believe it to be absolutely essential.

Trigger Control at Speed	
RULES: Drill	**Created By:** UNK
START POSITION: Aiming at target, trigger not prepped.	

PROCEDURE: On start beep, fire a single shot before end of beep.	**SCORING:** Limited
	ROUND COUNT: 1
	TARGETS: 1
	DISTANCE: Variable
	SCORED HITS:
	PENALTIES:
	NOTES:

Variable

Progressive Doubles

The Doubles Drill that USPSA champion Ben Stoeger created is one of my favorite experimentation drills. Although the course of fire is simple, there's a subtlety to the purpose of the drill that can be hard for people to grasp initially. In order to teach the drill in my classes, I came up with two preparatory drills I teach immediately prior to teaching Doubles. I find that this progression allows people to grasp the purpose of the actual drill.

Both preparatory drills are shot on a single target at seven yards. For the first part of the progression, the shooter draws their pistol at a comfortable pace and establishes a proper grip on the pistol. They then fire one round, aiming at a small point on the target. I usually use the letter A in the center of the A zone for this. The shooter then allows the pistol to rise freely in recoil, putting no muscular effort into the gun. The important point here is that the pistol should not shift in the hands at all, the grip should remain solid. The shooter then repeats this process at a deliberate pace for the remainder of the magazine. The intent here is to gather data on what the firearm does in recoil without any attempt at mitigating it. That will help your subconscious learn to drive the gun more efficiently when you do start mitigating recoil again.

The second drill in the progression begins the same way. On the first round fired, no muscular effort is exerted to control recoil. On each subsequent round fired, a little more effort is put back into the gun during recoil, until you find the sweet spot that returns the sights to your

258

point of aim and no further. Then you can work on replicating that feeling in the Doubles Drill, and in your shooting across the board. The shooting pace increases exponentially as well, with the goal being shooting as fast as you can pull the trigger.

After a magazine's worth on the second preparatory drill, we move on to the actual Doubles Drill, which I'll cover in the next section.

Progressive Doubles

RULES: Drill	**Created By:** Matt Little

START POSITION:
Hands relaxed at sides

PROCEDURE:	**SCORING:** Comstock
This is a 2 part drill:	**ROUND COUNT:**
1. Fire a single round deliberately, aiming at a specific point on the target. While keeping a proper grip, allow the gun to recoil fully, with no effort to control recoil. Repeat for a full magazine.	**TARGETS:** 1
	DISTANCE: 7 yards
2. Fire the first round as in 1 above, then each round put more effort into mitigating the recoil until you find the sweet spot where the sights return to the point of aim and no further.	**SCORED HITS:**
	PENALTIES:
	NOTES:

7 Yards

260

Doubles Drill

World Champion Ben Stoeger has been a huge influence on my shooting. I've trained with him multiple times and relied on him for brutally honest coaching and advice. His Doubles Drill is masterful in its simplicity. Shot anywhere from five to twenty-five yards on a single target, the shooter takes their time drawing and establishing a sound grip. Aiming at a specific point in the A zone, the shooter fires two rounds as fast as they can pull the trigger for ten yards or closer, slightly slower splits for further out. They then establish another sight picture and fire another pair of shots at the same speed, repeating this for six strings of four pairs each.

This is primarily an exercise in experimenting with grip shapes and pressures. Fine tune the placement of your support hand. Experiment with the bend and angle of your elbows. Explore which portion of your hands should exert the most pressure on the gun and in what direction.

A proper grip will allow you to maintain a fist-sized group at five to seven yards while pulling the trigger as fast as possible in each pair. The group widens and the splits slow the further out you go, but you'll be surprised at the level of accuracy at speed you can obtain if your grip and structure are correct. At twenty-five yards, two thirds A zone hits and the rest Cs with .30 splits is completely attainable.

An important point is that you should be aware of everything your sights do throughout the recoil arc. Paying attention to what your sights do in great detail will accelerate your progress. If your second shot tends to go low and to the support side, it's usually the result of moving the gun with the strong hand during the trigger press. If your second shot goes high and to the right, it's usually due to insufficient grip pressure from the support hand. Generally speaking, vertical stringing of your shots is preferable as an error to diagonal stringing and is usually the result of over or under driving the gun in recoil.

When ammo supply is sufficient, I often find myself expending up to two hundred rounds or more on this drill in a practice session. As simple as it is, it can improve your skill profoundly. Put the effort in on this drill, don't be afraid to experiment with your technique, and your accuracy at speed will improve drastically.

Doubles

RULES: Drill		Created By: Ben Stoeger	

START POSITION:
Hands relaxed at sides

PROCEDURE:	SCORING: Unlimited
Aiming at a specific point in the A zone, the shooter fires two rounds as fast as they can pull the trigger for ten yards or closer, slightly slower splits for further out. They then establish another sight picture and fire another pair of shots at the same speed, repeating this for six strings of four pairs each.	ROUND COUNT: 48
	TARGETS: 1
	DISTANCE: 5 to 25 yards
	SCORED HITS: 48
	PENALTIES:
	NOTES:

5 to 25 Yards

Experimental Transitions

I designed this drill to experiment with using vision to drive transitions. It's shot on two three inch circles at five or seven yards. The course of fire is as follows. Fire one round into each circle at a time, beginning at a deliberate pace, then continuing back and forth, working up to a reactive pace, and then a predictive one. Continue to increase the pace until you start to miss, then maintain that pace for the remainder of the drill, working on accuracy at that speed. Vary the distance between circles from one session to another.

The drill can also be shot on two small steel targets at ten to fifteen yards. This variation avoids any pasting or replacing of targets and enables you to get a large amount of quality repetitions done in less time.

I've found this drill to have huge benefits in my ability to take in visual information at high speed. It's also effective at learning to shoot subconsciously and simply being aware of the process. A third benefit is in eliminating unnecessary tension in your transitions.

There's no par time or accuracy standard per se on this drill. There's not even a set number of rounds. This is purely an experimental exercise. Use it to learn how transitions should look and feel, then learn to apply that to the rest of your shooting.

Experimental Transitions

RULES: Drill	Created By: Matt Little

START POSITION:
Hands relaxed at sides.

PROCEDURE:	
Fire one round into each circle at a time, beginning at a deliberate pace, then continuing back and forth, working up to a reactive pace, and then a predictive one. Continue to increase the pace until you start to miss, then maintain that pace for the remainder of the drill, working on accuracy at that speed. Vary the distance between circles from one session to another.	**SCORING:** Unlimited
	ROUND COUNT:
	TARGETS: 2
	DISTANCE: 5 to 7 yards
	SCORED HITS:
	PENALTIES:
	NOTES:

3 inch circles

5 to 7 yards

Walk Back Drill

One of the most common mistakes I see tactical shooters make is defaulting to the most precise aiming and trigger management techniques, regardless of shot difficulty or shot risk. The reason for this is two-fold. One part of the cause is that these are usually the only aiming and triggering techniques taught to beginners, and the other is that a zero-defect mentality is created in our training. We are taught that it's never ok to miss, even in practice. That may well be true in application, depending on context, but if we don't allow failure in training we can never know our limits, much less change them.

This drill is designed to eliminate that tendency by providing data for the shooter on the minimum necessary needed to see and do to get acceptable and optimal hits on a particular target. The idea is to attempt each shot pair with less than you think you need and then adjust based on the results until you have solid data for each target difficulty. The procedure is simply to fire reps of two rounds at the target and experiment with aiming and trigger management techniques until you are satisfied that you have an accurate concept of what is necessary for you at that target difficulty.

This is not a drill that needs to be done frequently, but since the minimum needed for a particular shot will lessen over time as your grip, index, and trigger management improve with training, it should be periodically revisited. The setup shown here is for pistol. For carbine the distances should extend further out.

Walkback

RULES: Drill	Created By: Matt Little

START POSITION:
Hands Relaxed at Sides

PROCEDURE: Fire 2-5 sets of 2 rounds each at each distance. Determine the minimum sight picture and trigger management needed to reliably get acceptable and optimal hits at each distance.	SCORING: Comstock
	ROUND COUNT:
	TARGETS: 1
	DISTANCE: 3-25 Yards
	SCORED HITS: Variable
	PENALTIES: None
	NOTES:

3 Yards

5 Yards

7 Yards

10 Yards

15 Yards

20 Yards

25 Yards

Shake & Bake Drill

If it weren't for my friend Frank Proctor, I would never have begun USPSA competition, and my subsequent growth as a shooter would never have happened. Frank was an instructor at the 20th Special Forces Group training detachment in Anniston, Alabama, teaching at SFAUC and SOTIC. He was also a USPSA Grand Master shooter who urged me to begin competition. I trained with Frank at SFAUC, and again when he became nationally known as a firearms instructor, and several times since, and he has had a huge impact on my development as a shooter.

This drill, that Frank calls Shake & Bake, is phenomenal for working specifically on dismounting and mounting the firearm at a threshold. Its benefits carry over to all movement with a firearm, especially in confined spaces. It can, and should, be run with either carbine or pistol. For carbine, either extend the distance or use paper targets for safety.

The setup for the drill is simple. One stack of two barrels centered approximately ten yards from two steel targets about a yard apart. The shooter begins standing behind the barrel stack at less than an arms length away from it. The course of fire is simple as well. The shooter then engages the appropriate steel target from each side of the barrel stack with one round and repeats this process for the length of the drill, engaging as fast as they can get appropriate visual confirmation for the shot.

268

This drill is for experimentation on how you can mount and dismount your firearm as efficiently as possible. Key points are eliminating excess and inefficient movement, and picking up the sights as soon as possible. Common errors to avoid are dropping or raising the firearm excessively, and inefficient presentation.

Spend time in your training on this drill, and use it to discover your optimal and most efficient technique.

Shake and Bake	
RULES: Drill	**Created By:** Frank Proctor
START POSITION: Standing less than one arms length from barrel stack	

PROCEDURE: Engage the appropriate target from each side of the barrel stack and repeat until drill is done. Focus on efficiently mounting and dismounting the firearm and acquiring the sights on presentation. Attempt to eliminate all unnecessary movement and tension.	**SCORING:** Unlimited
	ROUND COUNT:
	TARGETS: 2
	DISTANCE: 10 Yards
	SCORED HITS:
	PENALTIES:
	NOTES:

3 Yards Apart

● ●

10 Yards From Barrels

ISOLATION DRILLS

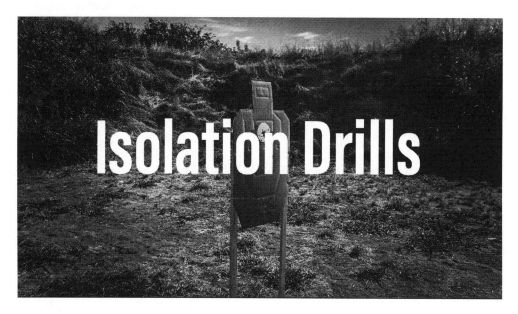

"It is not daily increase but daily decrease, hack away the unessential." - Bruce Lee

If experimentation drills are where you create your technique, isolation drills are where you refine it. To build high levels of performance on a skill, you need to practice it in isolation without other distractors. Isolation drills are where you push beyond your current level of on-demand skill. You have to give yourself permission to fail on these drills in order to improve. The important point here is identifying why you failed and working to correct it.

My typical practice on an isolation drill looks something like this. I start out with a repetition that is my cold on-demand effort. The goal here is not to lay back or be lazy, but rather to do the best I feel I can do without failing. Then each subsequent repetition I push a little further until I find my failure point. This isn't a mistake on an easier run, I'm trying to find the limit of my current skill. Once I find that failure point, rather than backing off, I try to work at that exact point for the next several repetitions and try to fix my technique at that pace. This is where the improvements come from.

The last important point is this. At least on the last drill of a session, whether dry fire or live fire, and in the beginning on every isolation drill you do, finish up with one last rep performed at your on-demand level of skill. That feeling of pushing is addictive. If you don't reset to your on-demand performance level, then you run the risk of pushing your shooting when you need to apply it, and that produces disastrous results.

Done properly, your isolation work can lead to rapid improvements in skill. Done incorrectly, you can damage your shooting and actually regress in skill. Be mindful in your practice, observe dispassionately what happens in each repetition in great detail. Every round fired in live fire, every trigger press in dry fire, should be a lesson learned. Otherwise you're just making gun smoke and spent brass, not getting better.

Bill Drill

Bill Wilson, one of the founders of both IPSC and IDPA, created this classic drill. The Bill Drill is typically shot from seven yards, although it should be practiced at distances from five to twenty-five yards. The course of fire is simple, draw and fire six shots on a single target. At seven yards, the goal is all A zone hits in under two seconds. This breaks down to a one second draw, and five .20 splits. Sounds relatively easy, but if you can do this consistently and on-demand then you are doing very well indeed.

This drill is a multipurpose isolation drill. You can use it to work on grip, sight tracking, predictive shooting pace, and other elements of shooting. At further distances it becomes a very challenging test of grip and trigger control. The main thing to guard against is excess tension, as it tends to build as you try to go faster.

Right now I am using the Bill Drill to work on relaxation while shooting. I tend to be overly tense when I shoot fast, and trying to drive my time on this drill down to 1.5 seconds requires relaxation. Because of the versatility of this drill, you should make it a regular staple of your practice. When using this drill for carbine training, try and really push the times down. You can get down to under 1.5 seconds with a little effort.

Bill Drill

RULES: Drill	**Created By:** Bill Wilson
START POSITION: Hands relaxed at sides	

PROCEDURE: Draw and fire 6 rounds. Standard distance is 7 yards, but should be practiced at 5-25.	**SCORING:** Virginia Count
	ROUND COUNT: 6
	TARGETS: 1
	DISTANCE: 7 Yards
	SCORED HITS: 6
	PENALTIES: Miss = -10
	NOTES:

7 Yards

273

Strict Bill Drill

This is a drill I created to force extreme accuracy under time pressure. It has become my favorite drill for that purpose. From five yards, draw and fire six rounds into a three inch circle in three seconds or less. This requires a precise index and proper grip on the draw in order to be successful. In order to get under three seconds, you have to be able to shoot this at a predictive pace. In order to do that, everything has to be solid from the draw.

Currently, I am averaging 2.8 seconds cold and on-demand and my personal best is 2.27 seconds. Once I'm warmed up I can shoot splits of .2 seconds or so, but the draw requires sufficient confirmation that I am very happy if the first shot is under 1.25 seconds. Basically, all of the extra time from a traditional Bill Drill should be on the draw, and you use your grip and structure to keep your hits inside the circle.

I find that when going back to the standard Bill Drill after working on this my accuracy is much improved while maintaining the same sub-two-second pace. This drill also builds confidence for shooting difficult shots at a predictive pace. Give this drill some time in practice, and your accuracy at speed will improve significantly.

Strict Bill Drill

RULES: Drill	**Created By:** Matt Little
START POSITION: Hands Relaxed at Sides	

PROCEDURE: From 5 yards, draw and fire 6 rounds into a 3 inch circle in 3 seconds or less.	**SCORING:** Limited
	ROUND COUNT: 6
	TARGETS: 1
	DISTANCE: 5 yards
	SCORED HITS: 6
	PENALTIES: Miss = Fail
	NOTES:

5 Yards

Four Aces

Four Aces, and it's less effective cousin One-Reload-One, are extremely popular drills on social media. I use them in my classes to teach efficient technique for the reload, but truthfully I feel these should be rarely done in your own live fire training. The weapons handling of the draw and reload can be built almost entirely in dry fire. Periodically use this drill as a confirmation that your dry fire is correct and you haven't let any flaws creep in to your technique, but it's not necessary to spend huge amounts of time and ammunition on it.

This drill is typically done at seven yards, although I think it's good to vary distances and target difficulty. Draw and fire two rounds, reload, and then fire another two. The reason this is a better verification than one-reload-one is because a proper grip is necessary for a rapid second shot to be accurate. It's too easy to cheat this when firing just one shot. A decent performance metric on four aces is all A zone hits in under 2.5 seconds. Truly good shooters can drive this down under two seconds. This drill should be periodically done with your carbine as well.

The main purpose for this drill in live fire is to gather data to inform your dry fire training on draws and reloads. Use it for that purpose and your weapons handling will get faster and more precise.

Four Aces

RULES: Drill	**Created By:** Ben Stoeger
START POSITION: Hands relaxed at sides	
PROCEDURE: Draw and fire two rounds, reload and then fire another two. The goal is 4 A zone hits in under 2.5 seconds.	**SCORING:** Virginia Count
	ROUND COUNT: 4
	TARGETS: 1
	DISTANCE: Variable. Typically 7 yards.
	SCORED HITS: 4
	PENALTIES:
	NOTES:

7 yards

277

Blake Drill

The Blake Drill is one of my favorite drills for working on transition speed. Named for Blake Miguez, a USPSA champion famous for lightning fast transitions and splits on closer targets, the drill's intent is to work on relatively close target transitions. The drill is shot on three targets, typically set at seven to ten yards and separated about a yard apart. There is value in shooting this drill at other ranges as well, but it begins to change the flavor of the drill if you're much closer or further than that.

The course of fire is to draw and shoot all three targets consecutively with two rounds each. The idea is that your splits should be as fast as possible, and your transitions should match your splits. This is intentionally a bit artificial. When you are applying your shooting, the transition speed is dependent on seeing what you need to see for each shot. This drill isn't shot that way. Instead, you're pulling the trigger at the pace of your splits and trying to make the gun move to the next target by the time the gun fires. Think of it as overspeed training, like a swimmer or sprinter does to learn new levels of speed. Try to really open up your vision and look precisely where you want the round to go on the target, and then see everything your sights are doing as the weapon fires.

You should practice this drill in both directions, left to right and right to left. You'll probably find that one direction is more comfortable than the other, but your times will probably be very close if not the same. This drill should be done with carbine as well.

Blake Drill

RULES: Drill	**Created By:**
START POSITION: Hands relaxed at sides	

PROCEDURE: Draw and shoot all three targets consecutively with two rounds each. Your splits should be as fast as possible, and your transitions should match your splits.	**SCORING:** Virginia Count
	ROUND COUNT: 6
	TARGETS: 3
	DISTANCE: 7 yards
	SCORED HITS: 2 per target
	PENALTIES:
	NOTES:

One target width apart.

7 to 10 Yards

279

Accelerator

My version of Accelerator is slightly different than the one created and popularized by Ben Stoeger. The target array is the same, one target at about seven yards, a second at about fifteen yards, and a third at about twenty-five yards, each separated laterally by about a yard. This array is meant to force you to mentally "change gears" between targets of varying difficulty. This is a difficult thing to do for many shooters, but developing this kind of "throttle control" is of paramount importance to your development as a shooter.

In his version, you shoot each target in sequence with two rounds each, reload, and then shoot each target again with two rounds each. In my version, I don't include the reload, and each repetition of the drill is just two rounds each on the three targets. I also like to change the engagement order up. One time I'll shoot near to far, or far to near; next time I might start on the middle target, or shoot the middle target last.

Ideally there should be little difference in your time regardless of engagement order. The main error to watch out for is getting mentally "stuck" on the shooting pace for one target when you transition to a different one. It's common to see a shooter go near to far, and push the pace too hard on the far targets, or shoot far to near, and shoot the close targets too deliberately. Unlike the Blake drill, where we intentionally set an artificial pace, on this drill let your vision dictate the transitions and splits. For carbine, you'll need to extend the target distances out for the same training effect.

Accelerator	
RULES: Drill	**Created By:**
START POSITION: Hands relaxed at sides.	
PROCEDURE: Draw and shoot all three targets with two rounds each. Vary the shooting order frequently.	**SCORING:** Limited
	ROUND COUNT: 6
	TARGETS: 3
	DISTANCE: 7, 15, and 25 yards.
	SCORED HITS: 2 per target
	PENALTIES:
	NOTES:

25 Yards

15 Yards

7 Yards

Distance Changeup

Distance Changeup, much like Accelerator, is an exercise in "throttle control," changing mental gears between targets of varying difficulties. Also like Accelerator, my version of this drill is slightly different than the original that I learned from Ben Stoeger.

For the setup, I use two USPSA targets at five yards, separated about two yards apart. Centered between the two targets at fifteen yards I put a piece of small steel. The course of fire is to shoot the USPSA targets with two rounds each and the steel with one. Just like Accelerator, I like to vary the engagement order and shoot every possible sequence.

On this drill, the main purpose of the five yard targets is to distract you, get your mental transmission stuck in the gear appropriate for extremely easy, close, fast shooting. Those targets are so close that centering the outline of the gun in the A zone is more than precise enough for an Alpha hit. Because of the relative difficulty of the fifteen yard small steel, you need a sufficient level of visual confirmation and trigger management to make that shot. This makes the drill a particularly effective exercise in throttling back and forth between widely varying target difficulties.

Distance Change Up

RULES: Drill	Created By:

START POSITION:
Hands relaxed at sides

PROCEDURE:	
Draw and shoot the USPSA targets with two rounds each, and the steel with one. Vary the engagement order and shoot every possible sequence.	**SCORING:** Virginia Count
	ROUND COUNT: 5
	TARGETS: 3
	DISTANCE: 5 and 15 yards
	SCORED HITS: 2 per paper
	PENALTIES:
	NOTES:

15 Yards

5 Yards

Shooting on the Move

In my classes, I teach shooting on the move laterally. In your own training, you should adapt this as you progress, but I find that this drill gives me the best introduction to shooting on the move for my students. Use this as a starting point, adding in targets of varying difficulty and risk as well as movement in every direction.

For this drill, you need two shooting positions marked. I prefer barrel stacks or Bianchi barricades, but you can use target sticks as fault lines or cones if that's all you have. I usually use five steel targets, although you can use paper as well. Set up your vision barriers or fault lines roughly five to fifteen yards apart, parallel to the backstop. Set up your targets ten yards down range. The concept here is that you shoot the first target with two rounds from outside one of the barricades, shoot the three middle targets on the move between barricades with two rounds each, and shoot the last target from the outside of the opposite barricade.

The first and fifth target are there to force movement. Without them people tend to walk at an unreasonably slow pace. If there's a reason you're shooting on the move, then you need to move with a sense of urgency while still getting acceptable hits on target. For this drill, you should be shooting your second round on the fourth target immediately before reaching the far barricade. It will surprise you how fast and accurately you can do this with a little practice.

284

Once you're comfortable with this basic drill, start varying the direction of movement and the target array widely in your practice sessions and build your skills.

Shooting on the Move	
RULES: Drill	**Created By:** Matt Little
START POSITION: Standing relaxed on the outside of either barrel stack	

PROCEDURE: Engage the first target with two rounds from outside of either barricade. Shoot the middle three targets with two rounds each on the move between barricades. Shoot the final target from outside the opposite barricade with two rounds.	**SCORING:** Comstock
	ROUND COUNT: 10
	TARGETS: 5
	DISTANCE: 10 yards
	SCORED HITS: 10
	PENALTIES:
	NOTES:

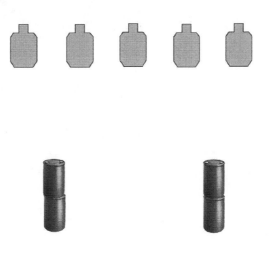

Position Entry and Exit

Rather than shooting *while* moving, position entry and exit work is moving *then* shooting. This can be further divided into easy and hard entries and exits, depending on shot difficulty and risk. These are fundamental skills for gunfighting yet they're often neglected or practiced inefficiently.

For an easy exit, fire at least the final shot fired, and more if possible, while "falling" out of position and then initiate the sprint by cross stepping with the outside leg. For a hard exit, finishing engaging all the targets at that position, then immediately initiate the sprint by turning the hips in the direction of travel and driving off the outside leg while taking a large step with the inside leg. In either case, glance quickly at *exactly* where you want to set up on entry at the the end of your sprint. This programs your subconscious and with enough practice will enable you to set up exactly where you want to be on your entry to the next position.

Once you begin to run, don't be afraid to pump your arms like a sprinter. Just avoid flagging yourself or anyone else in the process. And remember that there is a tactical or competitive reason why you're running, so run as fast as distance and traction allow.

The footwork for both easy and hard entries is the same. The only difference is when you can make your first shot. On an easy entry you can fire at least one round before you are fully settled and still. On a hard entry, you have to be completely stable before taking your first shot. As you approach the position use small choppy steps to bleed off momentum before taking a large step with the foot closest to the targets. At the same time, mount the gun, and aim at your target *through* the barricade. Turn the hips towards the target as you take a large step with the outside foot and then slide the inside foot into your shooting stance.

The drill is straightforward. Engage one target, or array of targets, from outside a barricade, sprint to the other barricade, and engage the other target or array from the outside of that barricade. Vary target difficulty and risk as well as run distance and direction. Do some practice sets with a reload during the movement and some without. The drill can be setup with cones or target sticks to mark the shooting positions, but it's better to use some sort of vision barrier such as barricades or barrels in order to learn to aim through the barrier as you set up into position.

Position Entry and Exit

RULES: Drill	**Created By:** Matt Little

START POSITION:
Standing relaxed on the outside of either barrel stack

PROCEDURE:	
PROCEDURE: Engage the first target with two rounds from outside of either barricade then shoot the second target from outside the opposite barricade with two rounds.	**SCORING:** Unlimited
	ROUND COUNT: 4
	TARGETS: 2
	DISTANCE: 10 yards
	SCORED HITS: 4
	PENALTIES:
	NOTES:

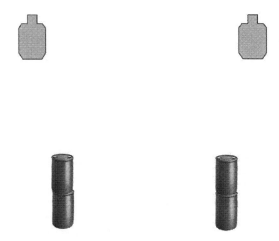

288

Short Movements

For shorter movements, under five steps or so, I don't usually take the support hand off of the gun. If I have to do another task during the movement, such as a reload, I'll typically do a crossover or walking step. If not, then a shuffle step variation, of which there are many, is faster. This is one area where footwork from striking heavy martial arts and combat sports can inform your gunfighting footwork. Experiment with a wide variety of movement patterns for this drill and see which ones enable you to shoot *sooner* in these short movements.

The drill setup is relatively simple. A barricade between one to three yards wide, and two targets, one for each side of the barricade. The procedures are to engage the appropriate target from one side of the barricade, move to the opposite side, and engage the appropriate target from there.

Vary the movement distance and direction from practice session to practice session. Make sure to do an appropriate amount of repetitions that include a reload. That is especially important on this drill since it typically alters the ideal footwork pattern.

Short Movements

RULES: Drill	**Created By:** Matt Little

START POSITION:
Standing relaxed on the outside of either barrel stack

PROCEDURE: Engage the first target with two rounds from either side of the barricade then shoot the second target from the opposite side of the barricade with two rounds.	**SCORING:** Unlimited
	ROUND COUNT: 4
	TARGETS: 2
	DISTANCE: 10 yards
	SCORED HITS: 4
	PENALTIES:
	NOTES:

Barrel Drill

The signature drill my friend Tim Herron, top-10 USPSA Grand Master, uses in all his practical shooting classes is his Barrel Drill. Tim designed this simple but deceptively difficult drill to work on target transitions while shooting on the move. The setup is three targets spaced one target width apart set at four yards from two barrel stacks. The barrel stacks are also a target width apart, with the opening centered on the middle target. The course of fire is moving laterally in either direction, engage the A zone of each target with one round from each of the three positions for a total of nine rounds. In order to pass the drill, all nine rounds must be A zone hits, and all eight transitions must be within a tenth of a second of each other. This is deceptively difficult, but once you can do it you'll be able to start seamlessly blending shooting positions with efficiency and accuracy.

Barrel Drill

RULES: Drill	**Created By:** Tim Herron

START POSITION:
Hands relaxed at sides, standing on either side of barrel stacks, facing targets.

PROCEDURE:	**SCORING:** Virginia Count
Fire one round in the A zone of each target from all three shooting positions. All target transitions must be within a tenth of a second.	**ROUND COUNT:** 9
	TARGETS: 3
	DISTANCE: 4 Yards
	SCORED HITS: 3 Per Target
	PENALTIES: Anything but A Zone = Miss
	NOTES:

Targets are one target width apart.

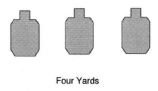

Four Yards

Barrel stacks are one target width apart and centered on middle target.

292

Zig Zag Drill

My friend, former SWAT cop, and multiple-time national and world shooting champion, Robert Vogel, invented this drill to work on movements in tight spaces around obstacles. It's extremely effective at working the ability to maneuver in close quarters efficiently and is very applicable for tactical as well as competitive environments.

The setup is fairly simple. Two targets about six feet apart, either steel or paper, and four stacks of two barrels each, centered on the targets in a perpendicular line starting at about seven to ten yards and spaced about a barrel's width from each other. The course of fire begins with the shooter standing directly behind the barrel furthest from the target and facing down range. The shooter draws while stepping out from behind the barrels to either side and shoots the available target on the move while weaving their way between the barrel stacks in a zig-zag pattern, shooting the appropriate target twice on each exposure. Once they reach the front of the barrel stacks, they continue the process moving back up range, ending their repetition when they reach their starting point.

A common failure point is for the shooter to move at a constant speed. They should slow down enough to stabilize the sights while shooting, then move as rapidly as possible until the target presents itself again. It's very easy to fall into the trap of either shooting while moving too rapidly and missing, or moving at their "shooting on the move" pace when not actually shooting. Both of these errors should be avoided.

Spend some significant time on this drill in your training, and both your ability to shoot on the move and negotiate obstacles while moving with a firearm will improve dramatically. Don't neglect running this with carbine either, focusing on mounting and dismounting the gun.

Zig Zag Drill

RULES: Drill	Created By: Robert Vogel

START POSITION:
Standing directly behind rear barrel stack.

PROCEDURE:	
The shooter draws while stepping out from behind the barrels to either side and shoots on the move while weaving their way between the barrel stacks in a zig-zag pattern, shooting the appropriate target twice on each exposure. Once they reach the front of the barrel stacks, they continue the process moving back up range, ending their repetition when they reach their starting point.	**SCORING:** Unlimited
	ROUND COUNT: 16
	TARGETS: 2
	DISTANCE: 7 to 15 yards
	SCORED HITS:
	PENALTIES:
	NOTES:

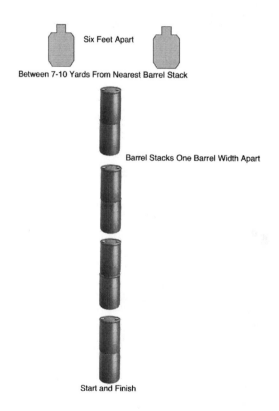

Six Feet Apart

Between 7-10 Yards From Nearest Barrel Stack

Barrel Stacks One Barrel Width Apart

Start and Finish

MXAD

X-Ray Alpha owner and instructor, Matt Pranka, a retired special operations soldier and USPSA Grand Master, designed this drill. The setup is simple, one open USPSA or IPSC target at five yards from the shooter, and a second one at fifteen yards. These are set up so that the lateral transition from target-to-target is minimal and the transition is almost entirely in depth. On the start signal, draw and engage the five-yard target with six rounds, then engage the fifteen-yard target with two rounds.

This is a phenomenal drill for working on visual precision during target transitions. The initial six rounds tends to draw your vision into the movement of your sights instead of your eyes remaining target focused and stationary on your initial point of aim. This makes it difficult to move the eyes rapidly and precisely to your specific aiming point on the second target. Fighting against this tendency will help you learn to stay target focused and drive your vision precisely.

This is also a good drill for preventing excess tension. Tension tends to creep up during the initial six rounds on the close target. If excess tension develops it can interfere with the transition and accuracy on the far target.

A productive variation of this drill is to engage the fifteen-yard target with six rounds first, then transition to the five-yard target and engage it with two rounds. Running it in either direction offers valuable lessons in training. Add this into your training rotation, and your transitions will become more efficient and precise.

MXAD	
RULES: Drill	**Created By:** Matt Pranka
START POSITION: Facing downrange, hands relaxed at sides, pistol loaded and holstered.	
PROCEDURE: On the start signal, draw and engage the 5 yard target with 6 rounds and the 15 yard target with 2 rounds. Targets may be engaged in either order.	**SCORING:** Comstock
	ROUND COUNT: 8
	TARGETS: 2
	DISTANCE: 5 and 15 Yards
	SCORED HITS: 6 on 5 yard target, 2 on 15 yard target
	PENALTIES: Miss = 10 Point Penalty
	NOTES:

15 Yards

5 Yards

Designated Target Drill

USPSA Grand Master, practical shooting instructor, and nationally-ranked competitor Hwansik Kim designed this drill, which has become my favorite drill for working on target transitions in the context of a complex target array. The setup for the drill requires a target array of varying distances and difficulty, ideally ranging from immediately in front of the shooter out to ninety degrees on each side. The drill can be done with as few as three targets or as many as the shooter prefers. Five seems to be the sweet spot.

The procedure for the drill is as follows: for each string of fire, pick one target from the array as the designated target. This target will be engaged first, last, and in between each of the other targets in the array. Labeling the designated target as DT, and the others as T1 to T4, it would look something like this: draw and engage DT, T1, DT, T2, DT, T3, DT, T4, and finish by engaging the designated target a final time.

This drill is an excellent way to practice a wide variety of complex target transitions in the scope of a single repetition. It can be used to isolate and work visual precision in transitions, as well as physical and mental relaxation in the same context. Add this to your training, and watch your transition speed and accuracy improve exponentially.

Designated Target Drill

RULES: Drill	Created By: Hwansik Kim

START POSITION:
Arms Relaxed at Sides

PROCEDURE:	
Set up 3-5 targets of varying difficulty, risk, and distance. Choose one as your "designated target." Engage the designated target, engage T1, transition back to the designated target and engage it, engage T2, engage the designated target, engage T3, and so on until all non-designated targets have been engaged, and finish the string on the designated target.	SCORING: Comstock
	ROUND COUNT: 18
	TARGETS: 5
	DISTANCE: Variable
	SCORED HITS: Variable
	PENALTIES:
	NOTES:

Sample Target Array

COMBINATION DRILLS

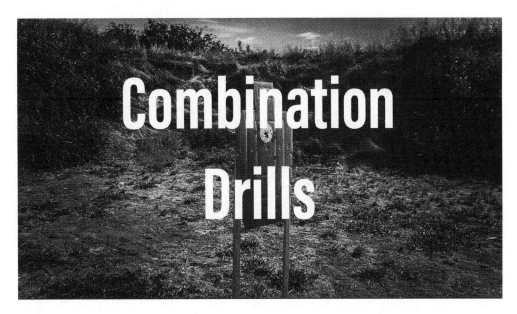

"The most complicated skill is to be simple." - Dejan Stojanovic

Differentiating between isolated skill work and drilling skills in combination is one of the cornerstones of my training philosophy. It's a relatively recent insight for me, and one that I wish I had realized long ago. This is how I build consistency and performance on demand in my training.

The idea behind this is that rather than pushing on one element of my shooting to build new levels of skill, in combination work, I try to execute all the component skills of the drill at the highest level I can without making mistakes. Over time, I'm looking to lower my incident rate or error, or in simpler terms, make fewer and smaller mistakes on average. I'm also looking to lower the performance gap between what I can do on each skill pushing in isolation, and what I can do on demand in combination.

When I work combination drills I typically limit myself three-to-five repetitions on any one engagement sequence. This is to avoid the "practice effect" where the sequence gets grooved in and performance improves. The idea is to build a better toolbox to solve shooting problems with, not just to get good at solving one particular problem.

Pay attention to all the data. Look at the difference between speed and accuracy elements between pushing on them in isolation, and performing them in combination. Evaluate patterns rather than isolated errors, but keep track of how often you make mistakes and how big those mistakes are.

Working combination drills correctly in training can make the difference between a shooter who can only perform well warmed up and when they "hook up" on a drill, and a shooter who can perform at a high level cold and on-demand.

Monticello Drill

The Monticello Drill is a drill I created as a young police officer. My theory behind this was that it was more difficult for an untrained shooter to track across their body when they drew than away from their body. Especially because most of the untrained shooters we encountered in Chicago shot strong hand only rather than with two hands. The other theory behind the drill was that at five to ten yards, in the absence of cover, it was better to press the opponent while advancing rather than retreating while firing. The course of fire was to draw while taking a large aggressive step to the right or left, and then advance to approximately three yards from the target while shooting on the move.

I practiced this drill extensively for several years, and then shortly after returning from a tour in Iraq I was placed in the exact situation I had theorized when creating the drill. I was in a gunfight in an alley of Monticello Avenue on the West Side of Chicago where the offender drew and fired at me from approximately seven yards. Since there was no cover, I responded exactly as in the drill I had created. The tactic worked as I had theorized, and I was able to win that engagement without being injured.

As a combination drill, the Monticello Drill combines lateral movement, drawing, and shooting on the move. It also represents a proven self-defense engagement sequence. I use this drill extensively in my Pistol Skill Applications class and believe strongly in its value.

Monticello Drill

RULES: Drill	Created By: Matt Little

START POSITION:
Hands relaxed at sides or at chest level

PROCEDURE:	SCORING: Unlimited
Draw while taking an aggressive lateral step and then shoot the target on the move, advancing uprange until you are approximately three yards from the target.	ROUND COUNT:
	TARGETS: 1
	DISTANCE: 7 Yards
	SCORED HITS:
	PENALTIES:
	NOTES:

7 Yards

302

Vice Presidente

I use the Vice Presidente Drill in many of my classes as an introduction to combination drill work. It is a simpler variant of Jeff Cooper's famous El Presidente Drill. In the classic El Prez, you start facing up range with your hands above your shoulders, turn and draw, shoot three targets set a yard apart and ten yards away with two rounds each, reload, and shoot each target with two more rounds each. In the Vice Presidente variation, you start facing the targets with your hands relaxed at your sides, omitting the turning draw.

This drill is an excellent introduction to working skills in combination. It includes a draw, a reload, splits, and transitions. No single element is particularly difficult and there are just enough skills involved to work on finding the proper mental gear for on-demand performance. I regularly include some variation of this type of target array and engagement sequence in my own training.

Vice Presidente

RULES: USPSA Rules	Course Designer:

START POSITION:
Hands relaxed at sides.

PROCEDURE:	
Shoot T1-T3 with only 2 rounds each, perform a mandatory reload, and shoot T1-T3 with only 2 rounds each.	**SCORING:** Virginia Count, 12 rounds, 60 points **TARGETS:** 3 **SCORED HITS:** Best 4 Per Target **START-STOP:** **PENALTIES:** Per USPSA Rulebook

Setup Notes:
Targets are set 1 yard apart and 5 feet high at the shoulders.

10 Yards

Calvinball

I was very fortunate when I finally started competing in USPSA. My training partner for the first two years I competed was my good friend, Les Kismartoni. Les is a top-twenty at nationals USPSA Grand Master and an IDPA national champion. His staple drill for working on consistency and what competitors call "match mode" is one he created and named "Calvinball," after the game without rules played by Calvin and his imaginary friend Hobbes in the popular comic strip that bears their names.

Calvinball is, in my opinion, the best combination drill for firearms training. It's also what prompted my thought process about categorizing drills as either combination or isolation, and led to the three drill categories I currently use. More than anything else, running this drill regularly with Les directly led to my current firearms training methodology.

For Calvinball, set up five barricades or barrel stacks, four on the corners of an imaginary square about ten-to-fifteen yards or so on a side, and the fifth in the center. Once you have a sound grasp of the drill, you can vary this setup, but this is the standard one. For targets, use a variety of steel targets, whatever you have on hand. The target array is variable, and should be different every time you do the drill. As a safety note, make sure there is at least seven yards from each steel target to the nearest shooting position to avoid fragmentation.

The drill is run with at least two shooters. More than five and it becomes unwieldy. The first shooter picks one shooting position and designates a string of fire from that position. As long as it is safe, the course of fire is entirely up to the shooter calling it. They can designate one hand shooting, awkward positioning, any challenges they see fit. The shooter who called the position then shoots it first. Their score is their time but, and this is important, any misses (even if made up) and the rep is a fail. In order to set a valid time the run must be clean.

Each shooter, including the one who called the position and set the initial par time, then gets three chances to set the fastest time and win that round. This is also important. The requirement of a clean run without makeup shots builds consistency, and having three chances prevents the shooters from being too conservative. This helps the shooter's develop the proper mental gear for shooting performance on demand.

Using steel for the drill instead of paper targets is also important. It allows all the shooters to instantly identify a miss. This not only keeps the drill running rapidly and efficiently, it helps create the requisite psychological pressure needed to develop on-demand performance.

The shooter with the fastest time on the first round then calls a course of fire with two shooting positions and movement between. They do not need to repeat the first round's position unless they choose to, this can be an entirely new course of fire. The same procedure is followed to determine the winner of the second round, who then calls a new course of fire with three shooting positions. The drill continues in this fashion until the session ends, or until no shooter can finish a round shooting clean.

Just as any missed shots are a failed rep, so is an error in following the course of fire. Shooting the wrong targets or moving to the wrong positions all invalidate a shooter's time. This builds the mental bandwidth required to string multiple tasks together under stress.

Pay attention to all the data when you run this drill. Over time, your performance on each component skill should get closer and closer to your best performance when you isolate that skill. Draws, transitions, splits, reloads, movement. All of those metrics should improve as you narrow the performance gap between what you can do in isolation, and what you can do when you combine skills together.

I can't overstate how valuable this drill is. Put it into your training program and you will improve your on-demand performance level exponentially.

Calvinball

RULES: Drill	Created By: Les Kismartoni

START POSITION:
Variable

PROCEDURE:	SCORING: Virginia Count
This drill is shot with two or more people. First shooter calls a course of fire from a single position and shoots it to establish a par time. All shooters then get three chances to beat the par. Any misses, even made up, and that run doesn't count. The shooter with the fastest time then calls a course of fire with two positions, and the procedure starts again. Continue adding positions each round until no shooter can complete the course of fire clean.	ROUND COUNT:
	TARGETS:
	DISTANCE: Variable
	SCORED HITS: Variable
	PENALTIES: miss = no score on run
	NOTES:

Target array is variable. Use steel targets only.

USPSA Classifiers

The USPSA classifier stages are courses of fire meant to be set up to the exact same specifications and then shot at matches. The stages being the same for everyone allows scores to be compared between everyone who shoots them in order to rank shooters by skill. The classifiers serve as excellent tests of shooting skill, but they can also be used in your practice sessions as combination drills. The stage diagrams are freely available on the USPSA website, as is the performance data to see where your runs compare to other shooters. I'm including a few representative examples of easily set up classifiers on the next few pages, but there are many more. The older ones tend to be primarily stand-and-shoot exercises, but most of the newer ones incorporate movement as well.

CM 99-48 Tight Squeeze

RULES: USPSA Rules	**Course Designer:** Joe Hudson

START POSITION:
Standing in shooting box, both wrists above respective shoulders.

PROCEDURE: Engage T1-T3 with only 2 rounds each, perform a mandatory reload, and engage T1-T3 with only 2 rounds each.	**SCORING:** Virginia Count, 12 rounds, 60 points **TARGETS:** 3 **SCORED HITS:** Best 4 Per Target **START-STOP:** **PENALTIES:** Per Current USPSA Rulebook

Setup Notes:
Set targets 5 feet high at shoulders. Hard cover is set at outside edges of A zone. No-shoots are set at edge of A zone, and one foot from centerline of stage.

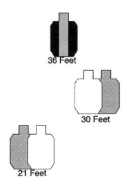

36 Feet

30 Feet

21 Feet

CM 99-46 Close Quarter Standards

RULES: USPSA Rules   **Course Designer:** John Wells

START POSITION:
Standing in appropriate shooting box, both hands above respective shoulders. PCC - stock on belt, muzzle down range.

PROCEDURE:
String 1: From box A, shoot T1-T3 with only 2 rounds each, perform a mandatory reload, and shoot T1-T3 with only 2 rounds each.
String 2: From box B, shoot T1-T3 with only 2 rounds each *strong hand only.*
String 3: From Box C, shoot T1-T3 with only 2 rounds each *weak hand only.*

SCORING: Virginia Count, 24 rounds, 120 points
TARGETS: 3
SCORED HITS: Best 8 Per Target
START-STOP:
PENALTIES: Per Current USPSA Rulebook

Setup Notes:
Shooting boxes are 3 feet by 3 feet. Targets set 5 feet high at shoulders.

5 Feet   5 Feet

15 Feet

C

21 Feet

B

30 Feet

A

CM 18-06 For That Day

RULES: USPSA Rules | **Course Designer:** USPSA Nationals Design Team

START POSITION:
Handgun: Standing inside shooting area, wrists above respective shoulders. PCC: Standing inside shooting area, weak hand on forearm, strong hand below belt, muzzle pointed downrange.

PROCEDURE:
String 1: Engage T1 with only 6 rounds, reload, and engage T3 with only 6 rounds *strong hand only*.
String 2: Engage T2 with only 3 rounds, reload, and engage T2 with only 3 rounds *weak hand only*.

SCORING: Virginia Count, 18 rounds, 90 points
TARGETS: 3
SCORED HITS: Best 6 Per Paper
START-STOP:
PENALTIES: Per USPSA Rulebook

Setup Notes:
Shooting box is 3 feet by 3 feet. Targets are 3 feet edge to edge and 5 feet to top. Top of no-shoot is set at bottom of letter A in A-zone. Hardcover is set to outside edge of A zone.

15 Yards

Stages

An action shooting competition like a USPSA or IDPA match is composed of a series of shooting problems to solve known as stages. Each stage is a course of fire that can include movement, barricades, obstacles, props, moving targets, and other elements. Some are fairly straightforward, and others can be quite complex.

Simpler stages can be set up in practice and used as combination drills. One of my favorite ways to train skills in combination in my own training is to set up a simple stage that can be run several ways and run it each way for three-to-five repetitions each. When you design your training stages, have an intent—a desired training effect—that you're creating with the design.

I'm including several representative stage designs from a couple of friends of mine who are a top-notch match directors and USPSA Grand Masters, Max Klatt and Alex Acosta, on the next few pages as examples. Your training stages don't need this level of complexity, but the design principles remain the same. Once you run a few, setting up your own becomes very intuitive and straightforward. If you don't do any of this type of training, I highly recommend you experiment with it in your own training. It will make you a better and more consistent shooter in short order.

RULES: Practical Shooting Handbook, Latest Edition **COURSE DESIGNER:** Max Klatt

START POSITION: Both hands touching any barrel. Gun is loaded and holstered.	
STAGE PROCEDURE	**SCORING**
Engage targets from within fault lines	**SCORING:** Comstock, 24 rounds, 120 points **TARGETS:** 9 Metric 6 MPP **SCORED HITS:** 2 Best per Metric, Steel down = 1A **START-STOP:** Audible - Last shot **PENALTIES:** Per current rulebook

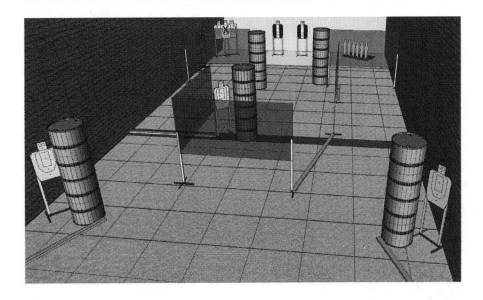

RULES: Practical Shooting Handbook, Latest Edition**COURSE DESIGNER:** Max Klatt

START POSITION: Anywhere with both feet on red line, Wrist Relaxed at sides, gun is loaded and holstered	
STAGE PROCEDURE Engage targets from within fault lines	**SCORING** SCORING: Comstock, 25 rounds, 125 points TARGETS: 11 Metric & 3 poppers SCORED HITS: 2 Best per Metric, Steel down = 1A START-STOP: Audible - Last shot PENALTIES: Per current rulebook

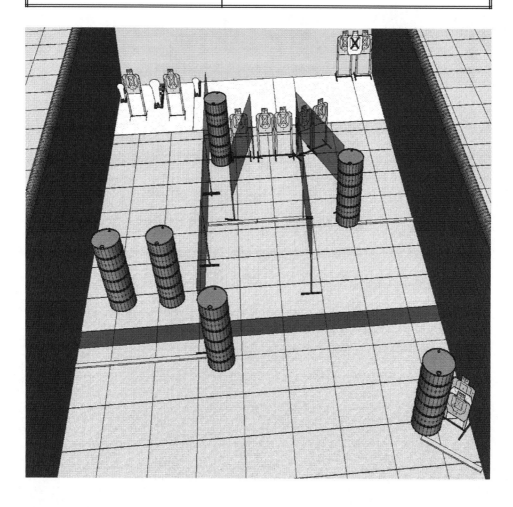

A Time to Pew

RULES: USPSA Rules   **Course Designer:** Acosta

START POSITION:
Standing anywhere within the shooting area.
Handgun: On the barrel, muzzle facing downrange, magazine inserted, chamber empty.
PCC: On the barrel, muzzle facing downrange, magazine inserted, chamber empty, safety on

PROCEDURE:	SCORING: Comstock, 16 rounds, 80 points
On the audible start signal engage targets from within the shooting area as they become visible. Popper P1 activates swinger S1.	TARGETS: 7
	SCORED HITS: 16 rounds / 80 Points
	START-STOP: Audible / Last Shot
	PENALTIES:

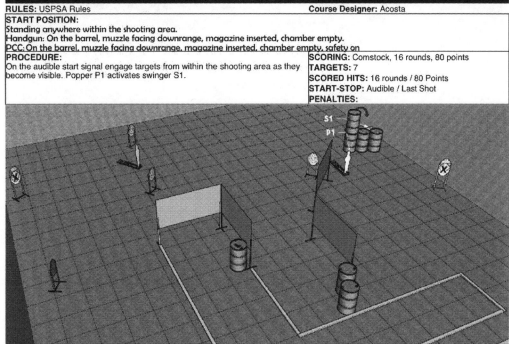

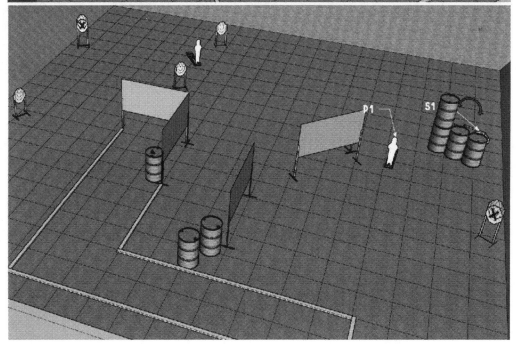

315

DRY FIRE PRACTICE

"Practice like you've never won." - Michael Jordan

Dry fire is of necessity where the bulk of your training repetitions should occur. It is simply impossible to match the volume or frequency possible through dry practice with your live fire practice. And even if you could do that amount of live fire, I honestly believe it would still be more productive to do the bulk of your training dry rather than live. Some skills, such as draws and reloads, I prefer to isolate exclusively in dry fire, and only occasionally verify in live fire.

You can translate any live fire drill into a dry fire drill. With sufficient live fire experience, even drills focusing on recoil management like Doubles or Bill Drills can be productively practiced in dry fire. You can isolate trigger control, grip, weapons manipulations, transitions, movement, and more. You can in many cases focus your isolation even tighter in dry fire than you can in live fire. You can eliminate the trigger press when doing draws, reloads, and transitions, and work just to the sight picture.

Isolation work tends to be most people's primary focus in dry fire, but dry practice lends itself just as well to combination drills, up to and including mini stages. You're limited only by your space and your creativity.

The same aspect of dry fire that is the most crucial, being truly and ruthlessly honest with yourself about what you see in your sights on each repetition, is also this type of training's greatest strength. Because there is no recoil, you can much more easily see any extraneous movement in the sights, and learn to correct your errors more quickly than in live fire training.

With dry fire, daily practice is easily achievable. Frequent practice sessions have been proven to be one of the keys to mastery in any field of endeavor, and for shooting this is only possible with a properly constructed and implemented dry practice regimen. Put an unloaded gun in your hand every day, and see how rapidly your skill improves.

SHOOTING SKILL TESTS

"Testing leads to failure, and failure leads to understanding." - Burt Rutan

You should regularly include validation drills in your live fire training sessions to test your progress, and seek out tests run by others, such as competitions or organized challenges. Testing yourself is a vital part of training. It creates the feedback loop for informing your future training. Testing is how you diagnose the areas of your performance that need improvement or modification. You then take that data and use it to focus on exactly the areas you most need to improve. Without valid and accurate testing, your skill will stagnate in practice and improvements will grind to a halt.

What makes a test valid? How do we construct them so that they give us an accurate and detailed conception of where our skill level actually is under stress and on demand? There are a few hard and fast rules we need to follow.

The test needs to be relevant and understandable. A slow fire B-8 at 25 yards is an appropriate test for pure marksmanship fundamentals, but it does not measure shooting at speed. The USPSA classifier "Can You Count" with targets at six and ten feet measures weapons handling and trigger speed but doesn't challenge accuracy. Both are good tests for specific skills, but you have to understand what is being tested.

The test needs to induce stress. Skill degrades under pressure, so to get an accurate measure of your true skill level, you have to be tested under that pressure. How do we create that stress? We can do this in several ways, ideally a combination of them all. The test should be final. In other words, no re-shoots or do-overs. Performance on-demand, not the best of several runs. The test should have consequence. There has to be a penalty or reward. This can be created as simply as performance rankings. The pressure to win is real and tangible. The test should be public. Knowing that others can see your results is an immense stressor.

The test needs to create measurable and applicable data. The more relevant data points you can collect about your performance, the more detail you can then apply to your future training. On a FAST Drill, as an example, I want to collect not just my overall time, but my draw, splits, and reload times. I can then take this data, and isolate my deficiencies in practice in order to improve efficiently.

Seek out tests. Go after the "tactical" performance awards. Get classified in USPSA, IDPA, and Steel Challenge. Learn how good you actually are, on-demand and under pressure. Then use that knowledge to get better.

3:45 SKILL CARD

This is my signature skill test that I use in my classes. The 3:45 Drill is intended to be a test of high level performance with a pistol. It's shot on a target consisting of three 3" circles. The drill consists of four strings of fire shot at five yards. All four strings are shot from the holster with a 3.45 second par time. If drawing from concealment or a level three security holster an additional .25 of a second is allowed per draw. If reloading from concealment or retention top magazine pouches, an additional .25 of a second is allowed for the reload.

In order to pass the drill, all four strings must be shot back-to-back in this order:

1. Recoil Control: Draw and fire 5 rounds onto the center circle

2. Transition Drill: Draw and fire 1-1-1-1-1-1 alternating on the outside circles. (6 shots total, 3 per circle)

3. Reload Drill: Draw and fire 1, reload and fire 1 onto the outside circles. (2 total, 1 per circle)

4. SHO/WHO Drill: Draw and fire 1 strong hand only onto either of the outside circles, switch hands then fire 1 support/weak hand only onto the remaining outside circle.

A successful run on the drill results in 5 hits per circle. Line breaks are acceptable as long as the grease ring touches the line. The drill must be shot in my presence to receive the 3:45 Skill Card Patch. The target is available to download for free on my website so anyone can print it out and practice the drill.

GreyBeard Actual Three Forty-Five Skill Card Drill

Shot at 5 yards – all strings from holster with 3.45 second par
Must be done back to back in this order:
1. 5 rounds on center circle
2. Transition drill: 1-1-1-1-1-1 on outside circles (6 shots total, 3 per circle)
3. 1-reload-1 on outside circles
4. 1 strong hand only then 1 support/weak hand only on outside circles
Must be shot in my presence to win patch
.25 second allowance for draws and reloads from concealment
.25 second allowance for draws from level III security holster and reloads from retention pouches
1 "Mulligan" allowed per string for safety's sake if requested before a shot is fired
@greybeard_actual   www.greybeardactual.com

MODERN SAMURAI PROJECT BLACK BELT STANDARDS

Scott Jedlinski has been a friend since before I retired and started my training business. His Black Belt Patch standards are an extremely difficult test of on-demand performance with a pistol, in my opinion the hardest of the "tactical" shooting challenges. The standards consist of four strings of fire, all shot on a single USPSA target with a 3x5 index card in the head box. They must be shot in the specified order and consecutively. The listed par times are for either concealment or from an ALS retention holster. ALS + SLS gives a .1 second bonus to the times and an open top exposed holster adds a .1 second penalty to the times.

1. 3&2 Drill. 3 yards. 3 shots to the body A zone then transition to 2 rounds on the 3x5 card in the head box. Par time is 2.0 seconds.

2. 1 Shot Drill @ 7 yards. 1 shot to the body A zone. Par time is 1.0 second.

3. Bill Drill. 7 yards. 6 shots to the body A zone. Par time is 2.0 seconds.

4. 1 Shot Drill @ 25 yards. 1 shot to the body A zone. Par time is 1.5 seconds

For those who do not pass the standards at the Black Belt level, he gives standards for blue, purple, and brown belt levels as well, although there is no patch for those.

In order to earn the Modern Samurai Black Belt Patch, you must shoot the standards successfully in one of Scott's classes. At the time of this writing, only seventeen shooters have done so and earned a patch. I highly recommend his classes for the quality instruction he provides, so sign up for one, and see where you rank on his standards.

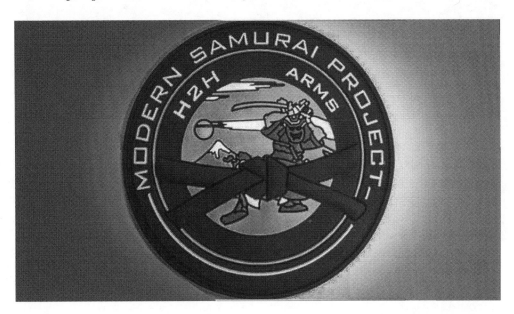

GABE WHITE'S TECHNICAL SKILLS TESTS

Gabe White is another top defensive shooting instructor who I consider a close personal friend. He was a true pioneer of AIWB carry for self-defense, and competition as training for tactical shooters. His Turbo Pin is an extremely sought after award in the tactical shooting community, and is a well thought out test of high-level defensive shooting skill.

His Technical Skills Tests, which is his official name for the courses of fire his performance awards are earned from, consist of four drills, which are also meant to mimic realistic engagement sequences in a self-defense incident. Over the course of his two-day class, each drill is shot for score twice. The highest scoring four out of the eight runs are counted for the performance award.

1. The Bill Drill (six shots to the body)

2. Failure to Stop (two shots to the body and one shot to the head)

3. Immediate Incapacitation (two shots to the head)

4. The Split Bill Drill (four shots to the body and two shots to the head)

All are shot on a single USPSA Metric or IDPA target or similar, with either a 4" circle or 3×5" card added to the head, at a distance of 7 yards. The shooter can start with hands at sides, hands at high torso, or a hands-up surrender position. At the start signal, the shooter draws and engages the target exactly as required by the drill. No extra shots are allowed. Your score is your time, with penalties added for shots outside the A/-0 zone. B/C/-1 zone hits add .25 seconds per shot. D-zone hits add 1 second per shot. Misses add 2 seconds per shot. Head shots that land in the body count as misses. Body shots that land in the head count as lucky shots and are scored.

He has three levels of performance awards for the drills, his Dark, Light, and Turbo pins. The Dark pin is considered a tactical level of proficiency in core technical skills of drawing and shooting; the Light pin represents excellence in core technical skills of drawing and shooting; and the highest award, the Turbo pin, is given for a highly developed level of excellence in core technical skills of drawing and shooting.

Dark Pin Standards

1. Bill Drill, 3.50 (Theoretical Breakdown: 1.50 + .40 + .40 + .40 + .40 + .40)

2. Failure to Stop, 2.90 (Theoretical Breakdown: 1.50 + .40 + 1.00)

3. Immediate Incapacitation, 3.00 (Theoretical Breakdown: 2.00 + 1.00)

4. Split Bill Drill, 4.70 (Theoretical Breakdown: 1.50 + .40 + .40 + .40 + 1.00 + 1.00)

Light Pin Standards

1. Bill Drill, 2.50 (Theoretical Breakdown: 1.25 + .25 + .25 + .25 + .25 + .25)

2. Failure to Stop, 2.25 (Theoretical Breakdown: 1.25 + .25 + .75)

3. Immediate Incapacitation, 2.50 (Theoretical Breakdown: 1.75 + .75)

4. Split Bill Drill, 3.50 (Theoretical Breakdown: 1.25 + .25 + .25 + .25 + .75 + .75)

Turbo Pin Standards

1. Bill Drill, 2.00 (Theoretical Breakdown: 1.00 + .20 + .20 + .20 + .20 + .20)

2. Failure to Stop, 1.70 (Theoretical Breakdown: 1.00 + .20 + .50)

3. Immediate Incapacitation, 2.00 (Theoretical Breakdown: 1.50 + .50)

4. Split Bill Drill, 2.60 (Theoretical Breakdown: 1.00 + .20 + .20 + .20 + .50 + .50)

This was the first of the "tactical" shooting performance awards that I pursued and achieved, and that achievement is still something I am proud of. Gabe is a phenomenal teacher and shooter, and I can't recommend his classes highly enough. Seek out his training, shoot his skill tests, and see which level of performance award you can achieve.

THE FAST COIN

The late Todd Luis Green, founder of the website pistol-training.com, developed a diagnostic drill he used in his training classes to quickly assess a shooter's skill level. He named the drill the FAST, which stood for Fundamentals, Accuracy, and Speed Test. For those shooters able to shoot it clean twice in five seconds or less, he awarded a numbered challenge coin. This was the first of the "tactical" shooting performance awards, and paved the way for the variety we have now, including mine.

The drill is simple, and consists of one string of fire at seven yards. From concealment or duty gear with retention, the shooter draws and shoots two rounds to a three by five index card in the head box, performs a slide-lock reload, then shoots four rounds to an eight inch circle in the torso.

After Todd Green's death, Ernest Langdon was given responsibility for awarding the FAST coins, and the only way to earn one now is by shooting the drill successfully on two out of three tries in one of his classes. Ernest is an excellent trainer, as well as having both high level military and competitive experience with firearms. I highly recommend seeking out one of his classes and seeing where you rank on the FAST test. To practice the drill, download the target from pistol-training.com.

The F.A.S.T. (Fundamentals, Accuracy, & Speed Test):
Range: 7 yards.
Start position: weapon concealed or in retention duty holster with all retention devices active; shooter facing downrange in relaxed stance with arms down at sides.

Drill begins from the holster, pistol loaded with exactly two rounds.

- draw
- fire two (and only two) rounds at the 3×5 box
- perform a slidelock reload
- fire four (and only four) rounds at the 8" circle

Scoring:
Open-top retention (ALS, SERPA) without concealment add 0.50 seconds to the final score.
Flap/retention mag pouch subtract 0.50 seconds.
Misses to 3x5 box add 2.00 seconds per miss.
Misses to 8" circle add 1.00 seconds per miss.

Ranking:
10+ seconds: **Novice**
less than 10 seconds: **Intermediate**
less than 7 seconds: **Advanced**
less than 5 seconds: **Expert**

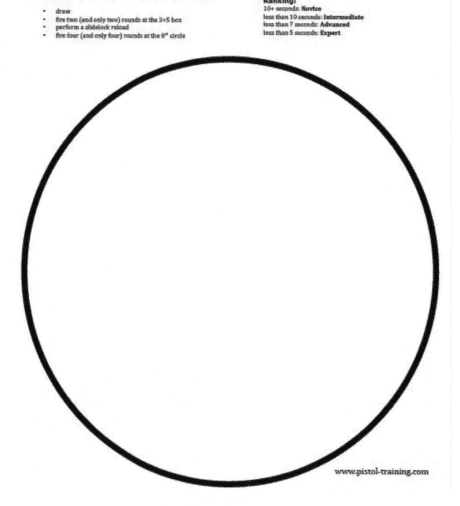

www.pistol-training.com

328

TIER 1 CONCEALED'S THREE SEVENS COIN

Jared Clawson, owner of the holster company Tier 1 Concealment, is an amazing shooter in his own right, and is famous for extremely difficult trick shots. He devised a shooting drill he calls the Three Sevens, intended to be an extremely high level test of concealed carry shooting skill. Anyone who can legitimately pass the drill on video receives a numbered challenge coin. This is a drill that requires a high level of accuracy at speed, and is extremely unforgiving. I'm proud to say I earned coin #33.

The target for the drill, available free of charge to download and print on the Tier 1 Concealment website, consists of four circles. Two of these are one inch in diameter, one is two inches, and one is three inches. The drill consists of seven shots at seven yards in seven seconds. The course of fire is as follows. From concealment, draw and fire one round into the upper left 1" circle. Transition to the upper right 2" circle and shoot it with two rounds. Then perform a slide lock reload, also from concealment, and shoot the bottom left 3" circle with three rounds, transition to the bottom right 1" circle and shoot it with one round.

Go to their website, print out the target, and test yourself on this extremely challenging drill.

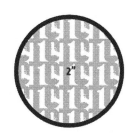

THREE SEVENS

This drill is to be completed at a distance of 7 yards, drawing from concealment, totaling 7 shots, within 7 seconds.

The shooter will draw and place one shot in the upper left 1" circle, transition to the upper right 2" circle, and place two shots inside it. The shooter will then conduct a slide lock reload and put three shots in the bottom left 3" circle, then transition to the bottom right 1" circle and place one shot inside.

This drill works on accuracy, throttle control, weapon manipulation and recoil management.

Any shots breaking the line are considered in.

This is a high-level CCW performance drill

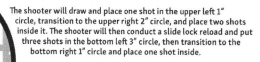

330

BILL WILSON'S 5X5

Bill Wilson, creator of the iconic Bill Drill and founder of IDPA competition, designed the 5x5 Skill Test to be a quick comprehensive evaluation of fundamental shooting skills. The 5x5 is also used by IDPA as a classifier, and is the course of fire I shot to make Master in IDPA with both carbine and pistol.

The 5x5 Skill Test is shot on a single IDPA target at ten yards. Shots to the highest scoring areas, the Down Zero zones in the body and head of the target add no time to your score. Shots to the Down One zones add one second each, Shots to the Down Three zones add three seconds each, and misses add five seconds to your score.

There are four strings of fire. All are shot from the holster with a pistol, and from the low ready with a carbine. Your cumulative time plus any penalties is your score.

1. 5 rounds to the body freestyle

2. 5 rounds to the body strong hand only

3. 5 rounds to the body, slide lock reload, 5 rounds to the body

4. 4 rounds to the body, 1 round to the head

IDPA classifies you as a competitor based on the following times:

Times for:	CDP	ESP	CO	SSP	CCP	REV	BUG	PCC
Master (MA)	19.18 or less	18.75 or less	18.47 or less	19.07 or less	19.60 or less	20.15 or less	23.25 or less	10.63 or less
Expert (EX)	19.19 thru 24.09	18.76 thru 23.28	18.48 thru 22.93	19.08 thru 23.49	19.61 thru 24.98	20.16 thru 26.78	23.26 thru 28.12	10.64 thru 12.98
Sharpshooter (SS)	24.10 thru 29.92	23.29 thru 28.80	22.94 thru 28.39	23.50 thru 29.36	24.99 thru 31.07	26.79 thru 33.34	28.13 thru 35.43	12.99 thru 15.82
Marksman (MM)	29.93 thru 37.63	28.81 thru 36.27	28.40 thru 36.18	29.37 thru 36.97	31.08 thru 39.26	33.35 thru 41.91	35.44 thru 44.65	15.83 thru 18.33
Novice (NV)	37.64 or greater	36.28 or greater	36.19 or greater	36.98 or greater	39.27 or greater	41.92 or greater	44.66 or greater	18.34 or greater

Effective as of Jan 1st, 2020

Whether or not you compete regularly in IDPA, this is an excellent test of your fundamental shooting skill. I definitely suggest you find an IDPA classifier match and get classified under match pressure. It will give you a good idea of where you stand as a shooter. I made Master in IDPA with both pistol and carbine and am proud of the accomplishment.

5x5

RULES: IDPA Rules	**Created By:** Bill Wilson

START POSITION:
4 Strings, each string starts with firearm loaded, holstered and shooter facing downrange, hands at side. PCC starts at low ready, at base of the target stand.

SCENARIO:	**SCORING:** Limited
PROCEDURE:	**ROUND COUNT:** 25
String 1: Draw and fire 5 shots freestyle.	**TARGETS:** 01
String 2: Draw and fire 5 shots using strong hand only.	**DISTANCE:** 10 Yards
String 3: Start with only 5 rounds in your firearm. Draw and fire 5 shots freestyle, conduct an emergency reload and fire 5 additional shots freestyle.	**SCORED HITS:**
	PENALTIES: IDPA Rules
String 4: Draw and fire 4 shots to the body and one shot to the head freestyle.	**CONCEALMENT:** No
	NOTES: Bay 6

Targets are 10 yds from fault line.
Target height is 5 feet.

P1

333

THE USPSA CLASSIFIERS

The USPSA classifier system is different than the IDPA process. Where the IDPA classifier is a single course of fire, USPSA has eighty-six active classifiers. Every local club typically has one classifier stage per match. The maximum score on a classifier stage is called the high hit factor, and is based off of the best score on record on that particular course of fire. A competitor's classification percentage is based on the best six of their most recent eight classifiers, and that percentage places them in their class. A percentage below 40% puts a shooter in D class, 40-60% is C class, 60-75% B class, 75-85% A class, Master is 85-95%, and Grand Master is 95% and above.

Classification Bracket Percentages

Classification	Percentage of Maximum Hit Factor
Grand Master	95 to 100%
Master	85 to 94.9%
A	75 to 84.9%
B	60 to 74.9%
C	40 to 59.9%
D	2 to 40%

As we talked about in the section on combination drills, the USPSA classifiers present a wide variety of shooting challenges. The classifier system isn't perfect, but anyone who legitimately achieves Master or Grand Master in USPSA can shoot at a level that is extremely high indeed. A Grand Master shooter has performed within 5% of literally the best in the world six times out of eight.

Regardless of your thoughts on competitive shooting versus tactical shooting, performance is performance. Shooting enough local matches to get classified will give you a solid set of data points showing you where your skill stands against the fastest and most accurate shooters in the competition world, and that is a very valuable training tool.

CM 13-08 — More Disaster Factor

RULES: USPSA Handgun Competition Rules, Current Edition **COURSE DESIGNER:** Robert Porter

START POSITION: Standing inside the fault lines, heels against the X's on the back of the shooting box. Gun is loaded and holstered.

STAGE PROCEDURE

Upon start signal and from within the shooting box, engage either the upper three targets or the lower three targets with only two rounds each, perform a mandatory reload, and engage the remaining three targets with only two rounds each.

SCORING

SCORING: Virginia Count, 12 rounds, 60 points
TARGETS: 6 Metric
SCORED HITS: Best 2/paper
START - STOP: Audible - Last Shot
PENALTIES: Per current edition of USPSA Handgun Competition Rules

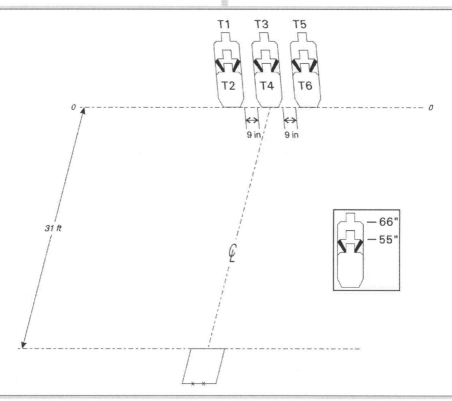

SETUP NOTES: Targets are set at 31 feet from the front of the shooting box, and are spaced 9 inches apart, edge to edge. The shoulders of T1, T3, and T5 are at 66 inches. The shoulders of the no-shoots are at 55 inches. Set the top edges of T2, T4, and T6 at 7.5 inches below the top edge of the no-shoot.) All targets must be aligned vertically, edge to edge. The shooting box is a standard 3 foot by 3 foot box. The X marks are to be 12 inches in from each side of the box.

New 10/24/2013

187

336

CM 09-14   **Eye Of The Tiger**

RULES: USPSA Handgun Competition Rules, current edition   **COURSE DESIGNER:** Russell Cluver

START POSITION: Standing in shooting area facing directly uprange, toes against the back of the box, hands relaxed at sides. Handgun is loaded and holstered as per ready condition in rule 8.1.1 and 8.1.2.

STAGE PROCEDURE

On signal, turn, then draw and engage targets with only two rounds each from the shooting area.

SCORING

SCORING: Virginia Count, 6 rounds, 30 points
TARGETS: 3 Metric
SCORED HITS: Best 2/paper
START - STOP: Audible - Last shot
PENALTIES: Per current edition of USPSA Handgun Competition Rules

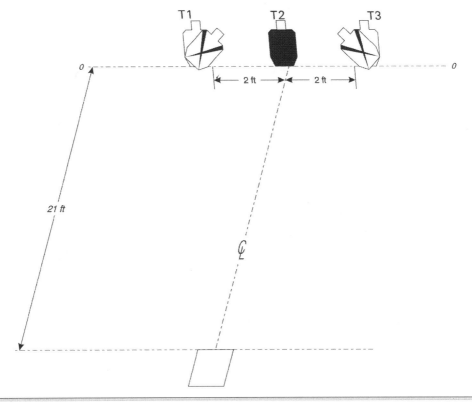

SETUP NOTES: Set paper targets to 5 feet high at shoulders. Shooting box is 3 feet by 3 feet. No-shoots are angled at 45 degrees to shoot targets. Overlay the top shoulder point of the no-shoots with the top shoul-der point of each target. The 45-degree shoulder angle should be parallel with the top horizontal edge of each target.

RULES: USPSA Handgun Competition Rules, current edition   **COURSE DESIGNER:** US Design Team

START POSITION: Standing in either Box A or Box B, both arms hanging relaxed at sides. Handgun is loaded and holstered as per ready condition in rule 8.1.1 and 8.1.2.

STAGE PROCEDURE

From Box A engage only T1-T3 with two rounds each. From Box B engage only T4-T6 with two rounds each. Start in either Box A or Box B. Upon start signal, from the starting box engage the appropriate targets. Move to the remaining box and engage the appropriate targets.

SCORING

SCORING: Comstock, 12 rounds, 60 points
TARGETS: 6 Metric
SCORED HITS: Best 2/paper
START - STOP: Audible - Last shot
PENALTIES: Per current edition USPSA Handgun Competition Rules

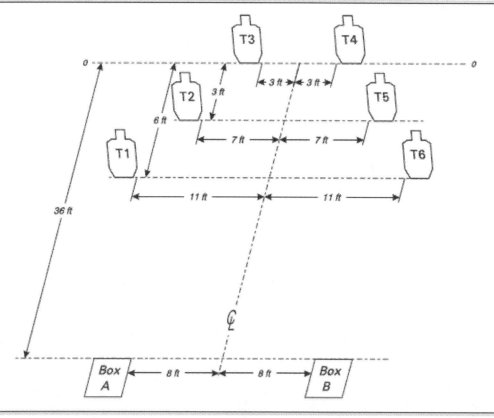

SETUP NOTES: Set paper targets to 5 feet high at shoulders. Shooting boxes are 3 feet by 3 feet.

MATCHES

I am a huge proponent of action shooting competition as training for the "tactical" shooter. The typical USPSA match can have anywhere from four stages for a weeknight local match up to twenty or more stages at a national championship, with each stage having a round count as high as thirty-two scored shots fired. The stages include such challenges as barricades, obstacles, movement, unstable surfaces and awkward shooting positions, moving targets, and more.

Matches make for an excellent test of shooting skills under stress. Especially major matches, where you have to perform consistently for twelve or more stages. The other valuable characteristic of major matches is the sheer variety and difficulty of shooting challenges they present. At major matches I've faced "hostage taker" headshots with a pistol at twenty-five yards from awkward shooting positions and moving targets with a pistol caliber carbine at sixty yards, all under time pressure and on the clock. I've included a few representative stages from the 2021 USPSA National Championship in this section.

A well designed USPSA match will quickly expose any weaknesses you have in your shooting skill. Don't shy away from that. Embrace it. Use it to inform your future training, and turn your weaknesses into strengths.

dieci dieci

STARTING POSITION:
Feet on marks, wrists below belt.

GUN READY CONDITION:
Loaded and holstered.

STAGE PROCEDURE:
Engage targets from within the shooting area. Popper 2 actives T5 which remains visible at rest.

SCORING: Comstock course of fire

TARGETS: 9 USPSA targets, 2 poppers | **ROUNDS:** 20

START/STOP: The start is audible

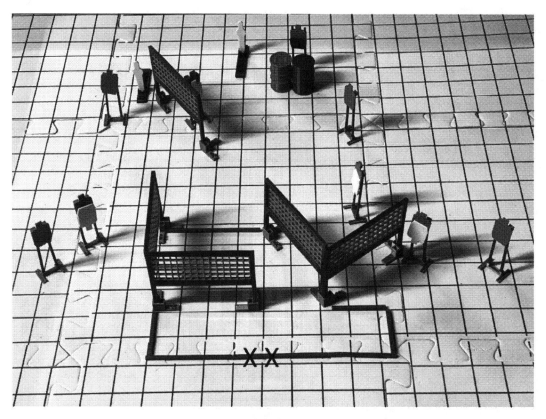

eh-leh

STARTING POSITION:
Hands on marks.

GUN READY CONDITION:
Loaded and holstered.

STAGE PROCEDURE:
Engage targets from within the shooting area.

SCORING: Comstock course of fire

TARGETS: 7 USPSA targets, 4 poppers | **ROUNDS:** 18

START/STOP: The start is audible

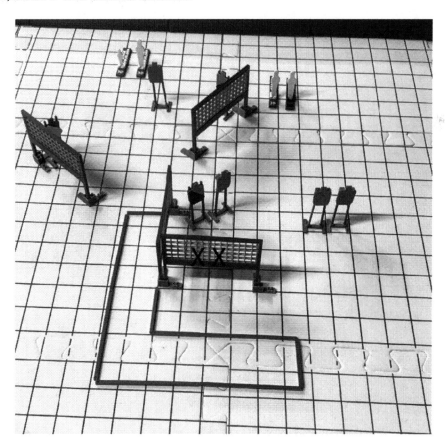

[STAGE 18] LOCAP NATIONALS / BAY C4

Quattro Angoli

STARTING POSITION:
Feet on marks, wrists above shoulders.

GUN READY CONDITION:
Loaded and holstered.

STAGE PROCEDURE:
Engage targets from within the shooting area.

SCORING: Comstock course of fire

TARGETS: 13 IPSC targets, 4 poppers | **ROUNDS:** 30

START/STOP: The start is audible

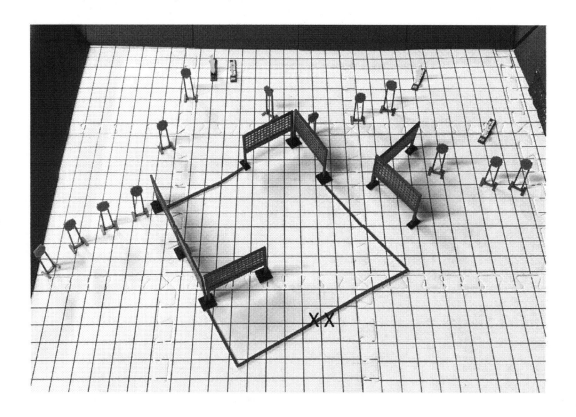

PROGRAMMING FIREARMS TRAINING

"The key is not the will to win. Everybody has that. It is the will to prepare to win that is important." - Bobby Knight

Most tactical and defensive shooters don't truly program their firearms training like athletes. The common tendency is to simply pick drills randomly to shoot rather than programming their shooting training in a goal-based progression. If you look at high-performing athletes, or even musicians, practice for skill development is done in a deliberate and mindful progression towards a concrete set of objective goals.

The first thing you have to do to program your training is set goals. To do this properly you first have to perform a needs analysis. How good do you need to be? That is a very personal decision, and it needs to be grounded in reality. What skills do I need as a patrol officer? As a SWAT officer? As a CCL holder interested in defending yourself and your family? You need to figure this out in a fair amount of detail and specificity. What does your draw need to be to an open target at seven yards? At fifteen yards? At twenty-five? What should your reload be shot-to-shot at those distances? How accurate do you need to be, and how fast should you be able to make your most accurate shots? You should have standards for all of this, as well as movement and target transitions.

If you're like me, and you're chasing the dragon, selecting your metrics is simple. I just base mine off of what the best in the world can do, and work to narrow the gap between my performance and theirs. But most people don't need that level of skill and that's ok. Most competent special operations personnel would be B-class at most if they shot USPSA, and I've never seen anyone who can shoot at a USPSA Master or Grand Master level that doesn't compete.

I'll add a caveat or two to your needs analysis and selecting your performance metrics. You need to build in a buffer of performance above your real-world needs into your metrics for practice. You'll always be able to execute at a higher level when you're comfortable and warmed up than you will when you are executing a cold on-demand performance. The other qualifier is this—in my opinion, if your job description includes hostage rescue, you don't have the luxury of picking lower goals. If you are on a team that conducts hostage rescues, there is no "good enough." You need to always strive to improve.

There's a flip side to your needs analysis that has to be accounted for when you pick the metrics to use as your goals. That's your level of commitment. How much of your resources, money and time, are you willing to commit to your skill development? If your level of commitment isn't commensurate to your goals, then they won't be attainable. You can't create world class levels of skill on weekend hobbyist levels of practice.

Once you have an idea of your performance goals, and your level of commitment, you can program your training appropriately. Like our fitness training, our shooting training should be planned out in training cycles, and further divided into macrocycles (long), mesocycles (medium), and microcycles (short). Microcycles are typically a week in duration, mesocycles anywhere from one to three months, and macrocycles are usually three, six, or twelve months.

The microcycle is basically your weekly training schedule. The amount of time you spend training daily and weekly adds up and determines where your skill level will be in a year from now. Your level of participation will determine this, of course. Just understand that the *minimum* weekly regimen for developing a high level of skill is about five dry fire sessions of at least 15 minutes each, and at least one live fire session a week. That amount of training can eventually get you to a very high level of skill compared to the average shooter. At one time before the overall skill level of the sport improved, that amount could maybe get you to

Master or Grand Master in USPSA if you had the requisite talent. These days it won't get you there, but it will get you to a level of skill far beyond most people who carry a gun.

The mesocycle is typically 4 to 12 microcycles. You choose the length based on your planned macrocycle length, and how many intermediate goals you are working on in that macrocycle. The macrocycle length is based on your next major testing event. For a top level competition shooter, the macrocycle would be based on the next national or world championship. It could be based around an upcoming training course where you're attempting to earn one of the tactical shooting skill awards such as the FAST coin or Turbo Pin, or a difficult military or LE training school. It can also be a completely arbitrary timeline you set for the achievement of personal skill goals.

One caution for law enforcement personnel doing their programming. LE officers have what I call "the burden of constant preparedness." Everyone else can program in an off-season then prepare for their peak performance in a gradual manner. Even soldiers get periods of less intense training as part of their recovery from one deployment and preparation for another. But law enforcement doesn't get that. There is no off-season, so you will need to adopt more of a conjugate periodization style where you work on various aspects of your shooting training concurrently.

Once you've planned out your training cycle length you can choose which skills or attributes to focus on in each mesocycle. This will allow you to select drills to work on the aspect of your shooting you're focusing in a microcycle. The way you should do this is not by focusing on one thing to the detriment of your other fundamentals. Rather, you should emphasize one particular aspect of your shooting while still working on everything else.

There are two natural progressions that should be adhered to in every training cycle and throughout your training lifetime for that matter. One is moving from block practice, where you divide up your sessions into discrete blocks focusing on one skill or attribute, towards interleaving practice, where you go back and forth between different skills throughout your session. In its classic form, if a block practice session focusing on skills A, B, and C looks like AAABBBCCC, then an interleaving practice session focusing on the same three skills would look like this: ABCABCABC.

For my shooting training, I tend to do interleaving practice slightly differently. Say I am focusing on reloads in a particular practice session. My sequence of drills might look something like this: Doubles, 4 Aces, Bill Drills, Blake Drills, 4 Aces, Transitions, 4 Aces,

Distance Changeup, Position Entry and Exit, 4 Aces. This way I continue to work on my fundamentals as a whole while still focusing on my reloads.

As you progress throughout your training cycle, and as you become more advanced in general, the proportion of your training time spent on the three categories of drills changes. As a beginner, almost all your training is experimentation, so that you can develop your personal technique. Over time, experimentation drills become less and less necessary as your shooting technique becomes well developed. If experimentation work is needed in your current training cycle, it should be predominantly at the beginning of the cycle, and then drop off in favor of isolation and combination drills.

As an intermediate shooter, isolation drills become the bulk of your training time, as you hone and polish the technique you developed through your early experimentation work. This is especially true towards the beginning of a training cycle. As the cycle progresses, and throughout successive cycles as your overall skill level improves, you steadily add in more and more combination drills until they become the majority of your training. The best in the world only do enough isolation work to maintain their technical level, and the rest of their training is all combination drills.

Throughout your training cycle you should periodically test your skill, and use the feedback from your performance to identify deficiencies and make course corrections in your training as needed. The end of each cycle should culminate in a test as well, and the data from that test is used to design the next cycle, and so on. The theory is to pick the small handful of weaknesses that will give you the greatest skill gains if improved. Then once that is done, pick the next lowest hanging fruit, and so on. This, if done right, should give steady incremental improvements in performance.

Program your skill training like an athlete's. Use the data, create a feedback loop, plan out your training appropriately, and watch your skill level improve as fast as your talent and level of participation allow.

GRAPPLING AND STRIKING IN TRAINING

"Everyone has a plan 'till they get punched in the mouth." - Mike Tyson

Skill at combatives needs focused effort and training, no less than shooting skill does. And the training can, and should, be organized in a similar fashion. We need to experiment in order to optimize our techniques in a way that suits our physiology and psychology. We need to isolate and hone our technique with focused effort. We need to work combinations of ever increasing complexity in order to build consistency under stress. And we need to test our techniques against noncooperative opponents. All of this should be done with an emphasis on footwork and positioning.

Simple and effective techniques should be prioritized. For striking, a good starting point is the jab, cross, hook, and uppercut for strikes with the hands. For close strikes, headbutts and elbows reign supreme. For kicks, all you really need as a foundation are straight and round kicks and the knee versions of those. A good source art for foundational striking technique is Muay Thai.

For grappling, You'll need a foundation of throws and takedowns as well as submissions. Hip throws, seatbelt tosses, leg reaps and sweeps, single and double legs are a good basic catalog of throws and takedowns. For submissions, start with arm bars and chokes.

Don't neglect footwork, positioning, and unbalancing the opponent. These can be drilled with a partner, and are the skill set that actually make the striking and grappling techniques functional.

Strikes should be worked on the heavy bag and focus pads, through shadow boxing, and with a partner. Grappling should be primarily trained with a partner, although a grappling dummy can have value. Sparring should be used relatively sparingly compared to solo and partner drilling, but is invaluable for real skill.

Shooting and gunfighting may be the focus of your training, but unarmed combatives are vital, especially for law enforcement applications and civilian self-defense. Don't neglect this skill set, it is absolutely essential.

EDGED AND IMPACT WEAPONS IN TRAINING

"The sword is the axis of the world and its power is absolute." - Charles de Gaulle

Edged and impact weapons bridge the gap between empty hand combatives and firearms. With an inert (unsharpened) training replica of the knife you carry, or an impact weapon, you can practice techniques solo, with a partner, and on a target designed to hold up to the repeated impacts.

It's important to understand the difference between hitting and cutting. For a strike with an impact weapon to be maximally effective, energy needs to be transferred from the weapon to the target. This feels like the "heavy hands" concept in empty hand striking. Edged weapons are different. Cutting involves drawing the edge along the target with the blade in proper alignment. Research this thoroughly in your training. It's a good idea to do at least some "test cutting" and learn the finer technical points required to make clean effective cuts with the knife you carry.

For complete skill development, some sort of noncooperative sparring is necessary. Padded and inert weapons make this possible with low risk of injury. Remember, though, that the lengthy "duel" type fighting with short blades seen in action movies is highly unrealistic. Real knife fights are short, violent, and brutal.

At least a passing level of familiarity with edged and impact weapons is essential for well-rounded combative skill. Spend enough training time and effort on this, and if the need arises you'll be sufficiently prepared.

TRAINING IN LOW-LIGHT

"We own the night." - John Lehman

That saying has become a military cliché, even if it's not wholly true anymore. Night vision has become more affordable and available, and the days of our complete technological dominance in darkness are over. But that doesn't change the necessity of operating in darkness. If anything, it means more skill is required of us.

In dry and live fire, work your tools. Lights and lasers are as important to learn to manipulate as your weapon itself. In force-on-force, pay attention to ambient light, backlighting, and backsplash. Practice using white light to control and disorient. Learn to move and shoot under night vision, both with passive and active aiming tools.

Work all of this diligently in your training. You're more likely to have to fight in a low light environment than a well lit one. Develop the skills and understanding needed to fight in the dark and win. If you fail to address this in training, you could pay a very heavy price in application.

FORCE-ON-FORCE

"You can only fight the way you practice." - Miyamoto Musashi

Without force-on-force, we cannot work our firearms-based tactics and techniques against noncooperative training partners. Just as martial arts styles become contrived and unrealistic without some sort of competitive aspect to their training, without properly conducted force-on-force drills and scenarios, our training for gunfighting will be just as artificial and ineffective. And with properly conducted force-on-force training, your ability to fight with a firearm can be developed to a very high level. I still remember being surprised at how easy my first gunfight felt compared to my training.

There is a flip side to this, of course. Without a high level of subconscious competence at weapons handling, marksmanship at speed, and movement techniques, force-on-force training can easily degrade into an expensive game of paintball. The hard skills have to be developed at a high enough level in order to receive the potential training benefits of force-on-force exercises.

The way most teams train force-on-force is incomplete. Most solely utilize scenario-based training, without devoting time to opposed drills. Scenario-based training is vital, but it's analogous to the testing phase of firearms training, especially when it's a large full mission profile exercise involving command and control. For optimal skill development, smaller more specifically focused drills should be run in force-on-force frequently, with the larger scenarios reserved for evaluating performance and creating a feedback loop for informing future training.

For civilians and others without access to force-on-force training, explore paintball and airsoft. Yes, they are games. Yes, they are not as realistic. However, they at least allow you to spar with mock firearms against uncooperative opponents, and learn valuable lessons from that competition.

Gunfighting is still fighting. And without fighting an opponent who is trying to defeat you, you will never reach your potential ability as a fighter. Embrace that. Learn from your defeats and victories in training, so that you won't have to learn those lessons when the fight is real.

BARRICADE FIELD DRILL

I was first introduced to the Barricade Field Drill by Ken Good, then Director of Training for Surefire. The barricade field is a powerful setup for drilling in force-on-force. It's a large open area with numerous randomly spaced barricades for cover. The field isn't used for scenario training, it's used for drills.

One element begins at one side of the field and the opposing element begins at the other. Each element can be as small as an individual and as large as is practical based on the size of the barricade field. The most common combinations are one-on-one up to four-on-four, but larger can be done if the training area can accommodate it. Usually the elements are evenly matched in size, but there can be significant training value in pitting a smaller element against a larger one.

When the drill starts, both elements engage each other using force-on-force. Unlike scenario-based training, where you fight through regardless of being hit, for the purposes of this drill any time you are hit, you're out of play for the duration of that round. The round continues until everyone from one element has been hit and that entire element is out of play.

The Barricade Field Drill allow you to work on many of the component skills and attributes needed for solo and team tactics. Use of cover, proper movement, situational awareness, verbal and non-verbal communication with teammates, understanding and using angles,

353

timing, and more all come into play. This drill enables you to "spar" in force-on-force against noncooperative opponents in an unscripted manner, which is essential if you want to develop true skill at fighting with firearms.

SHOOT HOUSE SPARRING

Much like barricade field drills, shoot house sparring in force-on-force training is intended to be unscripted and noncooperative. This drill is also run the same as barricade field work but inside a structure.

When the drill starts, both elements engage each other using force-on-force. Unlike scenario-based training, where you fight through regardless of being hit, for the purposes of this drill any time you are hit, you're out of play for the duration of that round. The round continues until everyone from one element has been hit and that entire element is out of play.

One of my favorite variations of this drill is one I did regularly for instructor development with my training staff at Chicago SWAT. One of my instructors, Paul Amelio, and I would go into the house as a two-man element and run force-on-force against a four or six-man element of students. Working this drill frequently, because of the increased need for processing and decision making, made conventional CQB much easier for us.

Another valuable variation of this is to conduct it using vehicles instead of a structure. This can be set up so that the start of the drill replicates either a traffic stop, vehicle takedown, or officer ambush. After the initiation though, the drill remains unscripted and noncooperative.

Don't neglect this sort of unscripted force-on-force drilling. If you put enough work into these sorts of drills, they will pay huge dividends for your skill and capability.

SCENARIOS

Scenarios are the type of force-on-force training most are familiar with. Scenario training is scripted, and unlike the other types of force-on-force drills we've discussed, if a "good guy" is struck with a marking round they continue fighting. The scenario can be as small as one student vs. a single role player, or as large as multiple teams or units including support and command and control elements. The scenario can replicate anything from the students' mission set—traffic or street stops, counter-ambush, entries, etc.—anything your training resources and ingenuity allow.

A couple of important points should be taken into account when running scenarios for your team or unit. The first is the quality of the role players. A bad role player can destroy the intended training effect of the drill. It's also valuable to cycle students through as role players, so they can experience their team's tactics from the receiving end. This leads to insights in how to improve the team's performance.

The larger scenarios involving multiple elements including command and control don't really offer as much value for improving the team's performance as smaller ones focused on the team do. The larger ones do have value, but they are primarily a coordination exercise to test command's ability to maneuver and control elements and don't allow the team itself to get enough focused repetitions for skill improvement. Smaller streamlined scenarios allow the team to focus on areas to improve and cycle through reps much more rapidly.

Proper scenario-based training does more than just build physical skill. It builds decision making, verbal and non-verbal communication, and most importantly the will to fight. While I do think scenarios are overly emphasized and drilling in force-on-force is neglected, properly conducted training scenarios are essential for individual and team development.

INCORPORATING COMBATIVES

Empty-hand, bladed, and impact weapon combatives should be incorporated periodically into scenario-based training. The ability to differentiate between tools and solve problems that don't warrant deadly force are crucial, as is the ability to combine firearms skills into this mix. All too often we treat firearms and combatives as two distinct options, but that's not the way it always works in application. Use of force is a continuum, and we need to be able to move up and down that scale seamlessly as the situation dictates.

With modern protective gear such as Red Man or High Gear, it isn't a difficult proposition to outfit role players sufficiently enough to incorporate combatives into your force-on-force scenarios. The appropriate care and control must be taken to minimize the risk of injury, but that's not substantively different than conducting force-on-force training in general. The benefits of including combatives regularly in your force-on-force training are numerous and extremely valuable for skill development.

TEACHING

"Even while they teach, men learn." - Seneca

I began instructing at an early age, teaching martial arts as a teenager. I've taught for the U.S. Army, for the Chicago Police Department, and for myself. I've trained civilians, police recruits, SWAT cops, foreign soldiers, and Green Berets. I love teaching because I love training. Student and teacher, trainer and trainee, coach and athlete. These roles are two sides of the same coin.

The best instructors act as coaches and guides, exploring performance improvement with their students rather than dictating from a position of authority. The worst simply regurgitate

357

institutional dogma without context, or focus on their own improvement rather than their students. The danger of sub-par instructors in this arena lies in the stakes involved. Improper tactics and techniques can literally cost lives. Even if the material being taught is tactically and technically sound, if the instructor is unable to teach them effectively enough for the student to perform them correctly, then the training is still counterproductive at best.

Teaching is a skill independent from the skills being taught. It needs to be practiced and honed like any other craft in order to master it. Let's explore the attributes and skills of a good instructor as well as common pitfalls to avoid.

Above all, a good instructor is a diligent and dedicated student. This is ongoing. There is never a moment when you "have arrived" and can learn nothing more of your craft. Even if you were at the top of your game operationally, once you move on from that role you still need to train and learn in order to maintain relevancy. I've seen famous instructors who I respect immensely become rigid and dated in their teaching, as if they are frozen at whatever the state of the art was when they left their operational role.

A good instructor is a high performer. You don't have to necessarily outperform everyone you teach, but you have to possess a high enough skill level to show that you understand how to reach excellence through your own training. You also need to be able to demonstrate every task to standard that you want your students to perform. I've actually seen LE instructors be taught that they should never demo in front of their students. This is a horrible practice. Barring some sort of injury or testing scenario, you should demonstrate everything you want your students to do. A good instructor is also confident enough in their skills and accomplishments to avoid the pitfalls of ego. You have to be secure enough to make mistakes in front of your students without it derailing your instruction.

A good instructor has a high degree of relevant experience. Contrary to what many LE and military institutions would like to believe, a forty-hour training course does not make anyone a subject matter expert. Would you study boxing from a coach who had never stepped in the ring themselves? My personal litmus test for teaching a subject is simple. If I haven't both trained hard enough at something to develop a high level of skill and also performed it operationally at a high level, I won't teach it. This is why I don't teach combat medicine or precision rifle shooting. I've trained in both and done both operationally, but not at a high enough level to feel like I should be teaching either. When there's a need for instruction in these, I bring in someone I know personally to have enough relevant skill to teach them well.

358

A good instructor is a good coach. Although sometimes necessary in institutional settings for purely logistical reasons, standing in front of a group and barking out instruction without providing individualized feedback is hardly a recipe for creating excellence in your students. Just like the best coaches know what cues to give each of their athletes to help them understand how to improve, a good instructor can diagnose and correct their students individually, even in a group setting.

Teaching is difficult, and teaching well more difficult still. But it is also extremely rewarding. In my opinion, teaching is an essential element for reaching true mastery in any craft. You never understand a skill as well as you will when you have had to teach another to perform it at a high level. Seek out opportunities to teach, and watch your abilities and understanding increase.

BOOK FIVE - THE FIGHT

INTRODUCTION - "THE MEDIUM AND THE MESSAGE"

"The truth is outside of all fixed patterns." - Bruce Lee

The medium and the message. I see these get confused all the time. I've seen it in the martial arts world almost my entire life. It's the primary failing of traditional martial artists. There is much of value in arts like Karate, Judo, and Aikido. But almost universally the proponents of these arts confuse the training drills with the fight. Instead of internalizing the message being transmitted, they adopt the medium being used to transmit that message as literal truth.

Thanks to my decades as an active cop on the streets of Chicago, I've been in countless physical altercations, and the lessons I learned from those traditional arts stood me in good stead in all of them, but not one of them looked exactly like the formal and stylized drills I had trained.

The same is true in the tactical world. I've been in gunfights overseas and at home, and the skills I gained on the flat range and in the shoot house served me well. But they served me well because I adapted those skills to the situation at hand, not because the drills that built the skills looked like the gunfights.

When people lack real world experience, this issue compounds. Over time the training gets more and more contrived and artificial. Eventually the medium becomes so corrupted that the message is lost, and the training loses its value. Even with real-world experience, without intense and objective analysis, affectation can still creep in to training and impair its effectiveness.

Even the best training is still to some degree artificial. It's designed to create skill, and will do so. But it's not the same as the actual fight, and cannot be. No fight looks like a kata. Conflict is chaotic, and the opponent gets a vote about how it unfolds. If you confuse the medium of the drills with the message they contain, you will be rigid and dogmatic instead of fluid and adaptable. Your techniques and tactics flow from your training and experience, they aren't constrained by them.

INITIATIVE

"This is the law. The purpose of fighting is to win. There is no possible victory in defense. The sword is more important than the shield, and skill is more important than either. The final weapon is the brain. All else is supplementary." - John Steinbeck

Initiative. This is the single most important factor in ensuring victory in any arena. Gaining and maintaining initiative is key. It keeps your opponents reacting to you, fighting your fight instead of their own. Regaining it once lost is also key. It puts the fight back on your terms instead of theirs. This is as true for armies and corporations as it is for individuals.

There have been many mental frameworks used to describe the process of initiative. The most common in tactical circles is undoubtedly USAF Colonel John Boyd's model of the OODA loop. In traditional Japanese martial arts, the concepts of "Sen" and "Go" are used to create a model explaining how to use initiative in conflict. Even the traditional CQB axiom of "speed, surprise, and violence of action" is actually an admonition to gain and maintain initiative. Let's examine initiative and some of the best frameworks used to understand it in greater detail.

Let's begin with the OODA loop. John Boyd was legendary as the fighter pilot who could win any dogfight in 40 seconds or less, but he was more than just that. He possessed a brilliant military mind as a strategist. He created the OODA loop as a model to understand how we win in conflict. Winning violent confrontations is about far more than just technique, resolve, or stamina. It is about employing the correct technique at the right time with initiative.

OODA stands for Observation, Orientation, Decision and Action. This is the cycle we move through in conflict. We observe our environment. Then we use our prior training and experience to orient ourselves correctly to the reality around us. We then decide on our next action based on that orientation. Then comes the action phase, where we implement our decision. We then begin the cycle again.

If we can initiate our cycles before our opponent does, and move through them more rapidly, or disrupt his cycles intentionally, we gain and maintain initiative. Everyone focuses in their training on the "Act" phase of the cycle, but the other three are at least as important, if not more so. You can use this model in your training to help you understand the ways you interact with your opponents. Study this, and you will be far more capable in conflict than you would otherwise.

The other of my favorite models for explaining the initiative process comes from the classical samurai arts of Japan. They used the concepts of Sen and Go to explain initiative. You can think of Sen as initiative and Go as reaction. The first category they use is simply "Sen." Think of this as an ambush, an overwhelming and/or surprise attack. Seizing the initiative immediately, then not relinquishing it until the conflict is over.

The second category is "Go no Sen." This is a counterattack that regains the initiative from the opponent. In its crudest and least desirable form, it is purely responsive in nature. In its best application it is luring the enemy into a specific attack in order to deliver your counter. You can do this by creating an opening for the opponent's attack, or feigning a specific weakness.

The third category is "Sen no Sen." This is using a feint to set up your true attack. Your feint has to be convincing enough that the opponent reacts to it, creating the opening you need for your actual attack. In the case of a skilled opponent, you may need a series of attacks to set up your opening. The whole point is to lure them in to the position you find advantageous.

The final and most sophisticated category is "Sen Sen no Sen." This is the preemptive strike at the opponent's moment of preparation. Think of the boxer who reads his opponent's intent and lands his punch before the other fighter can deliver his. This is when the police officer or CCL holder reads the situation well enough to draw his weapon before the opponent does.

Both of these models help you understand initiative and how to apply it. If you truly understand this, you will be much more effective at handling all kinds of conflict. These concepts apply universally. They are as relevant to business and legal matters as they are to battlefield strategy and civilian self-defense. Study this thoroughly in your training, and learn to apply the principle of initiative in all aspects of your life.

SITUATIONAL AWARENESS

"Be always vigilant; there are many snares for the good." - Accius

The ability to process environmental information is a fundamental attribute for negotiating conflict. It may very well be the most important factor other than hard skills. We touched on John Boyd's famous paradigm for the mental process of handling conflict, the OODA loop, above. His concept illustrates the importance of awareness brilliantly.

OODA stands for observation, orientation, decision, and action. The action phase of the cycle is the one everyone focuses their attention on - the submission in grappling, the knockout punch or high kick in striking, the hostage shot in CQB. But the fight is usually won or lost in the other three phases.

Don't misunderstand, the hard skills used in the action phase are vital and need to be developed at an extremely high level, but without the ability to make sound tactical decisions based on an accurate evaluation of your environment, it is difficult to effectively apply those skills. And there's a flip side to this as well. Unless you have developed your hard skills to the level of subconscious competence, you won't be able to use your conscious mind to observe, orient, and decide. All of your mental bandwidth will be eaten up with the physical tasks you have to perform.

Situational awareness not only helps you win fights, it helps you avoid them, and set yourself up so that if you have to fight you are already in an advantageous position before the fight begins. Develop your situational awareness throughout your everyday life. Create a pattern of observations made, and quiz yourself on your knowledge of the environment around you. Play the mental "what if" game with yourself wherever you go.

The ability to maintain a current and accurate mental picture of your environment is an extremely valuable and truthfully rare skill. Cultivate this attribute, and it will serve you well, not just in conflict, but in life in general.

DISTANCE AND POSITION

"In strategy it is important to see distant things as if they were close and to take a distanced view of close things." - Miyamoto Musashi

We came upon a cave complex once in the mountains of Afghanistan being used as a base of operations for Taliban fighters. Rather than clear it, against potentially heavy resistance, we backed away outside of small arms range and called in an air strike from a position of safety. The JDAM leveled the cave complex, rendering it unusable for the enemy.

This is in essence no different than the striker who slips his opponents jab and places himself at their flank, in an advantageous position where his opponent is vulnerable to his counterattack. Or the gunfight I was in that inspired my Monticello drill, where my movement offline when my opponent drew allowed me to engage him without being shot myself.

Skillful manipulation of distance and positioning maximizes your ability to affect your opponent while simultaneously decreasing their ability to harm you. Use angles and range to your advantage, and to place your opponent at a disadvantage.

Understanding proper distance and position is vital for managing violence, even—and perhaps especially—before the violence even starts. Learn this principle and how it adapts to different environments and situations. Practice it at every fighting range, individually and as a team or unit if that applies to you, and you will significantly increase your ability to manage conflict of any kind.

DISTRACTION AND DECEPTION

"All warfare is based on deception." - Sun Tzu

A boxer's feint and a SWAT team's flash bangs, The wooden horse of the Trojan war and the mock amphibious invasion of Kuwait at the start of Desert Storm. These are all examples of distractions and deceptions employed to gain a tactical advantage.

At their heart, these stratagems are designed to impair the opponent's ability to make correct decisions in a timely fashion. Just as our ability to process the information from our environment and make the correct decisions rapidly is crucial for victory, our ability to prevent our opponent from doing just that can give us a profound tactical advantage.

This is an area of strategy that you must understand and exploit in order to maximize your ability to manage violent conflict. It applies to individual fighting and team tactics equally.

Explore this concept in all aspects of your tactics and combatives training, and internalize it. This principle can be applied in many situations outside of violent conflict. Master it, and it will serve you well in all aspects of your life.

CALMNESS

"Between stimulus and response there is a space. In that space is our power." - Victor Frankl

Panic is contagious. If unchecked it can wreak havoc on a team's ability to function properly in a crisis. The good news is that calmness is also contagious and is the antidote for panic. Calm, decisive leadership keeps a team focused and on task in the midst of chaos. This is why fighter pilots and SWAT officers cultivate an apparently unearthly calm in their voices when speaking on the radio. They understand the importance of remaining calm during conflict, and the influence of their calmness on their teammates.

The same principle holds true for the individual as well. We can combat panic through controlled breathing, correct self-talk, and the process focus cultivated through proper training. And it's not just panic our preprogrammed calmness protects us against. Fear, anger, desperation. All of these strong negative emotions can affect our ability to fight, often with catastrophic consequences.

This is a relatively simple skill, but that doesn't mean it's an easy one. We have to learn the proper techniques for cultivating calmness in conflict, and we have to practice them in stressful situations until they become automatic. This is where stress inoculation in training becomes essential. Learning to control our breathing and remain process-focused under external stress has to be practiced repeatedly for it to be effective.

This ability is a profoundly powerful one. It doesn't just give you an edge in combat, the skill carries over to all aspects of your life. Cultivate it and develop it, and learn to master your negative emotions rather than be their slave.

PRESSURE

"Do not allow the enemy to attack a second time." - Miyamoto Musashi

We must learn to bring psychological pressure to bear on our opponents. Get inside their heads. Make them angry and careless, or panicked, afraid and desperate. Take away their calm, their ability to remain process-focused. Impair their situational awareness and ability to make decisions.

The mechanisms we can use to bring psychological pressure to bear are limited only by our imagination. Physical pressure and psychological pressure are intertwined, but that is by no means the only way to press the opponent. The legendary samurai, Miyamoto Musashi, was by all accounts an expert at pressing his opponents and destroying their composure. His most famous duel, against Sasaki Kojiro, is a perfect example of this. Musashi knew the temperament of his opponent and exploited it masterfully. He was late for the duel, which is seen as an insult in Japanese culture. Then he arrived at the agreed upon location armed, not with his long sword, but with a wooden sword carved from the oar of the boat he took there.

Kojiro, already angered by Musashi's tardiness, became enraged by the wooden sword. He took that as an insult as well, as if Musashi didn't even respect him enough to use steel against him. In his rage, Kojiro drew his own sword and threw the scabbard into the ocean. Musashi taunted Kojiro, telling him, "You won't be needing that again, you've already lost."

Kojiro was unable to maintain his composure, and Musashi made short work of him, dispatching him with a fatal blow to the forehead from the wooden sword. Musashi's use of psychological pressure won him victory against his most skilled opponent.

Conflict is as much mental as it is physical. We need to understand that and use it to stack the odds in our favor, much like Musashi did in his duel against Kojiro. This doesn't just apply to violent conflict. The same principle holds true in office politics or a courtroom, anywhere you find yourself at odds with another. Master this, and it will serve you well.

AGGRESSION

"A good plan, violently executed now, is better than a perfect plan next week." - George S. Patton

Controlled and dispassionate aggression often carries the day. From your opponent's point of view, your aggressiveness should be overwhelming. From yours it should be controlled and allow you to remain process-focused. Finding this balance is crucial to maximizing your effectiveness in conflict.

Sports psychologists call this balance an athlete's optimal level of arousal. It's a very individual thing; no two athletes are the same. Learning your optimal level of arousal and building the ability to replicate it on demand is a hallmark of a champion athlete. This is no different for the tactical athlete.

Test yourself against noncooperative opponents in training. Find avenues to cultivate the correct level of aggression. Grapple, box, or kickbox, do force-on-force, or at the very least paintball or airsoft. Learn your optimal level of arousal and how to create it on demand in the training environment before you need it in the real world. Cultivate the correct amount of aggression and learn to call on it when you truly need it.

TAKE THEIR BACK

"In battle, if you make your opponent flinch, you have already won." - Miyamoto Musashi

In the mixed martial arts world, when one fighter gives the other their back out of fear or panic, the bout is almost always over in short order. My competitive fighting career was before MMA became a sport, but I often exploited this then. I knew if I could press my opponent enough to make them recoil and turn away, the match would be mine. Because of the assignments I held and the areas of Chicago I worked in, I was in literally hundreds of violent physical confrontations in my career as a police officer. Much as in my earlier matches, if I could make them recoil and turn, if I could take their back, I knew that as long as I kept the pressure on, I had won.

I had a gunfight as a cop where the surprise and fear my first round fired instilled in the offender caused him to recoil away from me while attempting to fire his pistol wildly. I knew in that moment that unless I let the pressure off I had already won that gunfight. I had taken his back with my pistol in the same way a Jujitsu practitioner controls his opponent with a rear mount and choke.

This is a very valuable lesson indeed. Once violence is inevitable, the time for negotiation and de-escalation is done. Your physical response should be legally defensible and proportionate

373

to the threat, but it should also be physically and psychologically overwhelming to your opponent. Break their will to fight. Make them recoil from you in panic and fear. Take their back and keep it until the fight is done, and they are no longer a threat.

This principle applies to teams and larger units as well in combat. Like all the other principles of conflict it's true on the small scale and the large one. Breaking the resolve of the enemy so that they lose discipline and cohesiveness assures victory. Fighting is fighting, and the will is all. Break the enemy's will and impose yours, and you will certainly prevail.

AI-UCHI

"Death never takes a wise man by surprise; he is always ready to go" – Jean de la Fontaine

Ai-Uchi is a concept in the classical martial arts of Japan that translates literally as "mutual strikes." It means simultaneous defeat, where both combatants are struck decisively by the other in the same moment. This was reportedly a very common outcome in duels between Samurai, even the highly skilled.

When two skilled opponents fight with effectively lethal weaponry, both landing a fatal or incapacitating hit is very possible. Even if one survives, the cost of victory can easily be a wound one never quite recovers from. I, and every other veteran of extensive combat or active police work I know, have injuries that never healed quite the same.

374

This simple fact is why those experienced at violence are not eager to enter into it unnecessarily. Once you truly understand how easy it is to be killed or seriously injured, regardless of your skill level, you reserve violence for when it is truly needed. Only the naïve or arrogant long for violence.

I'll be the first to admit that I once did just that. I eagerly sought out life or death situations in order to test myself in their crucible. Now that I have thirty plus years of that in my past, I understand how many of my victories were due to luck and audacity rather than skill. I now feel no need to ever personally engage in violence again unless forced to and would happily avoid it for the rest of my days.

The other effect this fact has on those with experience at violence is that they understand that you must always stack the deck in your favor. Once violence starts your response must be overwhelming and decisive. This can look excessive or brutal to the untrained eye.

This is the reality of conflict. To view it any way other than the truth is to invite serious injury or death. To understand this truth, and its implications, is to be truly prepared for violence if you're forced to meet it head on.

FIX AND FLANK

"Those skilled in warfare move the enemy, and are not moved by the enemy." - Sun Tzu

Flanking is probably the oldest and most universal of tactics. In its purest form, as an infantry tactic, one element fixes the enemy through effective fires, while a second element maneuvers to the unprotected flank of the enemy. The fixing element then shifts and lifts fires while the bounding element attacks through the enemy positions, overwhelming and defeating them. This principle has applicability in everything from business conflict, to CQB, to one-on-one armed and unarmed confrontation.

This is why points of domination CQB is more effective than strong wall. The L-shaped formation created in the room during entry is essentially fixing and flanking the opponent. It's the optimal formation for vehicle takedowns as well. If you examine the infantry ambush, this is why the L-shaped ambush is superior to the linear. This principle is applicable to far more than just team tactics however.

As a young man I trained and competed heavily in martial arts. In Karate, one of my favorite strategies was to press the opponent, fixing him in place for a moment, then shifting to his less defensible side and exploiting my advantage with either strikes or a takedown. This is at its heart simply fixing and flanking. In Judo, the principle of kuzushi is, in essence, a flank. In this you pull or push your opponent in one direction, and when his resistance fixes him in place for a moment, you unbalance him in a different, more vulnerable direction. In classical Jujitsu, a strike often precedes a throw for the same reason. The strike momentarily fixes the opponent so that you can exploit a more vulnerable angle. All of these are examples of fixing and flanking.

In a one-on-one gunfight, the opportunity for the classic fix and flank does sometimes present itself. But more commonly, moving laterally off the line of attack and then pressing the advantage from a more advantageous angle is once again the same as a flanking maneuver. Meeting force with force head on is seldom the best strategy for dealing with armed or unarmed conflict. Attack vulnerabilities with strengths instead.

This same principle can apply in interpersonal dealings as well. It can be used in debates and business conflicts with equal efficacy. Conflict is conflict, regardless of the medium it exists in. Whenever possible, utilize this universal principle. Press the opponent mentally, gain the initiative, and attack weakness with strength. Fix and flank.

AMBUSH

"The two most important rules in a gunfight are always cheat, and always win." - Clint Smith

A life or death struggle is not a fair fight. It is not a sporting event. There are no referees, no rules, and no guarantee of assistance or rescue. And there is no such thing as an unfair advantage.

Understand that you have to be prepared to articulate legal justification for your actions, especially in self-defense and law enforcement, but potentially in combat as well. If that justification is present though, exploit any and all advantage available to you.

There is a reason why the ambush is heavily relied upon as a military tactic, and that is how overwhelmingly effective it is. It is the infantry equivalent of a sucker punch and beat down. There are applications for this in CQB, LE vehicle takedowns, defense against home invasion, and more.

Exploit the advantage of surprise whenever possible, and follow it up with overwhelming force. If you can, always choose being in a shooting over participating in a gunfight.

THE LINE OF ATTACK

"In the middle of chaos lies opportunity." - Bruce Lee

The line of attack. This is a powerful way to conceptualize physical aggression. In striking and weapons-based martial arts a high training emphasis is placed on the ability to move just enough off line to avoid an attack, without moving so far that you telegraph your intent. Ideally, you can use this to place yourself in an advantageous position for your counterattack.

This principle is just as applicable to fighting with firearms. More so in fact. You can block a punch or parry a blade, but the same isn't true of a bullet. Understand though, you can't dodge one that's already in flight. We aren't talking about action movie choreography here. But moving off the opponent's line of attack can be a powerful strategy in a gunfight. It's one I've used, and it prevented me from being shot when I did.

Work this principle in training until you understand it and can employ it realistically. Use it when applicable, and it will serve you well.

SPEED KILLS

"Shooting at a man who is returning the compliment means going into action with the greatest speed of which a man's muscles are capable." - Wyatt Earp

Speed kills. For all the ongoing and never ending debate about speed versus accuracy, that is an incontrovertible fact. While it is true that you can't miss fast enough to win a gunfight, you can certainly hit too slowly and lose. It's not simply speed or accuracy, that's a flawed paradigm. It's speed *and* accuracy that you need to carry the day.

People in the tactical shooting community tend to use the FBI law-enforcement statistics to justify a wide number of training conventions, sometimes justifiably, sometimes not. Data is a powerful tool, if you understand the mechanism and purpose of its collection and evaluation. Otherwise you run the risk of the old cliché "lies, damn lies, and statistics" applying to your thought process. The FBI's annual report actually focuses on police officers killed or injured, not law-enforcement gunfights as a whole. This doesn't address civilian self-defense shootings, nor does it include shootings where the officer was uninjured.

A statistic which does have weight from the FBI's annual LEOKA report is that the distance of a fatal law enforcement shooting incident is overwhelmingly seven yards or less. This is matched, at least roughly, by the statistics from the NYPD and LAPD as well. The NYPD characterizes these shootings as being fifteen feet or less, or over fifteen feet. They found that only 36% were over fifteen feet. The LAPD broke their categories down at ten yards (or thirty feet), with half occurring within that distance.

For civilians, this is likely to differ to some degree, as police officers are often attempting to effect an arrest, or protect others, not simply defend themselves. The few relevant sources of data, such as Tom Given's data on self-defense shootings by his students, or the LAPD's records on off-duty shootings, show once again an overwhelming majority at seven yards or less, with most being inside of five yards.

What do these statistics mean for our training? At ranges under 10 yards, especially without the opportunity to use cover, the priority has to be getting acceptable hits on the opponent first. Gunfighting isn't boxing. You don't want to receive any hits from your opponent if at all possible. Once you get acceptable hits, you can drive your hits to the optimal area and end the fight. Getting hits on the opponent first requires speed. Close range gunfights are not, in my experience, about high levels of accuracy with acceptable speed. They are entirely about high levels of speed with acceptable accuracy.

CORNERS AND
THRESHOLDS

"To the ego, death is always just around the corner." - Eckhart Tolle

Fighting with firearms inside a structure, whether assaulting a building as part of a team or defending your home against an armed invader, requires a solid understanding of how to address corners. This is the fundamental problem that needs to be addressed for armed engagements inside a structure. Everything in a building involves this. Corners, thresholds, furniture, obstacles. Even stairwells consist of horizontal and vertical corners.

Some things need to be understood about this from a practical standpoint. Not all walls actually provide effective cover. Especially in stateside residential construction, most internal walls within a building are only concealment. Rick Rau, my team sergeant in Special Forces, once won a gunfight by shooting through the wall his opponent was hiding behind. Over-reliance on internal walls as cover can be a fatal error.

Having said that, most people tend to treat walls as cover, and in the moment and under stress, tend to not realize they can often put effective fire on their opponent through them. If you clear structures as part of your job, it's up to you and your team to weigh the advantages and risks when you decide which techniques to use in a given context.

Every corner inside a structure—whether clearing it dynamically, deliberately, or methodically—introduces a set of angles that need to be moved through in an efficient way. There's a tendency to minimize the importance of this during dynamic clearing and to relegate it to something only done when we "slice the pie" in deliberate or solo clearance. But optimizing the angles used to move around a corner or through a threshold applies regardless of the clearing speed and technique we choose.

Learn to play the angles. Study the geometry of tactics and maximize your ability to address corners individually and with teammates. This is foundational knowledge required to prevail in any sort of armed confrontation in and around a structure.

360 DEGREE SECURITY

"But the shield for the common good of the whole line." - Plutarch

One of the guiding principles underpinning small unit tactics is 360-degree security for your element. In the simplest terms this means your element should be prepared to react to an attack from any direction at any time. This principle shapes team formations and movement and dictates defensive positions as well.

Depending on factors like element size, speed of movement, and operational environment, full 360-degree security may be impractical or impossible, especially momentarily. There's a priority to giving security up. The rear, where we came from, is the first to be released, followed by the flanks if necessary, and our direction of travel or known threat direction is maintained as long as possible.

Another way this is applied when operating as part of a team is, in essence, no different than the way it was first applied in the Greek phalanx. In the phalanx, each soldier's shield didn't protect them, it protected the man to their left. Much the same way, our plates protect our teammates when we block where they are vulnerable.

The principle of 360-degree security does apply when you are not part of a team as well, but obviously can't be implemented the same way. Think of this as a triage process where you evaluate the potential threats and use your positioning, movement, and tactics to mitigate what risks you can. This does not work without a high level of situational awareness and training. Even with that, it will never be possible as an individual to address all potential danger areas.

Study and train until you truly understand this foundational principle and can apply it subconsciously. This will have benefits, not just in conflict, but throughout your life in general.

INTERLOCKING FIELDS OF FIRE

"Remember, upon the conduct of each depends the fate of all." - Alexander the Great

Anyone who spent time in the infantry or special operations is familiar with interlocking fields of fire and the importance of this concept in both defense and offense. The idea is simple. You want to set up your team formation to avoid a one-on-one gunfight if at all possible, and the more guns you have in the fight the better.

Your team's formation should be set up to allow for at least two guns to address any one threat. You never want it to be a fair fight. Instead you want overwhelming fire superiority if at all possible.

If you understand this, and apply it properly, you stack the odds in your favor. This principle, along with that of 360-degree security, are the heart of small unit tactics. Master these principles, and you'll master tactics.

SMOTHER

"When you decide to attack, keep calm and dash in quickly... attack with a feeling of constantly crushing the enemy, from first to last." - Miyamoto Musashi

I had a Judo teacher named Yoshinaga whose great strength was his newaza, his ground fighting. I was probably a foot taller and a hundred pounds heavier than him, but I swear when he pinned me it felt like he was parking a Cadillac on my chest. I couldn't breathe or move freely, and he was able to submit me with ease. Any ability I had to maneuver or counterattack was smothered by his masterful use of positioning and weighting.

Smother the opponent. Once you gain the initiative and dominant position, exploit that advantage. Overwhelm them physically and psychologically until you've won. Give them no space to move, no room to think, no opportunity to regroup. This works in grappling and striking, and is very effective for contact distance fighting with firearms. The underlying principle can be applied to solo gunfighting to great effect, as well as small unit tactics.

Learn to apply this, both in physical conflict and throughout your daily life, and it will make you a formidable individual indeed.

STRIKING WITH THE FIREARM

"This was the technique called 'buffaloing,' and it was Wyatt Earp's favorite when he became a marshal later on." - Thomas Berger

Unlike Wyatt Earp's practice of using pistol whipping as a less lethal force option, in today's climate we should reserve striking with the firearm to situations where deadly force is appropriate. This should also be reserved for fights at contact distance where the firearm is already in play. It is extremely important to maintain trigger finger and muzzle discipline as well to avoid a negligent discharge.

For the pistol, I like two main options. I use the top of the slide with the same body mechanics as a ridge hand strike from karate. Turn the palm down, and strike horizontally to the side of the head with the arm extended, driving from the hips to generate force. The other technique I prefer is to use the base of the inserted magazine and pistol grip like a hammer fist strike. I don't like muzzle striking with a pistol due to the very real possibility of inducing a malfunction.

For the carbine, I do like muzzle striking. It creates a significant impact force without the risk of malfunctions it creates in pistols. The other option is striking with the buttstock of the rifle, either as a thrust or in an arc. Both of these can generate significant force. With striking with the stock, be especially mindful of muzzle direction. It goes without saying for both techniques that trigger finger discipline is essential.

There is no real need to overemphasize these techniques in training. Your general combatives work should give you efficient body mechanics. Beyond that, routinely incorporating combatives into your force-on-force training should give you ample opportunities to test these techniques against a noncooperative training partner.

STRIKING WITH THE BODY

"Take things as they are. Punch when you have to punch. Kick when you have to kick." - Bruce Lee

When in an entangled gunfight, don't neglect striking with the body. Hands, feet, knees, elbows, even your head and shoulders can be used to great effect. There is no real technical changes from pure unarmed combatives, and your general combatives training should prepare you sufficiently for this. The important note here is to simply remember all of the tools at your disposal, and employ them all to the utmost. Anything less than that is risking defeat.

GRAPPLING IN ARMED CONFLICT

"Begin every engagement by denying your opponent the tools they need to impose your game upon you. Only then do you work to impose your game upon them." - John Danaher

Our unarmed grappling training should give us the proper technical base, but we still need to understand the difference between sport or unarmed self-defense grappling, and grappling in a weapons-based environment. Edged weapons and firearms change the priorities of work when grappling drastically. Control of the opponent's weapon and employment of yours is now what's most important over submission or escape. There is also the fact that your impact tools or edged weapons can be used as adjuncts to your grappling by making it easier to manipulate your opponent's limbs. Work your grappling applications throughly with inert training weapons until you understand this fully.

EDGED WEAPONS IN APPLICATION

"To die with a weapon not yet drawn is false." - Miyamoto Musashi

In modern armed conflict, the edged weapon is best suited as either a low-visibility option or as a tool to prevent your opponent from disarming you and taking your firearm. Simple repeatable techniques that can be easily employed while entangled with your opponent are best. Train so that you can employ your edged weapons and execute effective techniques subconsciously at a high level of skill, and you can prepare yourself for this.

BOOK SIX - THE LIFE

INTRODUCTION - "SELECTION IS NEVER ENDING"

"A warrior is fierce because his training is fierce." - Miyamoto Musashi

I've been through several selection processes in my life. Some extremely difficult, some less so, but all important to me. I've helped run two, both of which I considered extremely difficult for the organization they were used for. If there's one lesson I would share from that experience that applies to everyone, regardless of their profession or culture, it's simply this: selection is a never ending process. This applies academically, professionally and athletically. It applies to warriors and police officers alike. It applies to artists and politicians, to accountants and bartenders. It applies in relationships and rivalries. It is a universal truth.

The wrong person thinks that they have "made it," they have "arrived." The joke in my early days in the army was "I got mine," talking about tabs or skill badges. The right person knows that what matters for literally everything important is performance on demand. What can I do today to earn my place at the table? In easy times, some can skate by on past

393

accomplishments or bequeathed status. The moment times turn hard though, that falls by the wayside at a shocking pace.

I remember my selection for a contractor spot I held that took me to Iraq in 2004. Everyone in my class trying out for this job had some sort of SOF experience, and the cadre were all SMU vets. The shooting standards were by no means easy, and weeded out a large percentage of the candidates. A veteran SEAL failed his one allowed reshoot, and was told by a cadre member that he was done with the process. He objected, loudly enough for everyone to hear, that he was a sniper with combat experience and shouldn't be removed from the course. The cadre member placed his hand on the SEAL's shoulder and said kindly in a deep southern accent, "I'm sure you were Bubba. I'm sure you were a good one. But today, you didn't have it and you're done."

That has always stuck with me in the years since. You either have it today or you don't. Performance on demand. Your history and experience informs your performance. And, we can contribute in different ways in different places and times in our lives. But what matters, really matters, is what can I do when it counts. Not intent, not past successes, just successful action now. What can I do today to earn my place at the table? Selection is a never ending process.

FREEDOM AND COST

"I prefer dangerous freedom over peaceful slavery." - Thomas Jefferson

Freedom and cost. Today, as I write this, is September 11th. 9/11. Eighteen years after the towers fell. Eighteen years of war. Eighteen years of America's best and brightest spending their youth fighting for our freedom on foreign soil. Because of this war, I had the privilege of fighting alongside heroes the equal of any warrior class the world has ever known. Because of this war, I have seen and experienced and accomplished things I never would have had the chance to otherwise.

But my war is over now. I retired in March 2019 after a dual career that had me carrying a gun for a living for three decades. In April, I had a long conversation with my friend and mentor, Mike Pannone, about being retired and what that really meant. Mike said something that really struck a chord with me. After a lifetime in service, we were both finally free. But like everything else in life, that freedom had a price.

The interesting thing about that is that those entrusted with protecting freedom aren't truly free themselves. As a soldier you give up your freedoms as part of your service. As a police officer you are subject to greater scrutiny and restrictions than those you protect. This isn't a complaint or a criticism. I knew the deal going in and accepted it willingly.

What I didn't know was the cost. Not my personal cost. Like I said, I knew what I would be paying and entered into that with eyes open. And my price, while heavy, was worth it. For every ache and pain I feel now, there was a victory then. For every freedom I put on hold, there was a memory gained, a chance to be a part of something beyond just my own desires. What I bought with that coin was cheap at the price. I bought a life beyond the ordinary.

The full price wasn't paid by me though. The real cost of that life was paid for me by others. Friends and teammates, and many I never knew. We all put our freedom on hold, but we didn't all get to the payout at the end. They paid the cost for all of us. For everyone who served and everyone who didn't. And here's what that means. I don't owe them sadness or isolation. I don't owe them bitterness or anger. I don't owe them regret. They didn't pay that price for me, for all of us, so that I would imprison myself with guilt.

They paid that price so that I could be free. So we all could be free. What I owe them is the life they should have had. Experiences and accomplishments. Enjoyment and relationships. What I owe them is to live a full, rich life. I owe them my freedom, and the responsibilities and rewards it brings. I owe them an authentic life. And just as importantly, I owe it to myself. We all do. Each and every one of us can choose between just existing or living a life that is true to our real selves.

We are all free if we choose to be. Not free from responsibility or consequence. But free all the same. Live your life, savor it. Tomorrow is not guaranteed, so seize each day. Strive and achieve. Relish and enjoy all that life has to offer. Learn and grow and become. Be free. Regardless of the price. Freedom is always worth the cost.

PRIVILEGE, RESPONSIBILITY, AND INTEGRITY

"To command is to serve, nothing more and nothing less." - Andre Malraux

Leadership can be a sobering thing. The wrong person in a leadership role can cause missions to fail, can destroy careers, can end lives. The right person can make all the difference, though. The right leader can change everything and everyone around him for the better. The difference between the good and bad is often how they view the nature of leadership.

All too often, leadership is viewed as privilege. Rank and position become tools solely to gain more power and prestige. Leadership isn't privilege. Leadership is responsibility. Responsibility to the mission, and responsibility to those you lead. Mission success or failure is on you and you alone. The welfare of your subordinates, their professional development, their training and preparation, all those things become your responsibility.

The guy I'm pulling security on in this picture is my old team leader and company commander. When I think of leadership, of integrity, I think of Joe. He epitomizes what a West Point graduate and an SF officer should prioritize ethically. I've seen him make hard moral choices that hurt his career to protect his men. He always viewed his leadership as responsibility. To the mission, but equally to his men. Their welfare and careers were as important to him as his own. And his character has remained unchanged to this day.

In contrast to this, I've seen other leaders in both LE and Mil sacrifice their subordinates for their own gain. I've watched peers I once trusted change over time into people I no longer recognized. What enables some to remain true to their better natures while others degrade over time into worse versions of themselves? What allows the good leaders to remain true to themselves, to keep their way? In my opinion, it's the same trait that allows people to seek excellence at their craft rather than settle.

That ability to objectively self-analyze and work on weaknesses can be applied to your character as well. We all have flaws. We all have moments of mental, emotional, or ethical weakness. It's how we handle them that makes all the difference. If we treat our mental strength, our ethical base, as a skill to be constantly honed, then we can become better versions of ourselves rather than allowing our personal demons to win.

QUIET PROFESSIONAL

"Politeness is a sign of dignity, not subservience." - Theodore Roosevelt

In the SOF and tactical communities, much is said about being a "Quiet Professional." Does that mean we don't ever say anything about our service, our background? Does that mean we can't capitalize on our experience and skills outside of the military? In my opinion, that is a foolish expectation and an unfair one. Anyone with special operations experience, especially combat experience, has paid a heavy price for their skills and knowledge. Those things are valuable, and that investment should have its reward. Doesn't mean you boast, or overshare, or wear your service on your sleeve.

What does it mean to be a Quiet Professional then? The litmus test for me is as it always has been. I never want my actions or words to embarrass the regiment in any way. There is a standard you accept when you join its ranks, and it needs to be upheld in all you say or do from that moment forward.

In my opinion, what it means to be a Quiet Professional is simply this—that you present what you should, remain quiet about the things that you shouldn't share openly, and above all that your public communication is professional and dignified.

POINT OF VIEW

"Truth is not what you want it to be; it is what it is. And you must bend to its power or live a lie." - Miyamoto Musashi

As I write this, I have been watching for days as gun control advocates desperately try to spin a media narrative to justify their talking points following the stopping of an active shooter by a young man legally carrying a concealed pistol at an Indiana mall. Flawed and manipulated statistics and misrepresentations of local laws are being seized upon in a desperate attempt to shore up a point of view based on emotion rather than empirical evidence.

Our point of view matters. It the lens through which we view reality. And the inability to change our perspective as new data becomes available to us is dangerous. Holding on to a point of view that doesn't align with reality makes us more vulnerable, and basing our perspectives solely on emotion rather than data makes us easily manipulated by those who do not have our best interests at heart. We need the ability to shape our own perspective by thinking critically about the information we are given, especially when it's an appeal to our emotions.

This applies to training, to technique and tactics, no less than it applies to politics and morality. There are well known trainers who I respect greatly for their life experience who are "frozen" at the level of development tactics and techniques they were at when they retired, and others who never questioned what they were taught on any level. This leads to a rigid and dogmatic attitude that can stifle development of true skill.

Nurture the ability to maintain a objective perspective grounded in reality. Constantly challenge your own views through research and experimentation. Strive to think critically rather than dogmatically. Master your emotions rather than allowing them to control you. Never be afraid to change your point of view in order to align it with the way things actually are. Do this and your training will be better, your tactics and techniques will be sounder, and it will be harder to manipulate you.

ORDERS

"Blind obedience to authority is the real root of all evil." - Marty Rubin

"I was just following orders." The Nuremberg defense, known in international law as the Plea of Superior Orders. The former Nazi officers at the infamous Nuremberg trials, who offered this up in defense for atrocities and war crimes, were unsuccessful and convicted for their actions. This defense is much older than World War Two, dating back to at least the fifteenth century in the Holy Roman Empire, where it was used unsuccessfully to defend a knight named Hagenbach who was beheaded for war crimes.

I am proud of both my former professions, and the role I played in each of them. We are in disturbing times now though. At the time of this writing, we are well into two years of "two weeks to stop the spread." Governments and individuals seem perfectly content with indefinite suspension of individual rights and liberties over a disease with less than a two percent fatality rate. Canada just invoked emergency powers to not only arrest protesters but to seize their bank accounts. Australia has become a police state virtually overnight. Parts of the United States have enacted vaccine passports and severe restrictions on rights of assembly. Protests against these trends have sprung up across the world, leading many countries in Europe to backtrack from draconian mandates.

In my law enforcement career, I was no stranger to public protests and civil unrest. I can say with certainty however that we never violated the protestors' constitutional rights. In the last two years, I've seen things that trouble me deeply though. Police officers in New York detaining children because they didn't have a vaccine passport. Federal law enforcement stating that disagreement with mask and vaccine mandates is a form of domestic terrorism. Local law enforcement arresting people for simply congregating on their own property peacefully. Law enforcement in other first world countries arresting people for simply being outdoors.

If you get on the wrong side of history, simply saying "I was just doing my job" isn't going to help you. It won't help you legally, and more importantly it won't help you ethically. Don't compromise your oath and your ethics. Whatever price you pay in the short run to remain true to them pales in comparison to the price you'll pay in the long run if you don't.

HISTORY

"A generation who ignores history has no past - and no future." - Robert Heinlein

Anyone who spends any time talking to me knows that I am a student of warrior philosophy, culture, and history. We can get invaluable lessons about our craft, and more importantly about life, from learning about those who came before us and emulating those aspects of their warrior cultures that can help guide our way. That's the positive. Like so many other things though, there's a potential negative as well.

There's a phenomenon in our current warrior class where it's become fashionable to identify ourselves with our historical counterparts, or even fictional warriors. This is to some degree undoubtedly driven by social media and pop culture. There are instructors, soldiers, and SWAT cops on Instagram and Facebook promoting themselves as members of warrior classes long extinct, or in some cases warrior cultures that exist only in fiction.

There's nothing wrong with learning from our history. There is so much to gain from the examples of our predecessors. But there's a huge difference between studying history, and identifying with something you're not. I spent my entire life studying martial arts, but I'm not a Samurai. I'm a Green Beret. I love the stoic philosophy of the Greeks and Romans, but I'm not a Spartan or Praetorian. I'm SWAT. I'm of European ancestry, but I'm not a Viking or a

Templar. I'm an American soldier and cop. And as much as I love speculative fiction, I'm not a Jedi either.

When I was contemplating my retirement and thinking of starting my training business, I had a phone conversation with a trainer who is extremely popular on social media. He was giving me his advice on marketing and branding myself. He suggested that I pick a historical persona to identify with, one that embodied warrior ideals and performance at the highest levels. I remember thinking that he and I were Green Berets, why would we need a different warrior class to identify with than the one were already a part of?

We have a warrior class in our society now the equal of any that has ever existed. And if you want to be part of that, the opportunity is there. We were just at war for 20 years. Anyone who truly wanted to get in the fight has had plenty of time to do so. If you are a Raider, or a Green Beret, or a Ranger, or SEAL, or Combat Controller, you are already the modern version of what people try to emulate. There's no need to be anything but what you already are.

And if you didn't get in the fight, that's ok. There is absolutely nothing wrong with being a student of shooting and tactics for your own personal protection and growth. This is a martial art in the purest sense. There are huge benefits to be gained from its pursuit. And this is the very essence of the American warrior culture. If this is you, you are embodying the true spirit of the Second Amendment. However, you're not a Mandalorian. You're not the Punisher. And that's ok, too.

Training is serious business. A fight for your life is as grave as it gets. But that doesn't mean we have to take ourselves so seriously. And it definitely doesn't mean we can't have fun along the way. And we need to learn from our forebears, studying warrior philosophy and history is of immense value, and not just for our craft. It can teach us how to live an authentic and fulfilling life. But we need to keep it in perspective. Take the lessons, but leave the trappings and affectations aside. They will only slow your growth as a warrior and as a person.

ADDICTION

"The adrenaline and stress of an adventure are better than a thousand peaceful days." - Paul Coehlho

Addiction. I was just on Josh Froelich's podcast "Addicted," and the premise of his show made me do some self-reflecting. Josh is both a phenomenal athlete (world IPSC shotgun champion and former professional MMA fighter), and a recovered addict. His premise is that his addictive nature contributes to his success as an athlete and in life. To some degree a podcast about shooting, it is more a podcast about performance. In all aspects of life.

I have never thought of myself as an addict. How could I be? I have been an athlete, a soldier and a policeman for my entire adult life. And I was wrong. I am addicted.

For over forty years I have been addicted just as Josh describes it in his podcast intro. Addicted to the training process, the grind, the sweat and effort of getting better. Addicted to the challenge of proving myself.

And for over thirty of those years I have been addicted to two far more powerful drugs. Conflict and risk. I've been in gunfights. I have jumped from airplanes and driven under night vision. I have fast roped and parachuted from helicopters and ridden on their skids. I've hunted HVTs in Afghanistan and been IED'd in Iraq. I've been in countless police raids and UC operations, foot chases and vehicle pursuits.

I'm retired now. I still have the grind. I still have the process. I still train every day, albeit with different priorities. I am finding new skills to learn, new ways to prove myself, new outlets for that competitive drive. And I'm enjoying that process.

But I will most likely never go into harm's way again. And that's ok. At least rationally. But the addict in me will always yearn for the conflict, will always hunger for the risk. So it's up to me, like any other addict who's no longer using their drug of choice, to find something positive to satisfy that need.

And that's ok, too. Because that striving, that dedication to self-improvement, the grind, is not just the process. It itself is the goal. The secret of a fulfilling life is that the journey itself is, in truth, the only destination worth reaching. And the sweat and effort of that journey is very addicting indeed. I'm an addict after all. And I wouldn't have it any other way.

MOMENTO MORI

"You could leave life right now. Let that determine what you do and say and think." - Marcus Aurelius

I had a good friend nicknamed "Happy" on my team in Basra in 2004. In typical fashion, we called him Happy because he was dolorous and grim. Happy survived the ambush at "Green 19" and the day we got IED'd. He and I stayed close friends, and I got to see him actually become truly happy when he remarried and began to finally enjoy his life. After all his time at war, from Kosovo to Iraq, he was killed by a drunk driver walking across the street in Wisconsin. Another friend and teammate from Basra in 2004, "Dart," was killed on our deployment to Afghanistan in 2009, after surviving countless brushes with death in between. Death came to both with unexpected timing, random and capricious, with no regard for experience or skill.

For the warrior, the possibility of death is a very real and present thing. But, the fear of death, the desire to cling to life, interferes with the ability to act. In armed conflict, even more so than in other athletic pursuits, the ability to perform instinctively and subconsciously is vital. What the samurai called "mushin" or "no-mind," what sports psychologists call "flow" or "the zone," is the only mindset that will maximize the chance of victory. The other trait of this mindset, apart from subconscious competence, is what modern psychologists and performance coaches refer to as being "process-focused" rather than "outcome-focused." Focus on an outcome will interfere with completing the process, which will then quite probably prevent the desired outcome.

In an action shooting match, desiring to win will cause the shooter to "push." This in turn will interfere with the competitor's ability to perform the process of shooting at speed, which will in turn cause them to make mistakes and perform below their level of skill. In a life or death fight, the same paradox exists. The harsh reality of armed conflict, whether as soldiers, or law enforcement officers, or even as armed citizens, is that death is a very real possibility for us all. The same mindset is the key here as well. If the cause is important enough to risk your life, then it needs to be won. The way to win is to cultivate a process focus, to develop subconscious competence. The desire to live will crowd the warrior's mind with extraneous thoughts and fears, which will prevent him acting with the proper unconscious decisiveness. Consciously wanting to survive will only increase the likelihood of dying. Focusing on the process instead will maximize the odds of victory. As Munenori Yagyu, a famous swordsman of feudal Japan, wrote, "Once a fight has started, if you get involved in thinking about what to do, you will be cut down by your opponent with the very next blow."

How then do we cast aside the thought of self-preservation and do what needs to be done? As part of a military or law enforcement team, as an armed citizen protecting others, how do we develop a warrior outlook on performance and risk? How do we cultivate the process-focused mindset required for life or death conflict? For the answer, we can look at the training and traditions of warrior cultures throughout history.

Some samurai, as an exercise in proper mindset, would contemplate their death every morning in gruesome detail. They held that by keeping the possibility of death always in their mind they would rob it of its fear and power. Then in battle, they were used to the thought of their death, and could act decisively, unconcerned with their mortality. The risk of death for them no longer held priority in their minds. The legendary samurai, Miyamoto Musashi, famously wrote that "the way of the warrior is the resolute acceptance of death."

The Roman emperor and stoic philosopher Marcus Aurelius was fond of the phrase "Momento Mori." Remember that you will die. By meditating on his mortality and the transience of his life and accomplishments, Aurelius and the other Roman stoics could take decisive action based on competence and rationality rather than be paralyzed by potentially disastrous outcomes.

The stoic philosophy of Aurelius and the warrior zen of Yagyu and Musashi are often compared, and with good reason. These are practical philosophies born of lifetimes lived at war. But as practical and battle hardened as these men were, their outlook was neither bleak nor grim. In fact, this warrior's way of looking at life can give the objectivity needed to find peace within yourself regardless of circumstance or exterior strife. This is the origin of the oft-repeated ideal that the warrior's path is one of self-development.

"Momento Mori." Remember that you will die. Every moment is precious, and to be savored, and our struggles and accomplishments are ephemeral and temporary at best. To hold on too tightly to our fleeting life is to never learn to live at all. Instead of clinging to this brief mortal existence, exult in the experience of life and learn to truly live. And that is the greatest lesson that the training and life of a warrior can teach.

GOOD AND EVIL

"It's tempting to see your enemies as evil, all of them. But there's good and evil on both sides. In every war ever fought." - George R. R. Martin

As I write this, the Russian invasion of the Ukraine is less than a week old. Stories from the conflict are flooding social media and news outlets, both mainstream and alternative. With our society, and arguably the global one, as polarized as it has ever been in my lifetime, it's tempting to view this conflict and its political underpinnings in a zero-sum fashion.

Life and reality aren't that simple however. We can believe that the Ukrainians fighting for their country are courageous without agreeing with their government's stance on political freedom. We can believe that the Russian invasion is wrong without demonizing the individual soldiers. We can believe that economic and political pressure on Russia and aid to the Ukraine are the morally right acts for our country to take without wanting our military directly involved on a large scale.

Make no mistake, there is evil in the world. Any cop who has dealt with a sociopathic killer or any soldier who has witnessed war's atrocities can tell you graphically how very real it is. And there is good in the world as well. But failing to see the ethical shades of grey between both extremes is a crucial error of judgment, tempting though it may be, and a dangerous one. It is vitally important that leaders and warriors avoid making that mistake.

Demonizing the opposition, viewing your enemies as evil caricatures rather than real people, is exactly what allows good men to do evil acts. Understanding the shades of grey between the black and white extremes prevents us from doing evil in the name of good. It's what prevents us from losing our way. It is possible to do necessary violence without hatred or bullying. It is possible to be justifiably ruthless without becoming needlessly cruel. And that distinction is where the truth of good and evil actually lies.

THE SWORD THAT GIVES LIFE

"It is bias to think that the art of war is just for killing people. It is not to kill people, it is to kill evil. It is a stratagem to give life to many people by killing the evil of one person." - Yagyu Munenori

"Katsujinken, Satsujinken." Or in English, the sword that gives life or the sword that takes it away. This was one of the mottos of Munenori Yagyu, an accomplished and famous warrior of feudal Japan. The meaning behind this simple phrase has not lost its relevance in the centuries since Yagyu's time.

The sword that takes life is force without morals. An oppressor, a brigand, a criminal, or a terrorist can each be skillful at violence. But without an ethical underpinning, force is just force, and can be used to achieve horrible ends. Indeed, violence has been used many times in history to commit atrocities and injustices. Man's inhumanity to man is all too commonplace.

The sword that gives life, however, is force used for the common good. Force that takes some lives to save many more. Make no mistake, violence is still violent. It's ruthless and often ugly. But, just like the carnage caused by the surgeon's scalpel, violence can be used for a positive purpose. This is different than the old trope "the ends justify the means." That invariably leads even the well-intentioned down a very dark road.

The distinction between these two has not lessened in importance in the centuries since Yagyu and his samurai fought to reshape medieval Japan. Two decades of war have proven that. Good men should not shun necessary violence. But what they must always shun, if they wish to remain good men, is unnecessary cruelty and needless brutality.

Which sword do you want to wield? The sword that takes life? Or the sword that gives it?

PRIORITY OF LIFE

"Power is no blessing in itself, except when it is used to protect the innocent." - Johnathan Swift

As of this writing, our nation is reeling in the aftermath of a mass shooting in a rural Texas elementary school. Politicians, journalists, and activists are attempting to exploit the tragedy for their own agendas. Parents are grieving, and in their grief they are understandably questioning the law enforcement response. If accounts are to be believed, there was both heroism and risk aversion on display by law enforcement as the event unfolded. I can't speak to the truth of what happened, I wasn't there. But I feel very strongly about how such incidents should be handled.

When you take an oath as a police officer, you are accepting the responsibility of valuing others' lives above your own. Your response to an incident should be dictated by the priority of life doctrine, rather than concern for your own safety. Priority of life is a term used by SWAT teams for a doctrine that determines how the team will choose the appropriate tactic on an objective. In the priority of life template there are several levels of value placed on the lives of those on scene. The highest value is the victims and bystanders, followed by other law enforcement not on the team. Of next importance is the SWAT team, and the lowest priority is the life of the offender.

This scale of value is at its heart pragmatic. Why should you place the same value on an individual attempting to harm innocent victims as on the law enforcement officer honorably serving his community? It's pragmatic on the flip side as well. If I can't place the lives of innocent children above my own as a policeman, then I don't deserve the title.

What this doctrine means for decision making is that we assume more risk when we are protecting innocent life than when we are simply apprehending a violent criminal or executing a search warrant. If the mission is what's called a barricaded subject, where an offender or offenders is inside a structure but no hostages or non-combatants are present with them, why put officers' lives at unnecessary risk? In a narcotics search warrant, why place evidence at a higher priority than officers' lives? In these situations, it is completely rational and reasonable to make tactical decisions that prioritize officer safety.

In a hostage rescue, a SWAT team assumes more risk when they make entry, prioritizing the lives of the hostages above their own. And the decision to make entry is a balancing act. Assaulting too early or too late can lower the chances of successful hostage rescue, and the correct timing depends on multiple factors. But the decision to wait or not isn't based in officer safety at all. It's solely about the safety of the hostages.

And the most time-sensitive situation mission of all, an active shooter like the one in Texas, demands instant and aggressive response to save lives. Officers make entry as soon as they can, and move rapidly towards the sound of gunfire. Any other response costs innocent lives, and that is unconscionable. If you can't accept that responsibility you have no business wearing a badge.

CORRUPTION

"Power attracts the corruptible. Suspect any who seek it." - Frank Herbert

I spent my entire adult life until my recent retirement working for the government. That experience both reaffirmed my belief in what our republic stands for, and made me very cynical about the corruption of those ideals by the multi-generational ruling class that has arisen in our country. The events of the last several years have only served to show how vital it is that we course correct as a nation before we finish following the example set by Rome over a millennium ago and fade into history and obscurity.

Our founding fathers, despite the current political fashion of demonizing them, were brilliant men. They created a system of checks and balances within our government designed to prevent any one individual or group from gathering too much unilateral authority. They understood human nature and the corrupting influence of power.

The last couple of decades have seen a progressive undermining of those ideals by people who give them lip service, and cry about "existential threats to our democracy" while they themselves subvert the democratic process, commit crimes with impunity, and initiate politically motivated criminal investigations and prosecutions to persecute their opposition and prevent any challenge to the power they've amassed.

We have multiple government officials, including former Presidents, connected to a convicted sex trafficker who dealt in underage prostitution, and the client list was never released. The same sex trafficker supposedly committed suicide in custody, the latest in a long list of convenient deaths surrounding one presidential family. I am a combat veteran and retired Chicago cop, and in three decades of service had fewer people in my professional circles die than the Clintons have. Correlation is not causality, but that is statistically improbable in the extreme.

One political party laughs off destroying evidence in a criminal investigation regarding classified emails being kept on a non-secure server, yet conducts a search warrant on a former president's home over classified documents, citing a statute that has never been used in a criminal investigation or prosecution. When they were unhappy with losing a presidential election, they claimed it had been stolen. But when the other party echoes that claim, with some apparent justification, they cry sedition and insurrection. And meanwhile they flood our nation with illegal aliens and try to change voting laws, all in an attempt to curry more votes and amass power for themselves.

The same party continually attempts to chip away at the Bill of Rights. Free speech apparently means touting the party line, otherwise it's hate speech and racism. Any disagreeing opinion is censored or repressed. The Second Amendment is constantly attacked under the guise of "common sense gun safety." "Red flag laws" allow searches and seizures of firearms without due process, in direct violation of the Fourth Amendment.

We have elected and appointed officials turning a blind eye to public crime and violence, and even worse, weaponizing it for political gain. Public servants from both political parties selling out their constituents and becoming multimillionaires on salaries of under $200,000 a year, often from business dealings with foreign nations. At the same time, the IRS is being increased by enough additional agents to staff the combined police departments of New York, Chicago, and Los Angeles.

How do we turn this around? We are at what is undeniably a crucial point for our nation. If we can't rebuild the integrity of our public institutions and our citizens' faith in them, our republic is doomed to fail.

We need to hold government officials from both parties accountable. Our elections are not so compromised, at least in much of the country, that they have no effect. We need to use our votes to change the political culture of our government. Our elected officials must be made to understand that they must put their constituents first or be voted out of office. If we don't do this, if we don't manage to right our course as a nation, I am afraid we are in for dark times ahead.

THE GREATER GOOD

"A republic, if you can keep it." - Benjamin Franklin

The older I get, the less I care about public opinion. The older I get, the less I believe the government should have any say in how people conduct their lives. There's a balance there though, obviously. I should have the right to live as I please, but only if I don't impair anyone else's ability to do so. This also doesn't abrogate the individual of a responsibility to the greater good. But if the greater good isn't about the government, or imposing a way of life I find palatable onto others against their wishes, what is the greater good?

Robert Heinlein once famously wrote, "The basis of all morality is duty, a concept with the same relation to group that self-interest has to individual." If we construct our personal ethics rationally and logically, stripped of emotion, political demands, religious beliefs, and cultural trappings, it's not too hard to discern what is truly moral.

The greater good is not Christian, or Muslim, or any other religion. It isn't conservative or liberal, Democrat or Republican, black or white. It is a rational and logical concept. The greater good is what benefits the most over the long term while infringing on the fewest. The only true definition of immoral is harming another without valid justification.

418

My entire adult life, my job was applying force to others. People may not like that definition, but that is at the heart of what the soldier and policeman does. Apply force for the greater good. The thing I am proudest of, though, both as a soldier and as a cop, is that I never did violence to another unnecessarily. It was never for revenge, or pleasure, or ego. It is far too easy to be jaded by what you see, to be seduced by the ability to apply force on behalf of the state. To become cruel and a bully. But when you do so, you perpetuate injustice and tyranny. You create enemies where there need be none. I never shied away from violence. It was part of my job. And violence, contrary to political correctness, is often necessary. But violence just because you can always sows the seeds of future conflict. Likewise, anyone in law enforcement who enforces unconstitutional mandates, with or without overt force, is no longer serving the common good. My oaths were to the constitution and the public, not to a mayor or a president.

I avoid commenting on politics and current events as a rule. It invariably leads to arguing with fools, a hobby I have no interest in. But I have never seen our country so divided. Allegiance to a country is different than agreement with a government. Our country, for all its faults and mistakes, is truly a unique and unprecedented thing in history. A republic designed to allow the true power to remain in the hands of the people. The First and Second Amendments alone are crucial to preventing the natural tendency of governments to descend into tyranny over time. Which is why they so often fall under political attack.

If we remain as divided as we currently are, we run the risk of losing the republic the Constitution has given us, just as Benjamin Franklin cautioned. I have seen true oppression, real tyranny and poverty, and I have seen the effects of war. These are things no living American has truly experienced at home. All the "boogaloo bois" chomping at the bit for a civil war are wishing for something I would give my life to avoid, a war at home. That doesn't mean we aren't morally obligated to fight tyranny if it comes to that. We are. I just pray it never has to happen. But if we don't learn, and quickly, to be Americans first and contribute to the greater good of our nation rather than fight amongst each other over political or religious ideology or race, then I am very afraid that is the direction we may be headed.

It is time to be rational and objective. Time to heal wounds and move forward, rather than spark further dissension and strife. Contrary to what the media would have you believe, it isn't the police vs. the poor, or conservatives vs. liberals, or black vs. white. If you are for individual freedom instead of government tyranny, if you understand the duty to the common good, if you can make ethical decisions based on fact instead of emotion, then your allies are others who can do the same, regardless of occupation, race, or political affiliation. Seek and serve the common good, and do no unnecessary harm.

TO KEEP AND BEAR ARMS

"To disarm the people is the most effectual way to enslave them." - George Mason

There has been a lot of political drama in our country regarding the Second Amendment. There are strong emotions on both sides, but deciding where we stand on issues based upon emotion rather than reason is dangerous. Not just because it leads to poor decisions as a general rule, but especially because it makes us easily manipulated.

Anytime a person in power makes an appeal to emotion rather than using logic and reason I'm suspicious. There is a Latin phrase that perfectly captures the litmus test I use on emotional appeals. "Qui Bono." This means "who benefits," and asking yourself that question whenever you're evaluating someone's statements or actions is a powerful tool for discerning their true intent.

In the case of the Second Amendment, I see this through the lens of my experience. I have seen true repression and tyranny in other countries. I have seen those in power abuse it because there are no checks and balances in place to prevent it. Stateside, I have seen the aftermath of violence against the innocent who were powerless to defend themselves. Even in large municipal jurisdictions where you're never far from a police officer, violence is sudden and unexpected, and the police often can't get there in time to intervene. My understanding of violence and its cost isn't academic, it's real and personal.

The proponents of gun control in our country use emotion like a weapon in their arguments. They point to tragedies that understandably horrify good people and use that horror and outrage to shore up their position. But mass shootings, as tragic as they are, make a poor case for gun control when evaluated based on the actual data. The FBI data on active shooter incidents, which excludes gang violence and other crime-related shootings, shows that far fewer people are killed or injured in mass shootings than by either medical malpractice or vehicle accidents.

Thirty-eight people, excluding the shooters themselves, were killed in such incidents in 2020, the most recent year the finished report is available for. If you include all firearms deaths, even suicides which account for over fifty percent, the number for 2020 rises to 45,222. By contrast, the number of deaths related to medical errors is estimated at between 22,000 - 98,000 yearly, depending on which study you believe. You are at least as likely to die at the hands of your doctor than you are to be shot and killed by another. Compare this to traffic crash fatalities for 2020, which were 38,824, and once again it's a higher risk of death than violence with a handgun if you exclude suicide. And although raw numbers of firearms-related deaths have risen, per capita they are lower than in the 1970's.

In my opinion though, these statistics are actually irrelevant to the debate. The Second Amendment isn't about sport or hunting. It isn't even about self-defense. The Second Amendment is about one thing, and one thing only—the ability of the people to resist and overthrow tyranny. The Framers of the Constitution hadn't just returned from a hunting trip. They had defeated an empire and earned our nation's independence.

This understanding of the Founder's intent behind the Second Amendment nullifies much of the gun control rhetoric. It's why their claims about "weapons of war," magazine capacity, "assault weapons," and so on are irrelevant. The Second Amendment is at its core about war. One of the incidents that triggered the revolutionary war was an attempt at gun confiscation by the British. In 1774, General Gage confiscated arms and ammunition throughout Boston via warrantless searches by British soldiers.

This triggered a series of events that led to the first Continental Congress, and eventually to the colonies successfully fighting for their independence. It was also the genesis for both the Second and Fourth Amendments. The Founding Fathers drafted the Constitution and its Amendments specifically to guard against our government becoming the type of tyranny they had freed themselves from.

The truth of the Founding Fathers' intent and understanding has been born out time and again. One of the first things Hitler did when he rose to power was to put strict limitations on gun ownership, as did Mao, Stalin, and Lenin. In this century, we've seen strict gun control immediately precede genocide in Sudan and social upheaval in Venezuela. Australia confiscated firearms, and during the pandemic changed from a free nation to an oppressive one.

The lesson is this. A disarmed populace is powerless to resist tyranny. This is a lesson our politicians understand, as evidenced by the fact that the elected officials pushing hardest for gun control here in the United States are the same ones advocating loudest for sending arms to the Ukraine so that its citizens can resist Russian invasion.

The counter argument against this premise is that resistance against a modern military would be futile with semiautomatic rifles and pistols. This is a faulty argument on a couple of levels. Any Special Forces soldier can attest to just how effective guerrilla warfare can be. And this argument on the part of gun control advocates, when looked at through the lens of the Constitution and the Founders' intent, actually invalidates many of the current restrictions on firearms ownership such as the NFA. It also makes the "weapons of war" argument from gun control proponents immaterial on it's face, as weapons suitable for waging war are the very items the Second Amendment is written to guarantee access to.

Another common assertion by the politicians who want to remove public access to firearms is that the Second Amendment is a collective right, not an individual one. This is based on the use of the word "militia" in the amendment, and claims that the Second Amendment was written to only apply to institutions like the National Guard. The problem with this argument is that it is historically inaccurate. At the time of the adoption of the Bill of Rights, no such institution as the National Guard existed, and the term "militia" simply meant every able-bodied male citizen of fighting age.

So if deaths by firearm violence are statistically far less significant than we have been led to believe, and if the intent behind the Second Amendment was to safeguard against our government devolving into tyranny through the guarantee of an individual right to keep and bear arms, then why the political push for disarming our populace? Once again, I believe the answer to that can be discerned by asking ourselves "qui bono," and examining who truly benefits from such measures.

The people advocating hardest for gun control, despite the constitutional protections of the Second Amendment, are protected around the clock by people armed with guns. Their safety is reasonably assured. They aren't worried that those in power will abuse it, because they are in power. How then would they benefit from our right to keep and bear arms being abolished?

The only logical conclusion is that they understand exactly the Founding Fathers' intent behind the Second Amendment, and that the truth of it is exactly why they want to abolish the right. They don't want the checks on their power that an armed populace creates. They themselves aspire to the sort of absolute power that the rulers of other nations enjoy, unfettered by accountability. And if we want to maintain any semblance of the Republic our Founding Fathers envisioned, we must guard against that at all costs.

WAR

"Who wishes to fight must first count the cost" - Sun Tzu

I feel I have some relevant knowledge on the topic of war. I have a master's degree, but I don't think of college as my education. It was a project I did as an adult, not where I learned the things that define me. I went to a very different school. We majored in insurrection and rebellion, with minors in sabotage and violence. We learned diplomacy, language, and technology, too, but all of it was intended to enable us to master our trade.

Our trade, our calling, our profession was war. We were intended to be used to topple regimes and end bloodlines. And we did. In deserts and among mountains far from home, we did just those things. We were the masters of our craft, and found fierce joy and a strange fulfillment in the chaos. We loved war like a dark bride, and she loved us back.

Our battles were won at a great cost, though. We all paid that cost, with our bodies and our souls. Many of the finest men I've ever known paid that price with their very lives, and no one who danced with war remained unchanged. For better or worse, we will never again be who we were before war's seductive embrace. As high a price as we paid, it pales next to the cost of war for the people of those far off lands. Countless lives lost, not just through death, but shattered by poverty and despair as well.

When we were done, we journeyed home, seeking peace. We struggled, all of us, with the beast that war had woken inside of us. Most of us found ways in time to lull the beast to slumber and turn our hearts to peaceful pursuits. The beast sleeps fitfully, but sleep it does, only occasionally reminding us with random dreams and errant thoughts that it still lives within us.

We are in a dangerous time as a nation. We have never been so divided as a people, nor had the level of organized public violence we have now. I fear for our country. If we aren't very careful, a war at home is possible, maybe even probable. And those of us who loved war know her far too well to ever want a war at home. Make no mistake, the beast we put to bed when we came home seeking peace should never be woken, and it sleeps lightly at best.

No one who has been to war, even those of us like me who loved war and reveled in her embrace, wants her dark desires to follow them home. We want to hang our swords above the fireplace and be at peace. But the beast sleeps lightly at best, and without caution it may again wake.

AFTERWORD- "THE GREYBEARDS"

"Beware of an old man in a profession where men usually die young." - Kevin Lacz

By the end of my SF career, my team was one of the oldest in group. Probably one of the oldest in the regiment. My team sergeant had hunted SCUDs in the gulf war in Fifth Group, and my commander holds the regimental record for continuous time in command of the same ODA. First as a captain, then as a warrant. A record that will never be broken, because they've changed the rules to prevent it. By 2009, probably half the team was over 40, and a couple were around the half century mark. Staying operational that long is not an easy thing to do in this profession, and my elders on the team were my mentors, passing along hard lessons learned.

During that 2009 deployment, we had a capture-kill mission on an HVT. During the hit, our blocking position came under fire from small arms and RPGs. We called in air support a couple of times as we wrapped up SSE on the objective and made our way across the village to exfil. Dave and I took two squads of Afghans and moved out to secure an LZ for the chinooks while the rest of the team remained in covered and concealed positions. We set in a perimeter and just before calling in the pilots, our interpreter came running up to me. He had just heard the Taliban saying on the radio that they would attack our position and get revenge for their brothers we had killed. Dave and I put the Afghans on alert, told the rest of team to stand by, and settled in for more fighting.

My interpreter came running up again with a disheartened look on his face. "Commander Matt, I am so sorry. The Taliban they say, 'It is the Greybeards, everyone go home and hide your guns. No more brothers die today.'" As we exfilled without any further fighting, I thought about that intercepted transmission. Much like active cops in the US, the bad guys gave us a street name. Life expectancy in Afghanistan is short, and anyone who lives as long as we had is seen as wise. And in our case dangerous. My beard wasn't grey yet, but I was lucky to fight alongside and be mentored by senior teammates with the breadth and depth of experience mine had. The lessons they taught and the decisions they made kept us alive.

Now that I'm older than my senior leadership on the team and in the regiment was then, now that my beard is grey with the weight of experience, I've adopted our Taliban "street name" for my training company. I can't ever repay those who came before me for the lessons that kept me alive. But I can pay it forward. I can pass that wisdom along to the next generation of warriors and add my own lessons learned to it. More than any victory overseas, more than any arrest as a police officer at home, that is the legacy I want to leave. Knowledge and wisdom. Given to me by those who came before. Added to and passed along to the ones who come after so that they too can one day be old, and grey, and wise. Then the next greybeards can add what they have learned and pass it on in turn. And so on down the line.

ACKNOWLEDGEMENTS

This book is the culmination of a lifetime of seeking knowledge from those who came before me. The list of those I've learned from is too long to cover completely here, but I'll do my best to thank everyone I can. I would not be who I am, and this book would not exist without everyone mentioned here, and many others there's no room to name.

My father, Thomas Little, fighter pilot and federal agent. I am far more like him that I ever thought as a young man. He taught me to shoot and filled my head with stories of the Wild West and the gunfighters that tamed it. My mother, Mary Tucker. She taught me to follow my own path regardless of what others thought or believed. My step-mother, Lynn Little. She taught me how to be a good cop long before I ever went to a police academy.

My teachers and mentors in martial arts who set me on this journey from the beginning. Soke Tetsuzan Kuroda. Shihans Takayuki Mikami, Hiroshi Ikeda, Keith Moore and Takayuki Yoshinaga. Instructors Pat Jennings, Kevin Hankins, and Marsha Turner. These people, and many more from my dojo days gone by, showed me the path I needed to walk.

My supervisors who mentored me and my teammates who pushed me throughout the early days of my Army career. The Spec 4 Mafia I hated so much as a private and am so grateful to now for starting me out right. Doc Savage, 18D extraordinaire and training team NCO at the old A/2/20. Tim White and Jody Beck, mates from the training team and the closest of friends. The nasty guard contingent at the Q-course, also lifelong friends—Ryan Ahern, Rick McCoy, Doug Bernard, and others. Will Summers, who would go on to be on the first team into Afghanistan after 9/11. Rob Caufield (RIP), who took the long walk soon after the Q. JK Davis, Tom Simmons, and others. My teammates at group, my brothers in arms, heroes all. Lenny Huff, Jeff Walsh, Rick Rau, John Hackett, Dave Klaus, and so many others whose names I won't mention here because they are still serving. Tom White, who saved my life and remains one of my closest friends. Frank Proctor, who introduced me to shooting competition, and the other SOT-D instructors. The ones we lost in Afghanistan: Chris Robinson, Sev Summers (Will's brother), Alex Granado (my teammate in Iraq as well), Don Luce, Bill Woods, and Matt Pucino.

Team Wichita from my State Department tour in Iraq. Shane Schmidt (RIP) and Jim Erwin, who taught me a lot about being a good teammate and made me a better SF soldier for it.

Derek Davis, Trooper, Rob Prevost, John Holschen, and my other mates. The ones we lost at Green 19: Robert Pole, Robert McCoy, Ronald Hyatt, and Ryan Young.

My supervisors, coworkers and subordinates on the Chicago PD, and from my early cop days in Louisiana. Scot Toups, Rowdy Long, Wilce Gilbert, and Troy Smith (RIP). My partner and lifelong friend, Vince Jamison. Legendary Gang Team Sergeants Eddie Yoshimura and Marvin Bonnstetter. Bosses like Mike Rigoli, Matt Tobias, Leo Schmitz, and many others. The officers of the 011th and 014th Districts. My fellow supervisors, and the officers and detectives who worked for me in the Organized Crime and Detective Bureaus, especially the Citywide Gang and Heavy Weapons Teams. My officers and fellow supervisors at SWAT, far too many to name here, and many still serving.

The instructors and shooters, both competitive and tactical, who've mentored me on my way. Ken Good, force-on-force and low light pioneer. Rob Trivino, retired SMU sergeant major. Mike Pannone, one-eyed Green Beret whose accomplishments alone would fill a book of this size. My old USPSA training partner, Les Kismartoni, USPSA Grand Master and national champion. Other shooting friends like Eric Kamps, Jay Carillo, Joel Park, Riley Bowman, Alex Acosta, Jeff Rockwell, AJ Zito, and too many more to mention. Ben Stoeger, world champion shooter and internet troll extraordinaire. Robert Vogel, also a world champion shooter, and a good friend. Tim Herron, another amazing coach, top competitive shooter, and a genuinely great human being. Gabe White, close friend, AIWB ninja and martial philosopher supreme. Scott Jedlinski, who paved the way for the current RDS revolution and mentored me when I started my training business in ways I can never repay.

I've only scratched the surface. The list of people I've learned from and been enriched by knowing is far too long to list here, and I can only hope I've not offended any of the countless people who helped me on my path by omitting them. I am sincerely grateful to each and every one of you.

BIBLIOGRAPHY AND RECOMMENDED READING

- Aurelius, M. (175). *Meditations.*

- Avery, R. (2019). *Practical Shooting.* Digital Shibumi.

- Brown, L. and Ferrigno, V. (2005). *Training for Speed, Agility, and Quickness.* Human Kinetics.

- Bassham, L. (2011). *With Winning in Mind 3rd Ed.* Mental Management Systems.

- Clausewitz, C. (1832). *On War.*

- Colvin, G. (2009). *Talent is Overrated.* Penguin Books.

- Coyle, D. (2008). *The Talent Code.* Bantam Books.

- Dintman, G. and Ward, B. (2003). *Sports Speed.* Human Kinetics.

- Department of the Army. (2020). *Ranger Handbook.* U.S. Army.

- Enos, B. (2012). *Practical Shooting: Beyond Fundamentals.* Loose Cannon Enterprises.

- Ericsson, A. (2016). *Peak.* Houghton Mifflin Harcourt.

- Everett, G. (2009). *Olympic Weightlifting.* Catalyst Athletics.

- Gladwell, M. (2008). *Outliers.* Little, Brown, and Company.

- Hogan, S. (2021). *Built From Broken.* Salt Wrap.

- Horschig, A. and Sonthana, K. (2021). *Rebuilding Milo.* Victory Belt Publishing.

- Howe, P. (2011). *Leadership and Training for the Fight*. Skyhorse.

- Kilgore, L. Hartman, M. Lascek, J. (2011). *Fit*. Killustrated Books.

- Kurz, T. (1994). *Stretching Scientifically*. Stadion Publishing.

- Lamb, K. (2008). *Green Eyes & Black Rifles*. Trample & Hurdle Publishers.

- Lamb, K. (2011). *Stay in the Fight*. Trample & Hurdle Publishers.

- Lee, B. (1975). *Tao of Jeet Kun Do*. Black Belt Communications.

- LeFavor, P. (2015). *U.S. Army Small Unit Tactics Handbook*. Blacksmith Publishing.

- Machiavelli, N. (1513). *The Prince*.

- Mackenzie, B. Codoza, G. (2012). *Power Speed Endurance*. Victory Belt Publishing.

- Musashi, M. (1645). *The Book of Five Rings*.

- Osinga, F. (2007). *Science, Strategy, and War: The Strategic Thinking of John Boyd*. Routledge.

- Pearlman, S. (2006). *The Book of Martial Power*. Overlook Press.

- Perez, C. (2004). *Anatomy of a Hostage Rescue*. Naval Postgraduate School.

- Rippetoe, M. and Kilgore, L. (2009). *Practical Programming for Strength Training*. Aesgaard Company.

- Starret, K. (2013). *Becoming a Supple Leopard*. Victory Belt Publishing.

- Stoeger, B. (2019). *Breakthrough Marksmanship*. Amazon KDP.

- Stoeger, B. (2018). *Skills and Drills Reloaded*. Amazon KDP.

- Stoeger, B. (2017). *Dryfire Reloaded*. Amazon KDP.

- Stoeger, B. (2016). *Practical Pistol Reloaded*. Amazon KDP.

- Stoeger, B. (2020). *Match Mentality*. Amazon KDP.

- Stoeger, B. and Park, J. (2021). *Practical Shooting Training*. Amazon KDP.

- Thibaudeau, C. (2006). *The Black Book of Training Secrets*. F. Lepine Publishing.

- Tsatsouline, P. (2001). *Relax Into Stretch*. Dragon Door Publications.

- Verkoshansky, Y. and Siff, M. (2009). *Supertraining*. Verkoshansky.

- Yagyu, M. (1634). *Family Traditions on the Art of War*.

- Zatsiorsky, V. And Kramer, W. (2006). *Science and Practice of Strength Training*. Human Kinetics.

INFORMATION RESOURCES

- Brian Enos Forum   forums.brianenos.com

- GreyBeard Actual   greybeardactual.com

- Pistol Forum   https://pistol-forum.com

- Practical Shooting Training Group   www.practicalshootingtraininggroup.com

- Primary & Secondary   primaryandsecondary.com

EQUIPMENT SOURCES

- AimCam   aimcam.com

- Ben Stoeger Pro Shop   benstoegerproshop.com

- Lone Star Armory   www.lonestararmory.us

- Practical Performance   www.practicalperformance.org

- Stand 1 Armory   stand1armory.com

- Tactical Shooting Pro Shop   tacticalshootingproshop.com

- Vulcan Machine Werks   vulcanmachinewerks.com

GLOSSARY

18D - SF Medical Sergeant

AAR - After Action Review.

AIWB - Appendix Inside the Waistband. Carrying a concealed pistol inside the waistband forward of the hip bones.

BJJ - Brazilian Jujitsu.

CAT - Combat Application Tourniquet.

CCL - Concealed Carry License.

Comms - Communications.

CQB - Close Quarter Battle.

DEVGRU - Naval Special Warfare Development Group. Also known as SEAL Team Six. The US Navy's counterterrorism SMU.

ECQC - Extreme Close Quarter Concepts. Excellent training course on entangled gunfights from Craig Douglas of Shivworks.

EDC - Every Day Carry. The weapons and tools you customarily have on you each day.

Exfiltration (Exfil) - The part of a mission involving returning from the objective.

FID - Foreign Internal Defense. Training allied military personnel.

GPP - General Physical Preparedness.

GWOT - Global War on Terror

HVT - High Value Target.

IDPA - International Defensive Pistol Association.

IED - Improvised Explosive Device.

IF - Intermittent Fasting. A dietary strategy involving restricting eating to a reduced daily time window.

IFAK - Individual First Aid Kit.

IIFYM - If It Fits Your Macros. A dietary strategy prioritizing daily macronutrient amounts over food types.

Infiltration (Infil) - The part of a mission involving movement to the objective.

IPSC - International Practical Shooting Confederation.

IR - Infrared.

IWB - Inside the Waistband. Carrying a concealed pistol inside the waistband. Usually refers to strong side carry behind the hip bone.

JCET - Joint Combined Exercise Training. Joint exercises between SOF units and foreign military.

JDAM - Joint Direct Attack Munition.

Kata - In classical martial arts, a set sequence of techniques used as a training methodology.

LCC - The last covered and concealed position prior to the objective.

LE - Law Enforcement.

LZ - Landing Zone.

MACP - Modern Army Combatives Program.

Metcon - Metabolic conditioning workout.

MIL - Military.

MMA - Mixed Martial Arts.

MOUT - Military Operations in Urban Terrain.

ODA - Operational Detachment Alpha. Special Forces "A-team."

Operator - Commonly used term for special operations personnel.

Operational - In a combat role as a special operations soldier, or an enforcement role as a SWAT officer.

OWB - Outside the Waistband. Carrying a pistol, either overtly or concealed, in a holster outside the waistband.

OODA - Observation Orientation Decision Action. John Boyd's model for the mental process of managing conflict.

PNF - Proprioceptive Neuromuscular Facilitation. Stretching technique involving isometric contractions of the muscle being stretched.

PTS - Post Traumatic Stress. Also known as PTSD or post traumatic stress disorder.

Q-Course - Special Forces Qualification Course. The primary school soldiers must pass to earn the Green Beret and be assigned to the U.S. Army Special Forces.

QRF - Quick Reaction Force. A reserve force standing by to respond if the element on the objective is in danger of being overwhelmed.

ROE - Rules Of Engagement.

RPG - Rocket Propelled Grenade.

Shoot House - A facility constructed for live fire CQB training.

SF - Special Forces. Specifically U.S. Army Special Forces.

SFAS - Special Forces Assessment and Selection. A grueling one month tryout prospective Green Berets must pass to be allowed into the training process for US Army Special Forces.

SFAUC - Special Forces Advanced Urban Combat Course.

SFOD-D - Special Forces Operational Detachment Delta. The US Army's counter-terrorism SMU.

SME - Subject Matter Expert.

SMU - Special Missions Unit. A military special operations unit tasked with highly classified missions. SFOD-D or "Delta Force" is the most well known SMU.

SOCP - Special Operations Combatives Program.

SOF - Special Operations Forces.

SOPMOD - Firearms modified for SOF use.

SOTIC - Special Operations Target Interdiction Course. SF sniper school.

SSE - Sensitive Sight Exploitation. Collection of potential intelligence from an objective.

Special Forces - U.S. Army Special Forces. The "Green Berets."

SPP - Specific Physical Preparedness.

Stoicism - Greek school of philosophy emphasizing self-control over emotions.

SUT - Small Unit Tactics

SWAT - Special Weapons and Tactics. Law enforcement special operations unit tasked with hostage rescue and high risk warrant service.

TCCC - Tactical Casualty Combat Care.

TTP - Tactics, Techniques, and Procedures.

UC - Undercover.

UFC - Ultimate Fighting Championship.

USPSA - US Practical Shooting Association.

Zen - Branch of Buddhism emphasizing self-control over emotions.

ABOUT THE AUTHOR

Matthew Little is a US Army Special Forces veteran with combat experience in Afghanistan on an SFODA and in Iraq for the U.S. State Department. His military awards include the Bronze Star and the Combat Infantryman's Badge. Matt is also a retired Chicago Police Officer with extensive law enforcement experience in a variety of assignments, including serving as the training coordinator and an operational supervisor on full-time SWAT team.

Additionally, Matt is a lifelong martial artist and black belt who has trained extensively in a variety of disciplines and is a former national level competitor. He is also ranked as a Master Class shooter with pistol and carbine by both the US Practical Shooting Association and the International Defensive Pistol Association. He has earned many tactical shooting skill awards including Gabe White's Turbo Pin, the Tier 1 Three Sevens coin, the RE-factor Kill Card, 5.56 Training's Sicario Pin, and the Trigger Prep Vice Card.

He has instructed foreign and US military personnel and police officers in firearms, combatives, and tactics. This instructional experience was not solely academic, as Matt was usually then leading his students operationally either in combat or in arguably the most violent city in North America. In retirement he teaches law enforcement and military personnel as well as responsible armed citizens in firearms, tactics, and combatives through his company GreyBeard Actual LLC. This is his first book, but he has published several articles on shooting and tactics in nationally syndicated magazines.

Matt lives in the great state of Texas with his beloved wife, Angela Little, an accomplished shooter and athlete in her own right and the chief operations officer of their company, as well as their menagerie of pets which includes a beautiful Siberian Husky, a jealous Siamese cat, and a very entitled bearded dragon. When he's not training, teaching or writing, Matt's hobbies include picking up heavy things and putting them back down, making gun smoke and spent brass, reading extensively on a variety of topics, and watching obscure movies and TV shows.

Made in the USA
Columbia, SC
13 August 2024

f18f1073-ebf2-4850-8495-e7ac9a720734R01